TRANSFERRED ILLUSIONS

In memory of
Ian Donald Sutherland (1924–2006)
and
Julia Briggs (1943–2007)

Transferred Illusions
Digital Technology and the Forms of Print

MARILYN DEEGAN
King's College, London
and
KATHRYN SUTHERLAND
University of Oxford

ASHGATE

Published by
Ashgate Publishing Limited
Wey Court East
Union Road
Farnham
Surrey, GU9 7PT
England

Ashgate Publishing Company
Suite 420
101 Cherry Street
Burlington
VT 05401-4405
USA

www.ashgate.com

British Library Cataloguing in Publication Data
Deegan, Marilyn
  Transferred illusions : digital technology and the forms of
  print
  1. Publishers and publishing 2. Digitally printed materials
  3. Electronic publications
  I. Title II. Sutherland, Kathryn
  070.5

Library of Congress Cataloging-in-Publication Data
Deegan, Marilyn.
  Transferred illusions : digital technology and the forms of print / by Marilyn Deegan and Kathryn Sutherland.
       p. cm.
  Includes bibliographical references and index.
  ISBN 978-0-7546-7016-2
  1. Publishers and publishing--Technological innovations. 2. Newpaper publishing--Technological innovations. 3. Communication in learning and scholarship--Technological innovations. 4. Electronic publications. 5. Scholarly electronic publishing. 6. Digital libraries. 7. Library materials--Digitization. 8. Transmission of texts. 9. Books and reading. 10. Information technology--Social aspects. I. Sutherland, Kathryn. II. Title.

  Z278.D44 2008
  070.5'797--dc22

070.5797 DEE

2008034477

ISBN 978-0-7546-7016-2

Contents

Preface

As books do, computers measure, store and represent information; and as with books, it is still authors and readers who process this information as knowledge, making sense or nonsense of what the tool communicates. So far, computers cannot replicate common sense or creative thinking. The intelligence involved in processing information into knowledge is only a human skill. As Charles Jonscher puts it:

> A computer operation is performed at the mechanical level by a machine, but it is in reality a transaction between people. Except when human programmers or users give the data meaning, a computer no more processes information than if its keys had been brushed by a passing dog. Information has meaning only in the context of a human interpreter: lacking an intelligent entity to interpret the information it contains, an encyclopedia is just so many squiggles on a page ... The failure to distinguish between the symbol-processing powers of a computer and the human intelligence of its operator is at the heart of many misconceptions as to the role of information technology in society.[1]

To the extent that we overestimate the computer's powers or underestimate and under-engage our own, we risk what Manuel Castells has described as the likely fate of twenty-first-century man and woman, 'informed bewilderment'.[2] Informed bewilderment is currently as serious a threat as ignorance to the real enlightenment that reading brings. The apparent and much-vaunted democracy of the information age, where freedom is equated to the speed with which we follow links, can turn all too quickly into slavery – the opening of one more window. The degradation of the concept of cybernetic hypertext itself makes the point. In the early 1990s creative hypertext, a series of nodes and links stimulating multiple perspectives on a topic or on the non-linear procedures of narrative, was the new thing the computer promised to the arts. Now it is an aspect of text's function we all take for granted – the capacity of any point on the Internet to synapse with any other – and nothing special. There is more to freedom than action without constraint or the immediate satisfaction of desires. Moral freedom could not be so easily defined, involving as it does the capacity to follow reason and intelligence and to control passion. Similarly, there is more to reading than the manipulation of links. Choice

---

1   Charles Jonscher, *Wired Life: Who Are We in the Digital Age?* (London: Anchor, 2000), pp. 148–9.

2   Manuel Castells, *The Information Age: Ecomony, Society and Culture,* vol. 3 (1998), quoted in Jonscher, p. 256.

is not the same as judgement, width does not imply quality, and pick and mix or cut and paste, under the direction of a search engine, may not be the best way to reach a truly informed opinion on anything beyond the informationally trite. Good reading is a reflective as well as a sensational process which engages our abstract mental faculties, and we give it up at our peril. Part of the problem is the tunnelled vision that the latest, newest, most fashionable technology induces in us all: in seeing what is new, we see nothing else. Hence the bizarre situation of libraries filled with books and readers who sit at computer terminals never lifting a copy from the shelves that surround them, or bookshops transformed into Internet cafés. In Geoffrey Nunberg's view, digital media cannot be allowed to be understood as autonomous but among the media that together make public discourse.[3]

The point is an important one because, among other things, it suggests that in losing physical identity and constraints, electronic forms of communication also lose some of the properties and regulators that confer public status. The institutions of print and latterly those of broadcast media like radio and television have decisively shaped collective opinion, but a prime characteristic of electronic texts seems to be to deny their common status as public objects. We can now, if we wish, set up on our home page or blog an RSS feed to send us news only on topics that interest us and only from sources we select. We can customize how we read other people's websites so that they look as we want them to and give us only the information we want. With electronic newspapers, we can choose to receive only those articles or sections we want, download them and print them off as our personalized daily paper to take to read on the commuter train or bus. As scholars we can create rich electronic archives of great literature from which each reader can select their individually tailored edition or reading text, annotated and illustrated in the way they want – MyDickens or MyDavid Copperfield. We can invite others into this personal universe by writing blogs or through MySpace, but it remains our universe. We can personalize fiction using characters from known authors (Fan Fiction), and most fantastic of all, we can create whole new personalities or 'avatars' in Second Life. Common ground (we are not talking about truth or accuracy here so much as breadth of perspective) as signalled by a shared newspaper or the expertly stabilized, single text of a scholarly edition, is threatened with erosion.

Where the computer is concerned, our tunnelled vision is further compounded by amnesia. We have forgotten that print did not replace manuscript production and circulation in any simple sense or even in the long term. Not only was printing established slowly from beginnings in the late fifteenth century as the dominant means of reproduction, the terms of its adoption remained irregular centuries after the invention of movable type. Cross-fertilization and hybridization, whereby books combined manuscript and print, continued for 200 years into the seventeenth century. The single classification of manuscript and printed books

---

3   Geoffrey Nunberg, 'The Place of Books in the Age of Electronic Reproduction', *Representations*, 42 (1993), p. 33.

also remained common in libraries into the seventeenth century. Improvements in print technology – mechanized presses, stereoplate printing, Monotype casting and offset printing – did not drive out the older processes and methods; they sat alongside them. William Morris, Virginia Woolf and Stephen Spender all printed on hand presses long after they were replaced by newer technologies. It might be objected that this is to argue from special cases – the special cases that high literature tends to represent. But the fundamental error is to assume a culture of total replacement: not only does history not bear this out, it continually subverts it. For some purposes, the book, pliant but bounded, with edges we can see and touch, may remain a better tool than a website.

Considering change or replacement from another angle, we might say that it is in those moments when an older technology is challenged by a newer that the old comes into focus. Fifty years on, we hardly register the fact that the modern assessment of the 'coming of the book', with its attendant enquiries into the 'immediate and unforeseen' effects of print, shared a cultural moment with the widely predicted 'going' or 'death' of the book. Yet the transition from Lucien Febvre and Henri-Jean Martin's 'coming' (*L'Apparation du livre*, 1958) to Marshal McLuhan's 'going' and his damnable history of 'typographic man' (*The Gutenberg Galaxy*, 1962) was a matter of only four years. Both announcements, now given classic status in the history of communications, need to be recognized for their timeliness; both responded to the burden of modern media consciousness, by which the materiality of our traditional literary culture (the functions of type, paper, format, book structures, and so on) came into sharper focus, under threat from what Raymond Williams described as the 'new technologies of language' – in 1977, when Williams wrote, telephone, radio, television, and only emergently the computer.[4] Discussions of the 'going' and the 'coming' of the book are responses to a particular moment in modern technological and cultural time; and as professional readers we continue to live with the consequences of both coming and going, one of which, bizarrely enough, is the current digital fetishization of print objects. The digital gives us a point of comparison with print and so a means of understanding what kinds of thinking, social interaction and cultural production we believe print makes possible. We look anew at what we took for granted.

One of the subjects of this book is the threshold print media provide for digital. As a generation of social critics from the 1970s and 1980s reminded us, technologies 'are not mere exterior aids but also interior transformations of consciousness, and never more than when they affect the word'.[5] For the moment,

---

4   Lucien Febvre and Henri-Jean Martin, *L'Apparation du livre* (Paris: Editions Albin Michel, 1958) translated into English as *The Coming of the Book* (London: Verso, 1976); Marshall McLuhan, *The Gutenberg Galaxy: The Making of Typographic Man* (Toronto: University of Toronto Press, 1962); Raymond Williams, *Marxism and Literature* (Oxford: Oxford University Press, 1977), p. 53.

5   Walter J. Ong, *Orality and Literacy: The Technologizing of the Word* (London and New York: Methuen, 1982), p. 82.

the technological transformation of our mental landscape that writing effects has calibrated our expectations of the next technological transformation as digital to print. Not only are we programmed to replace one invention by another – print by digital – failing to learn from history that it is rarely one thing or the other – but we are shaping the new by the old and familiar. Briefly in the early 1990s hypertext was hailed as the fourth 'primary form of literary discourse' (after poetry, drama and prose) and a tool for non-linear creation and interpretation – 'a new form concurrent with a new technology of textualization'.[6] Fast forward no more than a decade, and we are reading old books from screens. It is, however, the newspaper, print's dominant mass form for around 200 years, that currently and most persuasively shapes print's electronic remediation. Mass digitization initiatives, funded and wrapped round by online advertising, are recasting the book as the newspaper. This is unsurprising, given the shared democratic credentials of newsprint and computer digits. But here's an interesting thing: newsprint was and is everywhere; at the same time, it was and is ephemeral. In recasting the book, a robust technology, as the newspaper, under the old model the book's ephemeral other, we are, wittingly or not, using the new technology to reprioritize our literary relations. Digitized newspaper archives make the same point in reverse: suddenly the historical saturation of a particular and neglected print form is newly accessible, and its recovery requires us to reassess our past relationship to print. By contrast, publishers continue to invest in books, but they are now largely manufactured, from writer to almost the end of the production workflow, electronically. Libraries digitize them and, increasingly, we access them online. How do these changes affect the book's previously secure status as a cultural and as a physical object? And might pre-loadable electronic reading devices (e-book readers) herald the portable book collection much as iPods compress our CD libraries?

This book is about the forms and institutions of print – newspapers, books, scholarly editions, publishing, libraries – as they relate to and are changed by the emergent forms and institutions of our present digital age. Its focus is on the transformation of the old into the new and the shaping of the new by the old. Its subject and implied audience is the community we know best, that of scholarly libraries, writing and publishing, teachers and researchers in the arts and humanities, a community whose established expertise and authority are increasingly challenged by the methods of communication fostered by the Internet; and not least because the Internet loosens the bond between author/creator and product built up over the last two centuries. We have little to say about the exuberant or ironic popular creativity associated with that polemical and opinionated form, the blog, and nothing to say about social networking sites. Yet this is a book about the reach of the Internet, and it could not have been written without access to the Internet. This creates its own ironies: at least 50 per cent

---

6   Patrick Conner, 'Lighting out for the Territory: Hypertext, Ideology, and *Huckleberry Finn*', in Kathryn Sutherland (ed.), *Electronic Text: Investigations in Method and Theory* (Oxford: Clarendon Press, 1997), p. 75.

of our sources of information are websites, which we scrupulously reference in footnotes. We hope they will be there and live if our readers wish to follow the links. If they are not, then a different, no less pertinent lesson can be deduced. Our book contains two kinds of writing – one informational and the other more critical and reflective. Both are necessary responses, we believe, to this stage of the new technology and our relationship to it. We have tried to write accessibly in both modes and, where we can, to open doors between the two, in the belief that if we are to get the best out of the possibilities of digital technology for the arts and humanities, then we must learn to shape it and not merely consume it. As long ago, in digital years, as 1995, Jonathan Franzen wrote in the *New Yorker* of the bifurcation in our expectations of the new digital age: where 'visionaries of every political persuasion see empowerment for the masses', 'Wall Street sees a profit for investors'.[7] Currently there are more than 100 million blogs (and growing) on the blogosphere, with about 15 million active; there are, by comparison, a handful of data gathering and centralizing service providers, like Google and Facebook, funded by a near monopoly of online advertising. It is easy to see where the power really lies. Then again, the Internet is just another information space, sharing characteristics that have defined such spaces throughout history – wonderfully effective and unstable, loaded with valuable resources and misinformation; that is, both good and bad. Hence this book; for it is more important than ever that we, the writers, critics, publishers and librarians – in modern parlance, the knowledge providers – be critically informed and actively engaged in shaping and regulating cyberspace, and not merely the passive instruments or unreflecting users of the digital tools in our hands.

---

7   Jonathan Franzen, 'The Reader in Exile', *New Yorker*, 71 (2) (6 March 1995); reprinted in *How To Be Alone: Essays* (London: Fourth Estate, 2002), p. 171.

Acknowledgements

For answering questions, reading drafts, for information and advice, the authors would like to thank Jane Bird, Peter Dunn, Simon Horobin, Richard Ovenden, Simon Tanner, Peter Wilby and staff of the Centre for Computing in the Humanities at King's College London. Thanks too to graduate students in the English Faculty, Oxford, for contributing to our conversations and for participating in digital experiments. We are grateful to the English Faculty, Oxford, and to Harold Short and King's London for sabbatical leave in which much of the research for the book was completed.

A version of Chapter 2 was presented in March 2008 at the London Seminar in Digital Text & Scholarship, sponsored by the Centre for Computing in the Humanities, King's College London, and the Institute of English Studies, University of London.

Chapter 1
After Print?

San Serriffe

The consequences of technological change are rarely as self-evident or pre-determined as either their advocates or their critics imply. This is one reason why forecasting is so fraught with risk. By contrast, once new technologies are harnessed to institutions and naturalized as the expression of cultural choice, predictions about their effectiveness can indeed appear remarkably self-fulfilling; provided, that is, we do not underestimate the usefulness or, to animate the language of technology, the 'resourcefulness', of older technologies. In a pertinent essay, now some 15 years old, Paul Duguid considered what were then current prophecies of the 'death' of the book, to be ousted by electronic hypertext and multimedia alternatives. By way of illustrating the vulnerability of prediction, he noted the unanticipated survival of pencils and hinged doors: in 1938 the *New York Times* assumed that the heavily engineered typewriter would mark the end for the simple pencil; and since the 1920s a familiar filmic trope signalling 'the triumph of the future' has been the automatic sliding door. Speed of movement, the effortless transition from one space to another, the absence of recoil – these all make the sliding door a potent type of the future and of the liberation narratives written for its technologies. Yet as Duguid remarked: 'while the sliding door still appears on the futurological screen, the millennia-old manual hinge endures all around us (even on our laptop computers and cell phones).' What was difficult to imagine in 1994 was the sheer resourcefulness of the book, which is now flourishing thanks to the digitization of the production process, print-on-demand, web advertising, sales and reviewing, and the accessibility of high quality digital facsimiles. Not foreseen was the use of a new technology to revive an old.[1]

This said, we are surrounded by change. Whether we discover in the scale and speed of everyday cybernetic transformations signs of a newly diffused enlightenment or a deepening cultural twilight, we cannot fail to be aware of the vast and relatively sudden penetration of the new media into almost every aspect of our lives. Digital literacy, as it is sometimes labelled, is required in most areas of the job market and increasingly informs our non-work transactions and identities. For those of us teaching and researching in the arts and humanities, the audience to whom this book is addressed, these are pertinent if unexpected issues: unexpected

---

1   Paul Duguid, 'Material Matters: The Past and the Futurology of the Book', in Geoffrey Nunberg (ed.), *The Future of the Book* (Berkeley and Los Angeles: University of California Press, 1996), pp. 64–5.

because the traditional focus of our training – in literary and artefactual objects, in language and subjectivity, and in the cultural practices identified with older media – has not prepared us to meet or weigh the consequences of present large-scale technological shift; pertinent because our disciplines are nevertheless undergoing far-reaching change by virtue of the challenges offered to print by electronic text and information technologies. Not the least of such challenges is the newly imposed burden of media consciousness itself: it is really since the coming of the personal computer and the development of a computer culture in the humanities that students of literature have felt the need not only to grapple with an advanced form of technology in order to do our work, but also to comment on the effect it has on how we work, on the materials with which we work, and on the way technology (any technology) participates in creating meaning. Most unexpected of all is the way the materiality of our traditional literary culture (the functions of type, paper, format, book structures, and so on) has come into sharper focus in the new electronic environment; how the 'going' of the book and the 'coming' of the book share a moment in our cultural consciousness.[2]

Currently, the constituencies of print remain diverse and overlapping, while those of the new technologies of electronic media – of the Internet and the various storage and retrieval devices whose interface is the computer screen – are increasingly diverse. These constituencies also overlap, most of all with the diverse and overlapping constituencies of print. In the developed countries of the West, books remain at the centre of efficient education systems at all levels, despite predictions of the early 1990s that the classroom ten years on would be totally electronic. Those who read in one form usually read in another; so the book reader also reads periodicals and newspapers, though there is less evidence that this order of forms can be simply reversed and that those who habitually read news as regularly read books. And if there is evidence that surfing the Web and watching DVDs on computer screen now compete for our leisure time with television, there is less to suggest any accelerated exchange between watching screens of either kind and reading books for pleasure; while most scholars and other professional readers (a large category which includes journalists, lawyers and professional information researchers of various kinds) now work comfortably across print and digital media.

From certain perspectives, electronic communication systems like the Internet extend the possibilities (audio and visual display and diffusion) created by radio, television and the telephone in the course of the twentieth century. Something similar can be said of the electronic research tool in relation to the far older technology of print and the book where, in less than a decade from its wide commercial application, the computer refined the functionality of two of the oldest and most iconic book forms: the encyclopaedia and the dictionary. The family set of encyclopaedias held a privileged place in the Western home in the 1950s and 1960s, a proud sign of investment in knowledge as the future. To

---

2   Duguid, 'Material Matters', pp. 63 and 90 n. 1.

risk a small prediction, it is likely that, in their print forms, both encyclopaedias and dictionaries will largely disappear from everyday use, their search facilities already vastly enhanced and their cross-referencing functions better performed by electronic means. For most of us this will not be a cause for lament, even though both dictionaries and encyclopaedias, like newspapers, have been for centuries fundamental tools of our literacy. If we now return to the comparison with radio and television, we can qualify our sense of their similarity to the newer electronic medium by noting an important discontinuity in its principle of diffusion: computerized material is not really broadcast as their materials are broadcast; it is stored and available at command unless or until it is removed. We can distinguish more precisely among the various forms of telecommunication by noting that the technologies of radio and television share certain characteristics as one-to-many communicators, while the telephone is a one-to-one communicator, and the computer a many-to-many communicator, with some features in common with those multi-authored sets of encyclopaedias, the retrieval capabilities of which the computer releases so powerfully. Computers, much like encyclopaedias, store material which can be selected and interrogated in diverse ways and in personal time by the many and the individual. Computer-stored and -accessed material is there to be selected in a more specialized sense than the television programme chosen simultaneously by millions of viewers. As television is itself increasingly transformed by the newer digital medium, we see how its principle of counter-diffusion works: through gestures towards interactivity, through more, and more narrowly targeted, channels with smaller audiences, through programme viewing in personal time and the use of video and DVD recording and storage devices – all of which break down any simple sense of a broadcast medium. In fact, we might say, television programmes, through the impact of the new media, are becoming in terms of their availability more like the books on our shelves, which we take down and access at will; conversely, digital media combine the high informational tolerance and reader-centred functionality of print with the audiovisual display of television and the exchange capabilities of telephone. All of this enforces our sense that we live in a world of technological hybridity, in which systems of information storage and delivery borrow and reinterpret functions from one medium to another; and as readers, users and viewers we too conduct our lives between media.

At the same time, there is as yet a world of difference between the kinds of preferred use we discover in books and the various electronic media and in the quality of the experiences each provide. We say 'as yet', because there is no profound immutability in this state of affairs, just as there is nothing in our constitution as human beings that ties us inevitably to print and paper. No one is born a reader and, even in the history of reading, books are a relatively recent invention. The centuries during which in the West we bound so much meaning, so much of what constitutes ourselves, between parchment, leather and paper covers, guaranteed the authority of the book and encouraged us to mistake the object as natural, itself rooted in truths about human identity and society. We do this with the technologies of reading and writing because we see them as extensions of our selves; hence such compelling and distorting titles as *The Nature of the Book*.[3] After 500 years of print, we have largely suppressed any awareness of the book as material barrier, interpreting it as the representation of an authentic relationship that we make with meaning. We can see this exemplified in what only appear to be contradictory assertions: like Sartre's fetishistic biblio-form rebirth ('My bones are leather and cardboard, my parchment flesh smells of glue and mildew, and I strut at my ease across a hundredweight or so of paper ... I have at last become a complete man'); and Elaine Scarry's ambivalent, lingering rejection of imaginative literature's dependency upon its carrier. For her 'verbal art ... is almost bereft of any sensuous content. Its visual features consist of monotonous small black marks on a white page ... Its tactile features are limited to the weight of its pages, their smooth surfaces, and their exquisitely thin edges ... these attributes are utterly irrelevant ... to the mental images that a poem or novel seeks to produce.'[4]

Why in the diffusion and exchange of information, knowledge and culture should the transformation or substitution of one reading and writing technology by another matter? In particular, why might the loss of books matter? One answer is that in reading print we have learnt to filter out bibliographic data because, after centuries of acculturation, we take it on trust. From an aesthetically refined *and* from a common sense point of view, print forms (typography, paper, and other aspects of the text's material dress), do not make meanings, and the medium is not the message because, trusting the medium, we fail to see it as artifice. What else explains the loving attention Elaine Scarry pays to the physical features of the book, those exquisitely thin and smooth white pages that she nevertheless insists do not matter? The medium, then, is never truly neutral, which is to say that a text does not grow by a simulation of reality (nor, Sartre-like, is it physically co-extensive with our humanity) but by following the most arbitrary yet strict rules. Among these are the typographic and other visual signals which can change reference by convention, declaring that this is a newspaper and that is a collection of poetry and this other is an academic article. One reason why the earliest electronic texts simply rendered the features of book technology in electronic form is to do with these interrelated issues of trust and seeming neutrality.

Digital texts still largely serve as surrogates for printed texts and are often delivered, for preference, as print. Looked at another way, the technology that delivers the traditional paper book – a technology which encompasses the creative work of the author, the transportation and delivery of the text to the printer/ publisher, the design of the page, and the preparation of the data for transfer to

---

3   Adrian Johns, *The Nature of the Book: Print and Knowledge in the Making* (Chicago: University of Chicago Press, 1998). See also the title of Elizabeth Eisenstein's important book, *The Printing Press as an Agent of Change* (2 vols, Cambridge: Cambridge University Press, 1979).

4   Jean-Paul Sartre, *Words* (*Les Mots*) (1964), translated by Irene Clephane (1964), (Harmondsworth: Penguin Books, 1967), p. 122; Elaine Scarry, *Dreaming by the Book* (Princeton, NJ: Princeton University Press, 2001), p. 5.

film (that is, the entire conception and construction of the book) – is now from start to finish usually electronic – until the last step. The same is true of newspapers. In addition, it is important to recognize that the distinction conventionally observed in certain kinds of scholarly textual enquiry, between the authority and status of manuscript and print, cannot be assimilated in general terms to a distinction between digital and print documents. This is in part because, as an inscription technology, the personal computer functions *between* manuscript and print: by, for instance, providing a writing surface and print output. Until the personal computer, the manuscripts or typescripts that embodied acts of writing were discontinuous with the templates that guaranteed their reproduction as print; a writer's working manuscripts, in particular, as distinct from copies that circulated as manuscript, cut across or marked a break from the regulatory forces of reproduction. No longer. This further act of technological fusion or convergence assimilates the computer to what we know (both acts of writing and reproduction as printing) at the same time as it reshapes our understanding of those familiar and previously distinct technologies in new ways.

A useful way of thinking about the impact of communication technologies (the phrase here encompasses the processes of making, storage and transmission) is to address the thesis that the representational structures of any and all technologies (whether sound recording and reproduction, or cinema, or books, or computers) have implications for the formulation of knowledge and the reformulation of our critical engagements with it; that means of storage and reproduction and modes of understanding are related; that the medium is, after all, the message; and that changes in communication media provide simple clues to more profound changes, which they in turn promote and guarantee. This was Raymond Williams' verdict in 1977, a decade before the effects of computers began to be widely discussed. His contention was that the material conditions of production represented by the 'new technologies of language' developed through the twentieth century will work transformatively on the cultural practices that older technologies made possible; and that, with hindsight, high literature, as a privileged category, may turn out to be a function of print and therefore a phase, albeit a 'major phase', in our cultural history. He wrote:

> The principal changes are the electronic transmission and recording of speech and of writing for speech, and the chemical and electronic composition and transmission of images, in complex relations with speech and with writing for speech, and including images which can themselves be 'written'. None of these means cancels print, or even diminishes its specific importance, but they are not simple additions to it, or mere alternatives. In their complex connections and interrelations they compose a new substantial practice in social language itself, over a range from public address and manifest representation to 'inner speech' and verbal thought. For they are always more than new technologies, in the limited sense. They are *means of production*, developed in direct if complex relations with profoundly changing and extending social and cultural

relationships: changes elsewhere recognizable as deep political and economic transformations.[5]

Williams' point – his argument for the development of social language, and what he calls 'changing practical consciousness',[6] in history – is that our culture, being materially formed, is subject to change through the changing technologies which always constitute its fundamental processes. Textual adjustments in the broadest sense, like the appropriateness of particular literary genres to particular content and frames, are ideologically implicated in the efficiency of particular technologies. Scholars, for example, concede the connection between poetry and orality, that prose is the primary form established with writing, and that the novel developed in the context of a commercializing print culture. In providing new models of textual storage, presentation and exchange, the new media technologies of the computer in turn bring pressure to bear on old assumptions about texts previously taken for granted; in providing the conditions for a new understanding of transmission, they will influence in superficial and profound ways our thinking about the objects we imbue with cultural worth and the ways in which we imagine ourselves in relation to those objects.

Important recent books to engage with the new technologies of text largely take for granted the co-ordinates of Williams' immensely influential cultural materialism. Jay David Bolter and Richard Grusin's *Remediation* and Katherine Hayles' *My Mother Was a Computer* discover, in thinking about media developments, the frameworks in which we might think about ourselves, as twenty-first-century human beings. A shared insight across their writings attaches expository significance to what they see as recurrent practices within new technologies – of repurposing old technologies and the use of feedback loops. Bolter and Grusin label this feature of new media 'remediation'. New media are never totally new: they have antecedents, which they recall or re-present. This dynamic accounts for the complex interactions or filiations between apparently opposed and historically discrete developments which characterize a range of media technologies: a phenomenon that we have already described as reinterpretative. Rather than establishing new aesthetic or cultural criteria by which they will be measured, Bolter and Grusin argue that new media pay homage to, refashion, or 'remediate' older media: photography remediated painting, film remediated stage production and photography, and television remediated film, vaudeville and radio.[7] The term remediation is itself an interesting coinage whose other compelling usage in twenty-first-century North America is in environmental politics, to describe the process of cleaning up toxic waste or recovering brown-field sites. As examples of feedback we might cite the impact on print in the last ten years of the visual

---

5   Williams, *Marxism and Literature*, p. 54.

6   Ibid.

7   Jay David Bolter and Richard Grusin, *Remediation: Understanding New Media* (Cambridge, MA: MIT Press, 1999), pp. 53–62 and passim.

power of the electronic and the digitization of media other than print or the way television replicates the windowed world of the computer. Looking farther back, we might say that remediation has long been part of literary culture's complex ecology or resource efficiency, explaining the emergence, through imitation and experimentation, of new literary genres: for example, romance narrative from epic poetry and the novel from romance.

Katherine Hayles, in her turn, repurposes Bolter and Grusin's 'remediation' as her term 'intermediation' to include systems (language and code, analogue and digital) as well as modes of representation. For her, 'most importantly, "intermediation" also denotes mediating interfaces connecting humans with the intelligent machines that are our collaborators in making, storing and transmitting informational processes and objects'.[8] Hayles' argument, itself positioned intermediately to absorb insights from cultural criticism, on the one hand, and science fiction, on the other, imports from the worlds of fictional and scientific cybernetics the Raymond Williams-like insight, that '"what we make" and "what (we think) we are" coevolve together'.[9] Remediation, intermediation, information theory and modified notions of the human subject as either embedded in or constructed by intelligent information systems are all routes to understanding what Hayles calls the 'computational perspective' on our present reality.[10] Not our only perspective, the computational perspective is, nonetheless, seductive, intimidating and increasingly dominant across whole swathes of the humanities and social sciences (traditionally the home of a far different response). Grusin and Hayles are both professors of English literature; and the present writers share the same disciplinary background.

Hayles' title (*My Mother Was a Computer*) proposes a new natural narrative of our technological origins as human beings, one that challenges our earlier origin in print, as Typographic Man. As long ago as the 1960s, Marshall McLuhan, another English literature professor, offered a series of personal reflections on the effects of different communication media on European culture and human consciousness, under the titles *The Gutenberg Galaxy: The Making of Typographic Man* and *Understanding Media: The Extensions of Man*. Attention-grabbing phrases like the 'global village' and, already referenced above, 'the medium is the message', gave popular currency to his conviction that technologies refashion our identity. From the moment the invention of movable type was attributed to Gutenberg (circa 1450), McLuhan dated various powerful changes in the representation and circulation of knowledge and, in consequence, in our cultural self-awareness. These include: standardization, fixity, a foundation of certainty in which scientific rationalism could flourish, nationalism, loss of individuality, mass production and commodification, a downgrading of non-visual forms, and bad grammar; in short,

---

8   N. Katherine Hayles, *My Mother Was a Computer: Digital Subjects and Literary Texts* (Chicago: University of Chicago Press, 2005), p. 33.

9   Ibid., p. 243.

10   Ibid., p. 3.

an impoverishing unification of the field of knowledge, to be summed up in the phrase 'print culture'. Quirky and quarrelsome, McLuhan was also a man of his time: media savvy and an effective self-promoter. His style is characteristically aphoristic and repetitive; vatic and outrageous.

The damnable history of typographic man, the subject of *The Gutenberg Galaxy*, is presented as a sequence of brief notes assembled to drive home a battery of contentious theses, such as 'Schizophrenia may be a necessary consequence of literacy'; 'Literacy affects the physiology as well as the psychic life of the African'; 'Until now a culture has been a mechanical fate for societies, the automatic interiorization of their own technologies'; 'Typography tended to alter language from a means of perception and exploration to a portable commodity'; 'Nobody ever made a grammatical error in a non-literate society'.[11] Two years later, in *Understanding Media*, McLuhan pinned his hopes on the burgeoning 1960s' counter-culture and the rival technologies of electric communication to restore man literally to his senses. He admired the improvisational and the participatory in the 1960s' art scene, the new folk movement, 'happenings', and the complex punctualities of jazz, finding in their favouring of the auditory and the tactile in experience and the polyphony of speech aspects of traditional culture suppressed by print. In this context he distinguished between 'hot' and 'cool' media: the hot medium (print and film) discourages involvement ('hot media do not leave so much to be filled in or completed by the audience'); the cool medium (telephone, television) invites higher levels of participation.[12] In *The Medium is the Massage: An Inventory of Effects* (1967) he deployed a collage of graphic and typographic devices, akin to those used by Pop Art figures Andy Warhol and Roy Lichtenstein, to simplify and underscore the rebalancing of what he called 'the human sensorium' that the new electric age was bringing in.[13] His message is always startlingly messianic; if language led man into the Fall that was print, it would also lead him out:

> the world of visual perspective is one of unified and homogeneous space. Such a world is alien to the resonating diversity of spoken words. So language was the last art to accept the visual logic of Gutenberg technology, and the first to rebound in the electric age.[14]

---

11   McLuhan, *The Gutenberg Galaxy*, pp. 291–4, where the various theses of the book are helpfully listed.

12   Marshall McLuhan, *Understanding Media: The Extensions of Man* (London: Routledge and Kegan Paul, 1964), pp. 22–3.

13   Marshall McLuhan, *The Medium is the Massage: An Inventory of Effects* (Harmondsworth: Penguin, 1967), p. 125.

14   McLuhan, *The Gutenberg Galaxy*, p. 136.

Our new electric technology … extends our senses and nerves in a global embrace … Today computers hold out the promise of a means of instant translation of any code or language into any other code or language. The computer … in short, promises by technology a Pentecostal condition of universal understanding and unity.[15]

Ours is a brand-new world of allatonceness. 'Time' has ceased, 'space' has vanished. We now live in a *global* village … [McLuhan's ellipsis] a simultaneous happening. We are back in acoustic space. We have begun again to structure the primordial feeling, the tribal emotions from which a few centuries of literacy divorced us.[16]

McLuhan's narrative of technology is just that – a narrative. Like the most satisfying classic narratives, it is chiastic: typographic man, our forefather, was a sensorily deprived conformist, the victim of technology; the new phase in our technological development (a kind of electric orality) will reverse his trajectory, restoring him to pre-technological wholeness. The openly tendentious appeal of this reading rests on powerful urges in all of us: to idealize primitive cultures; to ignore or simplify the non-conformity of human behaviour in history; and to explain the past as obstructive of a better future that the present struggles to release.

Step back less than 200 years from 1960s' North America, to Britain in the politically and technologically turbulent decades 1790 to 1830, and a strikingly similar narrative is being written from the urgent awareness that society, its ranks and mutual relations, its modes of communication, and its fantasies, are being reordered by the printing press, McLuhan's original dark agent; and that something amounting to a revolution in consciousness was taking place. The dazzling rays of light emitted in popular iconography by the simple iron-frame hand-press, and presses which have morphed into gigantic striding figures, champions of the people – both notable images in the radical prints executed by the caricaturist George Cruikshank for William Hone's political satires of 1819–21 – witness to the contemporary conviction that 'the right application of the Printing Press was the remedy'.[17] Working-class autobiographies of the same years, though published much later (*The Life of Thomas Cooper, Written by Himself* (1872), *The Life and Struggles of William Lovett in His Pursuit of Bread, Knowledge, and Freedom* (1876)), attest to the near-religious illumination and magical salvatory powers of print. At this point in history, an explosive growth in the size of the reading nation[18] determined that the alternative to print was not social integration and total communication but disempowerment and dehumanization. Both radical and anti-

---

15 McLuhan, *Understanding Media*, p. 80.
16 McLuhan, *The Medium is the Massage*, p. 63.
17 *The Republican*, 7, 30 May 1823, p. 683.
18 William St Clair, *The Reading Nation in the Romantic Period* (Cambridge: Cambridge University Press, 2004), passim.

radical print propaganda represented print's unassimilated other, non-literate man, as pig-like, part of the 'swinish multitude'.[19] Identifying the nature and outer limits of a democratic press was crucial to the establishment of human inclusion and dignity in Britain in these years.

We can look at these events the other way, of course, McLuhan's way, and conclude that working man's and woman's discovery of themselves in print was simply a brief, bright episode in a larger narrative of loss; that literacy and the press were at one and the same time profoundly implicated in the emergence of working-class consciousness as a potentially revolutionary force *and* in its programmed absorption into a transformed model – which resubmitted, through print, print's initial opposition to the assimilative and conformist powers of the middle class. There is plenty of evidence that by the mid-nineteenth century the once radical goal of universal literacy was the precondition for political stability and conformity, and the surest social cement. Looked at this way, the emergence and appropriation of a popular press in the early decades of the nineteenth century offers the two halves of a narrative of human redemption and loss by interaction with and constitution through the communication technology of print – by finding and losing a voice, a point of view, an identity in print. We can track the theological implications of a thesis that shaped its own communications narrative by taking the second part of the old print narrative (loss) and welding it to the first part of a new narrative (redemption) to explain how we recover ourselves once again in electric technology. Put another way, McLuhan interrupted the old cycle of gain followed by loss, inverting the chiastic narrative written for the old media, in order to celebrate the new media – as a kind of second coming, now immune from historical exigencies.

McLuhan's new world was still analogue, brought into being by electricity and sound, as a simultaneous and universal conversation. To the digital devotees of *Wired*, the magazine and online periodical which began publication in San Francisco in March 1993, McLuhan became a counter-cultural, techno-utopian guru or 'patron saint', as the colophon of early issues proclaimed. For the first generation of literary critics exploring the so-called liberational effect of electronic technology on texts, he reintroduced into debate the lost distinction between rhetorical and written language, and legitimated the critical hype that greeted hypertext in the early 1990s. What neither McLuhan nor his 1990s' followers anticipated was the way in which further, unimagined, developments in electronic technology, like the Google search engine, the brainchild of two college students, would lovingly extend the culture of the book through instant delivery of high-resolution images of the pages of thousands of rare and previously hard-of-access volumes. How do we map this electronic rebasing in print onto McLuhan's narrative of redemption from print? Today the digitization of the world's books, within the last few years

---

19   Coined by Edmund Burke in his tract *Reflections on the Revolution in France* (1790), the phrase was taken up by conservative and radical propagandists in the battle over working-class rights.

a crazy and inconceivable project, represents the real revolution in the humanities, and our typographic origins seem even more secure. Except that we know the outlook can and will change again and in unpredictable ways.

***

On 1 April 1977, the *Guardian* newspaper alerted its readers to a significant event when it issued a seven-page supplement commemorating the tenth anniversary of the independence of the island republic of San Serriffe. In a series of articles, supported by advertisements from major companies Texaco and Kodak, the supplement explored the geography, history, government, cuisine and sport of San Serriffe, an archipelago consisting of two main islands – the more northerly Caissa Superiore (Upper Caisse), round in shape, and the more southerly Caissa Inferiore (Lower Caisse), also round but with a promontory extending southwestwards – with the overall appearance of a semi-colon. It described San Serriffe's leader, General Pica, its capital town of Bodoni, its major port, Port Clarendon, and one of its cultural jewels, the Ampersand String Quartet. In further reports over the years (the islands reappeared in the *Guardian* columns on 1 April 1978, 1980 and 1999), we learnt that San Serriffe has a thriving computer industry, based in Arial. A peculiarity of the islands is that they travel: they were initially sited off Tenerife, but their first properly reported location was in the Indian Ocean, and they are currently floating (according to observations on 1 April 2006) off the South Island of New Zealand. San Serriffe, which might plausibly be twinned with Swift's Laputa, the 'floating island' of *Gulliver's Travels*, has been described as one of the most successful April Fool's Day hoaxes of recent decades.[20] Peter Preston, the *Guardian* editor in April 1977, was inundated with official complaints from travel agencies and airlines claiming disruption to business from customers wishing to book flights and refusing to believe the islands did not exist. Readers who fell for the joke presumably did not realize the islands' origins in printing terminology: that San Serriffe is literally a republic of letters.

The first sanserif types appeared in William Caslon's specimen book of 1816, and they were given the name sanserif by the typefounder Vincent Figgins in his type specimen book of 1832.[21] The term distinguishes the new letter forms from all previous typefaced letters by their absence of serifs, the type representation of the marks which in traditional calligraphy with a quill pen finish off or attach to the tips of vertical strokes. Serifs, which characterize typefaces whatever their design before the early nineteenth century, are usually explained as helping the eye stick to the line and thus making reading easier, the extended tips of letters acting as connectors across letters as well as separating letters more clearly one from

---

20   Information derived from <http://en.wikipedia.org/wiki/San_Serriffe> and <http://www.guardian.co.uk/g2/story/0,3604,308487,00.html> (accessed 21 February 2007).

21   Michael Twyman, *Printing 1770–1970: An Illustrated History of its Development and Uses in England* (London: The British Library, 1998), p. 69.

another. Since they lack connectors, the proper use for sanserif faces was early judged as display work – advertisements, titles, labelling – usually in upper-case type. It was assumed that it would be more comfortable to read continuous text, a novel for example, in a serifed fount, and more eye-arresting to take in a message on a poster or to read tabulated numerals in sanserif. As a clear departure from the norm, sanserif was identified as a new typeface for an emergent and growing area of non-book textual or information transmission.

Sanserif types exploded into prominence in Britain in the early twentieth century, through the alphabets designed by Edward Johnston for the signs and printing used in the London Underground, and the types produced by his more famous pupil Eric Gill for the Monotype Corporation (Gill Sans). In Germany and elsewhere in Central Europe, where typographic innovation was more thoroughly implicated in the modernist struggle for simplicity and urgency in form and communication, sanserif represented 'the modern age of the machine' and, lacking the national connotations of the older German blackletter, 'the world of international exchange'.[22] As the twentieth century wore out, the shift to establish typography within the fields of psychology and cybernetics replaced an earlier emphasis on its craft and artistic origins. Univers and Helvetica, both products of the purism that dominated Swiss type design in the mid-twentieth century, take to extreme the constraint and impersonality in communication demanded by the advocates of sanserif. It was these faces which lent themselves to the shift from metal technology to photocomposition and lithographic printing in the 1970s and 1980s. Becoming staples of everyday printing, they eventually influenced computer-designed letterforms.

Sanserif founts are standard for body-text on screen, especially online, because, it is argued, they present with more clarity in this medium; the same applies to television screens, where serifs flicker. It remains generally the case, however, that what is screen-readable does not make for elegance on paper. Here the revived digitized serif faces of Garamond, Baskerville, Bodoni, and the popular Times Roman work better. That the electronic medium maintains this distinction from print at the level of visual representation, even as it subsumes so many of the processes of print, invites thought: print on screen is, after all, unprinted print; that it should also be unprint-worthy, on grounds of aesthetics and even cognition, is interesting. The only exceptions appear to be works of basic or remedial literacy, where sanserif is often preferred. In the 1980s and 1990s, digital founts exaggerated their sanserif features to declare their computerliness – to create an electronic look. Arial, the sanserif typeface and computer fount packaged with Microsoft Windows since the introduction of Windows 3.1 in 1992, is now among the most widely disseminated faces in the world. Designed in 1982, it combines (critics say that it pirates) features of Helvetica and Univers while inheriting none of their status. Thanks to the tyranny of Microsoft, Arial is ubiquitous on the Internet and

    22   Robin Kinross, *Modern Typography: An Essay in Critical History* (London: Hyphen Press, 1992), p. 92.

as one of two standard founts used for text assembly by non-professionals. Among those who value typographic elegance, however, it is held in low esteem. Other improved computer sanserif founts have followed: Verdana, released in 1996, and also bundled with Microsoft's operating systems; and the majority of the new founts issued with Windows Vista and Office 2007 (Calibri, Candara, Consolas, Corbel). Verdana currently rivals Arial as the preferred Internet fount, with claims made for its improved readability through the incorporation of more 'humanist' features and more space within characters.[23]

McLuhan's prediction of an electric media revolution, which would fragment the collective viewpoint of typographic man in an explosion of audiovisual stimuli, has not worked out, so far, in quite the way he imagined. His reading of changes in mass communication was undoubtedly supported in the 1960s by the impending demise of hot metal; but not only does society remain resolutely typographic, the computer, to date the most powerful of the electric media, is extending the reach of textual communication into areas previously held by non-textual media, for example, radio and telephone. In particular, the system of electronic communication enabled by the Internet makes a claim to be the new republic of letters: a remediated, virtual, international community of writers and readers, separated by geography, religious and political beliefs but sharing a commitment to learning and its pursuit free from interference and indifferent to boundaries. The pattern of private correspondence cementing alliances in the old republic appears to be revived in discussion exchange systems, like Usenet, and in blogs. Now we are all citizens of San Serriffe. But the instant expertise, which is a function of the speed and specificity of Internet searches, is deeply inimical to the élite concept of open-ended, incremental enquiry in which networks of scholars like Pierre Bayle, John Locke and Leibniz operated in the seventeenth century. The paradox within the instant expertise that rapid electronic searching of all kinds promotes is, of course, its suppression of what is special and exclusive in the field of knowledge: we cannot all be expert. In addition, as Gordon Graham shrewdly points out, 'we must be careful not to confuse the power of the Internet as a form of communication with its value as a conveyer of (epistemologically significant) information'. To blur the distinction between the system and the knowledge (worthwhile or otherwise) that it may or may not supply is not unlike mistaking the impression of type (print) for literature; or, as Graham puts it, the Internet is not 'a source of information at all, but only a medium'.[24]

By way of example, we type 'Republic of Letters' into our search engine (Google). We reach 'Common-Place Coffee Shop', an online discussion group.

---

23   Information on computer founts derived from <http://www.microsoft.com/typography/fonts/> and <http://neosmart.net/blog/2006/a-comprehensive-look-at-the-new-microsoft-fonts/>; and Mark Simonson, 'The Scourge of Arial' (February 2001) at <http://www.ms-studio.com/artlces.html> (accessed 21 February 2007).

24   Gordon Graham, *The Internet: A Philosophical Inquiry* (London: Routledge, 1999), pp. 90 and 91.

We are invited to click on 'Coffee House', and 'Coffee House' invites us to move to 'Greasy Spoon'.[25] The links are logical, ruthlessly so, and we do nothing perverse by following them; but the swift descent into a parody of open knowledge is inevitable. There is a pleasing moral shape to the parody – its searches and their results are genuinely demotic. By contrast, the limited hypertextuality of the encyclopaedia in its book form, as well as the more rigorous editorial procedures by convention brought to its assembly, saves us from spectacular nose dives in our search for information in the print medium. Only if we regard regulation and editorial authority as fundamentally inimical to electronic communication will such current problems persist on the Internet. In some quarters they are already being addressed. For instance, TimeSearch, launched in 2007 and described by its designer, Bamber Gascoigne, as 'an early example of the post-Google generation of online search tools', offers fine tuning (in this case within a recognizable disciplinary category of history) without sacrifice of chance discovery.

This is a book, conceived in conversation, written on screen and delivered as paper, which proposes to consider the interpenetration of print and electronic representations of text since the late twentieth century. It is about the potential in and consequences of expressive textual forms, and by extension it is about inceptive forms: why and with what consequences we translate into and out of print. One of the questions it will address, under a variety of heads, is what it may mean to shift the locus of our literate culture from page to screen. What difference does it make to function with and without the old connectors, our familiar cultural serifs in the world of textual representations?

Prophesying the Death of the Book

The challenge posed by electronic technology to the technology of the printed book, which had dominated Western textual practices since the close of the fifteenth century, seemed irresistible in the early 1990s. Divisions quickly opened among scholars, writers, publishers and general readers as they identified themselves as either enthusiasts or mourners. Both camps took it for granted that the shift was monumental, and that the boundaries of what we know and how we possess what we know were changed for ever. Celebrants and critics alike greeted the end of an old order in extravagantly millennial terms. For George Landow, Professor of English at Brown University, '[t]he democratic thrust of information technologies derives from their diffusing information and the power that such diffusion can produce'; and for Richard Lanham, Professor Emeritus of English at UCLA, '[t]he electronic word democratizes the world of arts and letters … value structures, markets ideological as well as financial and theoretical, will be

---

25   This search was performed on 21 February 2007.

reassessed'.[26] Against such exuberance stood George Steiner's nightmare vision that computers contribute to 'the crisis of the word' and the 'nihilistic logic and consequent extremity of the after-Word'; and Sven Birkerts' warning that '[w]here the electronic impulse rules, and where the psyche is conditioned to work with data, the experience of deep time is impossible'.[27] Without 'deep time', Birkerts argued, there could be no wisdom; the pursuit of data leads inexorably to the loss of wisdom. The plangent title of his book, *The Gutenberg Elegies: The Fate of Reading in an Electronic Age*, said it all. What was shared by these early exponents was the sense of the new technology as totally immersive; and, in consequence, also shared was a sense of how utterly transformed the narrative we would need to write to explain our identities within society and culture after the computer.

At the same time, it is fair to say that these opposed critical claims were situated in the previous leanings and preferences of their proponents; that their diverse responses to the new technology were shaped by something more than the technology itself. Landow, a specialist in nineteenth-century literature and an explicator of Thomas Carlyle's apocalyptic fireworks, was already the author of studies of secular prophetic prose and the iconology of human crisis; Steiner, steeped in an Arnoldian intellectual élitism, held mass enlightenment to be a contradiction in terms. Both were trained to anticipate and relish the grand event and to see culture dramatically poised to soar above or plummet headlong into the abyss. Their positions were in consequence morally and politically imbued. More particularly, in their arguments it appeared as if the technology itself would act upon text in certain ways, and that of itself this was good or bad for us; that of itself this would expand or curtail the range of knowledge, pitting the potential access of the many against the profound enrichment of the few. Among the assumptions in play here concerning the power of technology is a simply congruent relationship between a text and its mode of distribution: a suggestion that technologies are meaning constitutive of the texts they deliver. Such ideas, now commonplace, had been gathering force since the 1970s. D.F. McKenzie's Panizzi Lectures of 1985 offered a summative moment in their dissemination. McKenzie, a bibliographer and print historian specializing in the seventeenth century, brought to his discipline a refreshing breadth of vision, derived from diverse sources: from the French-influenced social and cultural History of the Book movement (the *Historie du livre*), from close analysis of actual printing-house practices and from study of the cultural effects of print beyond the Euro-centric notion of the book. His ideas to

---

26   George P. Landow, *Hypertext: The Convergence of Contemporary Critical Theory and Technology* (Baltimore and London: Johns Hopkins University Press, 1992), p. 174; and Richard A. Lanham, *The Electronic Word: Democracy, Technology, and the Arts* (Chicago: University of Chicago Press, 1993), p. 23.

27   George Steiner, *Real Presences: Is There Anything in What We Say?* (London: Faber and Faber, 1989), p. 115; and Sven Birkerts, *The Gutenberg Elegies: The Fate of Reading in an Electronic Age* (New York: Ballantine Books, 1994), p. 76.

date found condensed form in the British Library Panizzi Lectures, under the title 'Bibliography and the Sociology of Texts'.

As McKenzie explained it, we need to move beyond the naïve literary critical or common reader's understanding of a text as solely the product of an authorial intention, and beyond the bibliographer's so-called 'scientific' view that a text is the technical record of its transmission by printers and publishers. What should replace this disciplinary bifurcation was an interconnected field of study in which texts might be discovered as the mediated products of combined economic, social and literary meaning. In coining the phrase the 'sociology of texts', he wished to set textual interpretation within the whole network of production and the diverse specialisms of the many human agents (compositors, pressmen, booksellers or publishers, and not simply authors) who bring them into being. At the same time, he refocused attention away from print to the full range of newer forms challenging the book's status as exclusive or privileged text transmitter:

> I define 'texts' to include verbal, visual, oral, and numeric data, in the form of maps, prints, and music, of archives of recorded sound, of films, of videos, and any computer-stored information, everything in fact from epigraphy to the latest forms of discography. There is no evading the challenge which these new forms have created.[28]

> In the ubiquity and variety of its evidence, bibliography as a sociology of texts has an unrivalled power to resurrect authors in their own time, and their readers at any time. It enables what Michel Foucault called 'an insurrection of subjugated knowledges'. One of its greatest strengths is the access it gives to social motives: by dealing with the facts of transmission and the material evidence of reception, it can make discoveries as distinct from inventing meanings. In focussing on the primary object, the text as a recorded form, it defines our common point of departure for any historical or critical enterprise. ... [it] testifies to the fact that new readers of course make new texts, and that their new meanings are a function of their new forms.[29]

The distillation of McKenzie's thinking at this point, into the phrase 'forms effect meaning',[30] has been almost overwhelming in its persuasive appeal to a generation assailed not merely by shifts in book format – the tumbling of sizes, from quarto to octavo to duodecimo, that the late eighteenth-century print reader witnessed, or the proleptic appeal of paperback design in the twentieth century – but by shifts in text technologies. Unless we are determined to think of texts as no more than their linguistic codes (words, with only an accidental relation to their

---

28   D.F. McKenzie, *Bibliography and the Sociology of Texts* (1986; republished Cambridge: Cambridge University Press, 1999), p. 13.

29   Ibid., p. 29.

30   Ibid., p. 13.

material means of storage and presentation), we will recognize the contribution of formal processes, as determined by technology, to meaning. This will be the case whether by technology we mean the chiselling of shapes into stone, writing on vellum or paper, the impression of inked metal type on paper, or the storing of a string of binary data on hard disk or CD-ROM to be translated at need into a readable display on the computer screen. But are we now in danger of relinquishing too much to our anxieties by supposing that technology therefore determines meaning; that the technology is the text? What do we intend to convey when we say that an electronic text of *Paradise Lost* or *David Copperfield* is meaningfully distinct from its book text? And if it is, how is it? In his work on the texts of Congreve's plays, McKenzie seems to imply that a detail of technology – as small as a shift in typography, for example – is meaningful.[31] At the other extreme, the differences that appear when a literary source is turned into a screenplay adaptation and a film often receive critical praise for their faithfulness to an original print text. But no one is likely to want to make a case for the equivalence of the broad relationships within which the two – changes in typography and changes in medium – function. The difficulty of locating the effect of electronic text, however, was early perceived to lie in the uncertainty of the status of its visual knowledge – of words that strike our senses as images but whose origin or ontology is mathematical and of course electronic. Changes in typography constitute small visual effects, which we may or may not agree are important for meaning; but the transfer of text from page to screen early assumed the shape of a crisis in the world of literary production and meaning.

In prophesying the death of the book, the enthusiasts for the new technology and the elegists of the old recognized an undoubted truth that how we represent to ourselves what we value in art, music and literature is refreshed by and implicated in transformations in methods of production and communication. On one level, the pro- and anti-electronic technologists were rehearsing in terms appropriate to our times the opposed populist and élitist positions which have been central to our understanding of culture since the birth of print: can there be great literature, art or music if it is/is not available to the many? More specifically, the struggle was over the reach of knowledge in an age of information: does electronic storage and retrieval expand that reach or does it rather ensure that what we know remains external, mere information, to be manipulated? For elegists like Steiner and Birkerts, it seemed as if the unfixing of text from its printed fixity would destroy literature's traditionally valued capacity to enter and transform (to unfix) readers. Birkerts argued for a distinction between reading deeply and reading laterally, each the consequence of the spaces in which we encounter texts – inside a book or upon a screen; the shift from inked shapes on paper to electronic impulses on a screen denoting a momentous adjustment of our understanding of what reading is and therefore of who we are. To Birkerts' way of thinking, electronic technology does not liberate text into the reader's domain, as Landow would claim, but represses

---

31   Ibid., p. 21.

this very possibility. His fear was that computer storage would obviate the need to read, and since the subjective self and interior life develop through reading, then the death of reading would herald the death of the self. For Steiner, in a conscious echo of Socrates' lament (as written and preserved by Plato) that writing signalled the death of memory, even the technology of print as a mass medium posed a problem in its discouragement of 'learning by heart'. But this was as nothing in the face of the electronic threat. '[T]he electronic volume and fidelity of the computerized data bank and of processes of automatic retrieval will further weaken the sinews of individual memory.' Now 'the distinction is that between "consumption" and "ingestion". The danger is that the text ... will lose what physics calls its "critical mass", its implosive powers within the echo chambers of the self.'[32] Steiner and Birkerts made their case passionately and extremely; but they were (and are) not alone in recognizing the unavailability of electronic text for contemplation. The claim continues to be made.[33]

This interpretation could not be more wrong, declared the enthusiasts. According to Jay David Bolter, in *Writing Space: The Computer, Hypertext, and the History of Writing*, '[t]oday we are living in the late age of print. The evidence of senescence, if not senility, is all around us ... The printed book ... seems destined to move to the margin of our literate culture.'[34] Bolter, a classicist with a degree in computer science, equated the fixed organization and presentation of the printed book with a whole tradition of assigning authorship, verifying texts and mass production; and he used his understanding of the technologies of writing as stages in history to shed light on the expressive features of electronic technology as he saw it. The dynamic structure of the pre-literate Homeric text and the literary tradition of non-linear (albeit printed) narrative, exemplified in modern times by Sterne's *Tristram Shandy* and Joyce's *Ulysses*, appeared in different ways to strive against and point to the expressive limitations and therefore the historical limits of print. Thus contextualized, the hypertextual or non-linear features of electronic writing (and reading) could plausibly claim to refresh the conventions of both oral and print forms. Like orality, its distant ancestor, electronic writing and reading technologies would resist the multiplied conformity of identical copies that print promotes. Bolter went further: 'More effectively than the codex or the printed book, the computer reflects the mind as a web of verbal and visual elements in a conceptual space.' The diffusion and networked interconnectedness that critics like Steiner and Birkerts feared would imperil the internalization of knowledge became in Bolter's argument the external embodiment of the mind itself 'as a network of signs'. 'When the contemporary technology is electronic, our minds

---

32   Birkerts, *The Gutenberg Elegies*, pp. 87 and 138; Steiner, *Real Presences*, p. 10.

33   For example, in Susan Sontag's posthumously published plea for the moral superiority of the print-based novel over electronic hyperfiction (extracted in the *Guardian*, 17 March 2007, pp. 4–6).

34   Jay David Bolter, *Writing Space: The Computer, Hypertext, and the History of Writing* (Hillsdale, NJ: Erlbaum, 1991), p. 2.

become pulsating networks of ideas.'[35] Hypertext, the cybernetic phenomenon of dynamically linked text, far from disempowering critical functions, promised to simulate more closely the mind's workings and so to intensify them. In such an environment, reading would become a more complex exercise in critical comparison across several spaces and the reader, in consequence, more fully engaged.

Ted Nelson had introduced the term 'hypertext' in 1965 in its first print occurrence 'to mean a body of written or pictorial material interconnected in such a complex way that it could not conveniently be presented or represented on paper'.[36] Bolter, Landow, Lanham, Steiner and Birkerts were all driven by an urgent sense that the computer's capacity for hypertextual connection and composition would enact something momentous in human understanding by displacing the printed page. Their academic slant was reinterpreted at the popular level in books like Nicholas Negroponte's *Being Digital*. Founder of *Wired* magazine and director of the Media Laboratory at the Massachusetts Institute of Technology, Negroponte introduced his bestselling study of the future of communications with a short essay, 'The Paradox of a Book'. It begins with an admission: Negroponte is dyslexic and in consequence he dislikes reading. As a child, he preferred railway timetables to books. As an adult this has stood him in good stead: he knows what most of his fellow Americans might not, the exact geographic source of the bottled Evian water served up at a technology conference he attends in California in the early 1990s. But the real purpose of his 'Evian story', as he calls it, is to illustrate 'the fundamental difference between atoms and bits': how trade has traditionally consisted of atoms exchanged across huge distances, 'slowly, painfully and expensively'; and how even at the moment of writing (the mid-1990s) bits are still distributed and exchanged as atoms. The example he gives is digitally recorded music packaged on plastic CDs, with the attendant costs of transport, storage and distribution. This, he argues, is all about to change, because the shift from atoms to bits is 'irrevocable and unstoppable'.[37] So far so true, we must agree. But what are we to make of the curious preamble to his narrative, which threads together dyslexia, railway timetables and bits, as it rejects reading, literature and atoms? Negroponte's subject is the exponential change that computers (and bits) are making to our lives: 'Computing is not about computers any more. It is about living,' he enthuses.[38] But his medium for explaining this is, after all, the book – atoms not bits. Among his contingent reasons for preferring the book (the scarcity of digital media among the wider public, the primitive computer interface, his repurposing of material from the electronic columns of *Wired*) is a

---

35   Ibid., pp. 207–8.

36   Theodore Holm Nelson, 'Complex Information Processing: A File Structure for the Complex, the Changing and the Indeterminate', *Proceedings of the 20th National Conference of the Association for Computing Machinery* (New York, NY: ACM, 1965), p. 96.

37   Nicholas Negroponte, *Being Digital* (London: Hodder and Stoughton, 1995), p. 4.

38   Ibid., p. 6.

deeper, less fortuitous concern: 'multimedia leaves very little to the imagination'. 'By contrast, the written word sparks images and evokes metaphors that get much of their meaning from the reader's imagination and experiences.'[39] Being digital, in 1995, was best understood by reading books, a technology whose fundamental interactivity would convince us of what it will be like when bits replace books.

In the same years, within and outside the academy, the seductive appeal of the electronic representation of text was strengthened by the enlistment of the computer as an agent of postmodernity or postmodernism, the somewhat confused label which critics and commentators from various perspectives attached to the condition of contemporary life after, roughly, 1970. The postmodern direction in all fields of enquiry was from essentialism to pluralism; from analysis, definition and certainty to ironic juxtaposition and uncertainty; from the mechanical, specialist and restricted to the organic, distributed and interconnected. Postmodernism denies the possibility of a fundamental reason or core of truth existing separately from the contingent strategies for its perception. Its explanations emphasize instability, indeterminacy and the priority of signifier over signified. When it came to literature, the postmodern reader was a participating user. In philosophy, postmodern thinking admitted neither an external, impartial perspective nor a totalizing subjectivity, being as radically removed from the rational meta-narratives and enclosed systems of Enlightenment thought as from the alternative fundamental subjectivities of the Romantic Imagination. Thus cast adrift, there could be no overarching constructions of meaning, only the discomforting knowledge of the coexistence of what can neither be reduced (down) to nor theorized (up) to a unified truth. In literature, the shifting criteria of persuasion, performance and play dominated postmodern writing and reading agendas. In thinking about textual ontology, ideas of origin or source of meaning, as embodied in the concept of a primary witness, gave way to the open-ended, non-prioritized exchanges of the intertextual. Depthlessness was in vogue.[40]

The shift implied a loosening, too, of the moral imperatives of older expert systems of instruction, as the computer-born term 'edutainment' suggested, mimicking the contemporary blurring of a division between high and low culture. Many postmodern thinkers – Lyotard, Baudrillard, Jameson – were fascinated by non-print-based technologies of communication (radio, cinema, television) and new possibilities for knowledge and information production, dissemination and use. On the university campus of the 1980s and 1990s, the computer became the postmodern tool of choice. It suggested the practical modelling of the ideas on textuality of recent gurus – Roland Barthes, Julia Kristeva and Jacques Derrida – for those professors and researchers anxious to deploy their teachings. The contrast proposed by Barthes in *S/Z* between the 'writerly' and 'readerly' text (in which the reader is either the passive consumer of meaning or active

---

39   Ibid., p. 8.
40   See David Harvey, *The Condition of Postmodernity: An Enquiry into the Origins of Cultural Change* (Cambridge, MA, and Oxford: Blackwell, 1990).

collaborator in its creation), his re-expression of the formalist ideal of an open-ended literature, in which texts are woven from other texts, Kristeva's connected coinage of the term 'intertextuality', and Derrida's anti-bibliographic obsession with undoing or deconstructing the marginal details of text, all appeared to point (not in the minds of their begetters, but of their technologically disposed interpreters) to the liberational potential of the computer to release text from its book-bound constraints.

Why debate about the electronic representation of text was engaged so vitally in the 1990s was that electronic text appeared to enact the inclusiveness of text as postmodern theorists defined it. The new *fact* of electronic text became part of the renewed interest in what text is. Coinages like 'textuality', 'textness', 'texture' and 'intertext' offered a comprehensive register whose promiscuous use confirmed our cultural inscription: some would say our relationships were now only textual. For Barthes, the use of 'text' (as opposed to the old-fashioned term 'work') to describe a literary object (a poem, play, novel) signified a redistribution of control from the thing to the activity, from what is displayed ('a piece of merchandise') to a 'methodological field'; and from the author/writer to the reader. For the text as distinct from the work exists in the activity of its reception rather than its production: 'the work is held in the hand, the text is held in language'. 'Text,' Barthes proclaimed, 'is a magnanimous word.' Text is irreducibly plural, suggested in its etymology (from Latin *texere*, 'to weave'), which points to its entwined (textile), or combinatory state. Hence Barthes' distinction that if the 'image' of a work is 'an organism', 'the metaphor of the Text is that of the *network*'.[41] 'Network' is the preferred translation into English of Barthes' term *réseau* (web, tracery), with its natural as well as mechanical application. For Barthes and for Michel Foucault, whose sustained cultural criticism decisively effected the work-to-text shift, 'text' is adversarial, generous, liberal, polysemous and, above all, *situated* – within the complex of cultural practices, among the networks of social power. In part characterized by a disavowal of the authorized and of authority (for Foucault the 'author-function' served as a brake upon the proliferation of meaning[42]), and in part by a delight in the marginal, the subversive and the unestablished, the shift from work to text would be democratic – except that the act of suspending orthodox valuation (implied in uncovering the textual) and unpicking accepted classifications requires a special discrimination that seeks out the unfamiliar within the familiar.

41　Roland Barthes, 'From Work to Text', in *Image-Music-Text*, essays selected and translated by Stephen Heath (London: Fontana, 1977), pp. 155–64; and *Roland Barthes by Roland Barthes*, in Susan Sontag (ed.), *Barthes: Selected Writings* (London: Fontana, 1982), pp. 418–19.

42　Michel Foucault, 'What Is an Author?', in Josué V. Harari (ed.), *Textual Strategies: Perspectives in Post-Structuralist Criticism* (Ithaca, NY: Cornell University Press, 1979), p. 159.

For Kristeva, the 'literary word' is always '*an intersection of textual surfaces*
rather than a *point* (a fixed meaning)'. Within the three coordinates of textual space
– writing subject, addressee and exterior text – where all exists, the 'notion of
intertextuality replaces that of intersubjectivity'.[43] As in the dynamic use of 'text'
by Barthes and Foucault, Kristeva's 'intertext' extended the properties of text to
a range of codes which are social and not necessarily written or printed. What
is woven as text could be material *and* ideological across a wide range, and text
could now refer to many kinds of practices which demonstrate the primary and
secondary features of 'textness'. That is to say, practices which: (1) are considered
the result of what Barthes called 'a combinatory systematic' (the network, the
web); and (2) are amenable to analysis or close reading as though they were a
written record. Obviously, visual, oral and numeric data (film, music, recorded
sound, graphics, photographs) would be included; but also buildings, clothing,
dance, rituals of various kinds – those codes inscribed at a further remove from
the world of writing or print. Even if we choose to limit ourselves to a definition
of text which excludes many of these wider practices, after Barthes, Foucault and
Kristeva, the term carried with it a vast range of unsettling and, most importantly
for our argument, non-bookish meanings. These required that we consider the
unfixity of text, the promiscuity as opposed to integrity of its identity, its mobility
and openness to change across time and place, and its permeability – to other
social structures and other texts. In this climate, collage became a privileged form
of discourse.

    Around 1990 there were those who embraced computerized hypertext with
fervour, reading the signs and tokens of postmodernism's bisected and fractured
pages as evidence of print dissatisfaction and electronic longings: was not electronic
hypertext the ultimate expression of our postmodernity? In fact, the contrary
was true; and the early theories and implementations of digital hypertext relied
heavily on the perverse interpretation of habitual features of print as anticipations
of non-print rather than as what they were: evidence of the visual and material
sophistication of the medium's resources. At the same time, electronic converts
minimized the print reader's historically attested willingness to engage in reading
books as a non-serial procedure. J. Hillis Miller was guilty of pedantic literal-
mindedness in his misunderstanding of Derrida's playful anti-book *Glas* when
he argued that 'a hypertext linked textbase on CD-ROM' would be a 'much more
useful' way of presenting it.[44] Derrida's book-bound anti-bookishness belongs to
a long tradition of bibliographic wit and intentional obscurity that scribes and
printers working with manuscript codex and printed book in the Middle Ages knew
how to manipulate in the service of a polylogically decentred work. That *Glas*
(1974) and the personal computer shared a historical moment is worth attending

---

43   Julia Kristeva, 'Word, Dialogue, and Novel', in Toril Moi (ed.), *The Kristeva
Reader*, trans. Seán Hand et al. (Oxford: Blackwell, 1986), pp. 36–7.

44   J. Hillis Miller, *Illustration: Essays in Art and Culture* (Cambridge, MA: Harvard
University Press, 1992), p. 34.

to, as are Derrida's pronouncements on the end or death of the book; but Derrida's remarks were not the prophetic utterances Landow deciphered when he wrote of electronic hypertext as having

> much in common with some major points of contemporary literary and semiological theory; particularly with Derrida's emphasis on de-centering and with Barthes's conception of the readerly versus the writerly text. In fact, hypertext creates an almost embarrassingly literal embodiment of both concepts, one that in turn raises questions about them and their interesting combination of prescience and historical relations (or embeddedness).[45]

Neither Barthes' distinction between 'work' and 'text' nor Derrida's project to break down the divisions between kinds of writing implied ways of thinking about writing and print awaiting or dependent upon the possibilities of digital technology. The indeterminacy and instability of the perpetual field of production, which both point to as contextualizing all writing, are not brought any nearer, nor are they rendered less problematic, by electronic technology: they are always there, part of the conditions under which writing *is*. To assume otherwise, as many enthusiasts did in the 1990s, was to mistake the theoretical enquiry into the book as a principle and locus of comprehensiveness, and writing as its resistance, for a search for an empirical resolution to this tension.

In his remarkable essay 'Traveling Theory' Edward Said examines the kinds of movement possible when ideas travel between people, situations or periods in history. He asks whether 'by virtue of having moved from one place and time to another an idea or a theory gains or loses in strength, and whether a theory in one historical period and national culture becomes altogether different for another period or situation'. His conclusion is that ideas do lose strength and do transmute across time and space, and that there is a 'discernible and recurrent pattern to the movement itself'.[46] In the theory whose travels exemplify his general principles (he examines class consciousness), he observes a 'degradation', which he defines as a 'lowering of colour' and a 'loss of immediate force' from one situation to another. But he also reaches another, contrary, conclusion, of equal importance: that at the same time as its transposition in time and place imposes a limitation on the theory, the difference implied in the distance traversed also exposes the limits of the theory itself; as Said puts it, distance reveals 'the limits of a theory that begins as a liberating idea but can become a trap of its own'. He uses the insight to point to the importance, therefore, of distinguishing between critical consciousness and theory, where the former is 'a sort of spatial sense' or 'measuring faculty', to be employed in recognizing that 'no system or theory exhausts the situation

---

45   Landow, *Hypertext*, pp. 33–4.
46   Edward W. Said, 'Traveling Theory', in *The World, the Text, and the Critic* (London: Faber and Faber, 1984), p. 226.

out of which it emerges or to which it is transported'.[47] Said's examples show the impoverishment of theory as it travels; and they also illuminate the dangers of a theory (of any theory) over-conscientiously applied to the situation from which it emerges. The danger in computing the postmodern condition as digitally hypertextual is that it too risks such degradation. In this case, the theory has not travelled far enough to invest its uses with critical consciousness; on the contrary, the literalizing reiteration implied in its transfer from one frame of reference to another – from theoretical discourse to demonstrable technological capacity – is perilously parodic.

Nevertheless, and despite the frequent intellectual reductiveness of their application, early hypertext systems were important in testing the usefulness of the computer for something other than statistical analysis or 'scientific' quantification. Defining hypertext as the mechanical extension of the workings of the critical imagination was a way of establishing a connection between literature (and the arts generally) as subject of enquiry and the computer as the means to that end. This of itself was hugely significant; for in shifting the emphasis of computing on the arts campus from number-crunching analysis to cultural synthesis, electronic hypertext represented an important reassessment of the potential relationship between technology and non-scientific disciplines: at the very least, this promised to give arts professors more clout in the pseudo-scientific world of funding and grant applications. Not simply an omnivorous laboratory tube through which data might be fed, the computer, through its hypertextual function, could assume some of the characteristics of an interactive environment, adaptable to the desire of literary critics to explore aesthetic space. Imagined thus, hypertext promised non-prioritizing modelling of materials rather than their fixed and finite arrangement. Since its organization is dependent on electronic links and not sequenced pagination, the electronic hypertext would make available structured collections of textual and non-textual materials in multiple relationships one to another, and with no necessarily determining sequence by which the parts might be related. Sophisticated linking of textual elements and easily manipulable tools for combining other kinds of materials (maps, diagrams, photographs), as well as the extra fluidity and non-integrity of information in the hypertext, would establish a rich environment whose workings would both mimic and heighten the mind's associative grouping of ideas, and therefore the user's sense of connectivity. 'The point is,' as Jerome McGann optimistically summarized it:

> the hypertext, unlike the book, encourages greater decentralization of design. Hypertext provides the means for establishing an indefinite number of 'centers' and for expanding their number as well as altering their relationships. One is

---

47   Ibid., pp. 236; 238; 241–2.

encouraged not so much to find as to make order – and then to make it again and again, as established orderings expose their limits.[48]

The context of McGann's pronouncement is worth attending to, as well as its content. For if by 2001 there was a general sense that any and every electronic textual representation is hypertextual, the passing of postmodern theory around the same time conversely prepared the conditions for a more rigorous understanding of what it means to be digital. As the textual critic Paul Eggert recently put it, '[t]he standard dichotomies that have served so far by way of electronic theory are looking vulnerable now'.[49] Few observers of the new media continue to indulge in liberational euphoria; nor do they ignore or downplay the book's adaptability to discontinuous reading. It was not simply that developers in the early 1990s overestimated the hypertextual functionality of electronic literary packages (though of course they did; and of course our imaginations leapt ahead far faster than the machines and the software could keep pace). Early hypertexts were pedagogic tools (Landow's *Dickens Web* and *In Memoriam Web*), or they were tools for writing and presenting fiction (Eastgate's Storyspace); but they neither were nor are the kinds of critical tools we then imagined might model complex theories of intertextuality. One reason for this is that the immediate future turned out differently from the predictions.

Momentously, and unexpectedly, the World Wide Web made its appearance in the early 1990s as a way of processing and presenting digital information on a huge scale; and its emergence effected a step backwards in terms of hypertextual connectivity. One of Ted Nelson's chief criticisms of the Web is that it is not hypertext, 'it's DECORATED DIRECTORIES! What we have instead is the vacuous victory of typesetters over authors, and the most trivial form of hypertext that could have been imagined.'[50] Many of the early hypertext systems, at this stage local rather than distributed, offered functions far superior to anything the Internet, with its unpredictable remote systems and fragile linking mechanisms, could manage. Unlike the Internet, they were authoring tools, like Hypercard and Guide; importantly, they were simple to use. They only became feasible with the development of features which now we take for granted but which were revolutionary in the late 1980s: the WIMP (Windows, Icons, Menus, Pointing devices) interface. Of course, the fact that a system is simple does not of itself make for well-designed products. This also applies to the Web, which has three equally simple underlying principles: a Protocol (HTTP) that allows the networks

---

48   Jerome J. McGann, *Radiant Textuality: Literature after the World Wide Web* (New York and Basingstoke: Palgrave, 2001), p. 71.

49   Paul Eggert, 'Text-encoding, Theories of the Text, and the "Work-Site"', *Literary and Linguistic Computing*, 20 (2005), p. 427.

50   <http://ted.hyperland.com/buyin.txt> (accessed 29 May 2007). See Nelson's prototype for a different conceptualization of the Web as non-hierarchical and therefore less trivial, at <http://xanadu.com/zigzag/> (accessed 29 May 2007).

to exchange information; an address (URL) that allows the information to be found in the right place; and a language (HTML) for marking up the various features of web documents for display. This apparent simplicity is the reason the Web exploded into activity – anyone could do it. It is also undoubtedly the reason why the Web is loaded with so much worthless information and bad design. As with early hypertext authoring systems, it is difficult to make good websites; but it is the further levelling of effort and the removal of any requirement to model sophisticated linked text that makes it seductively possible for almost everyone to build their own website.

In the face of this lesser challenge, the earlier forms of hypertext have largely disappeared, relegated to some unlit electronic limbo. A good example is *CDWord: The Interactive Bible Library*, a pioneering application developed by Dallas Theological Seminary and issued on CD-ROM in 1989. It incorporated multiple English Bible versions, the Greek New Testament, a full Greek lexicon, full-text Bible dictionaries and commentaries. Readers could link and scroll together windows containing the same sections of text in different versions as well as perform highly complex lexical and annotative searches. Money and expertise were poured into developing *CDWord*, and it has not survived.

> Brilliantly conceived and state-of-the-art when it was released, *CDWord* is a classic example of the pitfalls of the incunabular age. A Windows 2.x application, *CDWord* was barely operable under Windows 3.0 and failed completely with Windows95. Too closely tied to a transitory hardware and operating system environment, the original was obsolete within five years of its introduction.[51]

A similar narrative can be written for the experimental hypertexts (Landow's *Webs*, for example) assembled within Brown University's Intermedia system. There is a forlorn Intermedia web page which currently reads: 'Sadly, after version 4.0, a funding cut and an incompatible update to the Apple operating system forced discontinuation of work on Intermedia. Brown University now uses Storyspace in its place.'[52] Storyspace, a hypertext writing environment developed and marketed by Eastgate Systems Inc., describes its products as 'serious hypertext', with its most highly wrought not available in Web form: Shelley Jackson's electronic fiction *Patchwork Girl*; and 'serious' versions of Landow's *In Memoriam Web* and *Dickens Web*. Eastgate's Hypertext Reading Room offers web-based versions of some products, but emphasizes the limitations of Web delivery in meeting the sophisticated demands of its Storyspace writers and users. Its much-

---

51   'Fiat Lux: The Electronic Word. Scholars' Workstations and Digital Incunabula: the 1980s and 1990s' at <http://www.smu.edu/bridwell/publications/ryriecatalog/xiii_3.htm> (accessed 1 March 2007).

52   See <http://elab.eserver.org/hfl0032.html> (accessed 1 March 2007).

invoked phrase 'serious hypertext', coupled with the unavailability of most of its products for Web delivery, speaks digital volumes.[53]

What the World Wide Web has given is standardization; so it is unlikely that the kind of obsolescence that befell *CDWord* will be a problem in the future. But there is a price to pay for standardization, and that can be innovation: standards cannot exist for what is just beyond the horizon. Much of the excitement generated by early hypertext was bound up with its promise to reconceptualize text. Its failure, we can say, was inevitable to the challenge it proposed. In implementing a more limited notion of hypertext, the World Wide Web has shifted attention from systems that burrow deep into text in this specialist sense and towards huge online collections, like *Early English Books Online* (*EEBO*), Google Book Search and NetLibrary. At their best these provide instant access to high resolution images of every page of thousands upon thousands of books and pamphlets, seamlessly combined with computer-searchable text – a virtual library in which content rather than high functionality is the aim. Currently it is in the more rarefied world of electronic text editing that a critical notion of hypertext persists. In electronic editions texts can be linked to notes, to variants, to other texts, even to graphics or sound or movies, or to themselves. Creating electronic research editions requires planning and considerably more work than scanning or keying a transcription of a printed version and providing some basic links. Hypertext archives like the *Rossetti Hypermedia Archive* and the *William Blake Archive* are annotated online editions of remarkable sophistication, but they are also accurate simulations of print and manuscript documents rather than experiments in cybernetic difference. The distinction is significant: manifesting some version of an editorial theory still entailed to the problems of print and the book rather than premised on literature's antecedent hypertextuality, these archives are not the kinds of burrowing experiments with text that early developers envisaged, if scarcely executed, in the early 1990s.

A second generation of digital scholarship is currently annexing the area of cultural studies developed as the History of the Book as the inevitable extension of their own proper activities. The shift (from hypertext to book) is ironic in its relocation of the earlier liberationist textual thinking in the situated electronic simulation of specific print objects. It seems that our attempts to understand how computers represent texts remain highly dependent on an understanding of how books and other dominant print forms, like newspapers, do so. When we create an electronic text, we are still likely to be determined in our representational choices by the representational filter of print forms – most obviously in the shape of some specific physical instantiation of the text we have in front of us, which functions as the Thing to be represented – the Real Thing – rather than as an alternative representation. You might say that in our relationship with electronic technology we are currently recovering amnesiacs. Our initial euphoria or trauma has yielded to a gradual refamiliarization with what we used

---

53   <http://www.eastgate.com/ReadingRoom.html> (accessed 2 March 2007).

to know, which has brought with it a reappraisal and a new appreciation of its richness. Far from dying, in its old age print is casting a long shadow across the digital generation.

Chapter 2
A Future and a Past for Newsprint

One of the debates of a decade and more ago that now seems less pertinent in its starkly oppositional form is that between the defenders of knowledge and the apostles of information.[1] Perhaps the scale of our dependence on digital technology has blurred the edges of what once appeared distinct categories of understanding – the blandness or pre-givenness of information and the troubling burden of labour or belief that knowledge entails, and the fear that in promulgating the former the computer would banish the latter. Perhaps, too, we have re-evaluated our relationship to the informational genres of print and to print's vehicles. The book is only one among these, just as the genres of high literature, which we too narrowly invoke when we speak of the 'death' of the book, are not the only forms inscribed within its hard or paper covers. As dictionaries and encyclopaedias, travel guides, recipe books and, from the twentieth century, phone books all attest, works of reference or information, in print, have been around a long time. In an important cautionary essay, Geoffrey Nunberg describes how our relationship to information has changed over the centuries and with it the phenomenology of the term 'information' itself. At some point in the early nineteenth century, information sloughed off its abstract connotations of critical engagement and the personal instruction that derives from active reading, to be replaced by a notion of passive consumption, according to which information inheres in content not in its acquisition. Information, Nunberg reminds us, rests on a particular social structure and is expressed in the particular forms that serve that structure. These are (or were until recently) the structure and forms that took root in the Victorian age. Taking his cue from Walter Benjamin, he points to the rise of industrial capitalism and the informational genres of print: timetables, work schedules, card catalogues, the mass newspaper and the modern novel, a form that is either 'parasitic on' or 'in violent reaction against' information. Among the persistent characteristics of informational forms are their uniformity, morselization and detachability, their objectification and their 'exhaustive representation of [their] domain' – all the news (*les informations* in French), the whole of human life, definitions of every

---

1   See the distinction invoked by Roland Barthes when he declares that 'reading is not a parasitical act ... It is a form of work', in *S/Z* (1970), trans. Richard Miller, (New York: Hill and Wang, 1974), p. 10. For a late discussion, see Kieron O'Hara, *Plato and the Internet* (Cambridge: Icon Books Ltd, 2002), an essay that considers how our definitions of knowledge, still largely based in Plato's epistemology, might need to change with the challenges and configurations of the Internet age.

word, and so on.[2] Indicative of information's exhaustive potential is its capacity both to colonize new media and to transfer its strong informational features from one mode to another. The print form of the newspaper, the sound and moving image of television, and now electronic media, in particular the Web, have been in turn 'informationalized'. The difference between print and digital forms lies not in what Barthes and others have distinguished as 'good' from 'bad' use, since mere consumption is powerfully rooted in printed information, but in the value *as* information of what we encounter on the Internet. By giving publicity and permanence to much that is private and ephemeral, the Internet is revising the relationship between information and other more openly subjective and local practices; for example, gossip. At the same time, the online newspaper is currently one of the best assimilated cross-over forms from print to digital. The multiple reading zones of the printed news page, its mix of text and image, its blurring of genres within a strong single format, and the dip and skip mode of reading which it invites, have all found easy accommodation within a variety of electronic forms. In setting a threshold for our digital encounters, the modern newspaper, the most widely disseminated print informational tool, is now implicated in new models of information. Some of these question the objective and collective character of information itself; others, by contrast, impose informational principles upon, or discover the properties of information within, forms which traditionally have resisted such classification.

Newspaper Publishing in the Online World

The desire to receive and share news is part of our social fabric: we all want to know 'what's new?' or 'what's up?' with our friends, families or neighbours, as well as what is happening on a local, national or international scale. As Mitchell Stephens observes, 'the frenzied, obsessive exchange of news is one of the oldest human activities'.[3] News is also information with a time stamp: if it is not new, it is not news but something else. The oldest form of news is oral: word of mouth which, before the advent of electronic media, could be conveyed only as fast as the fastest form of transport. Even before mechanization, this could be fast, and the stuff of legends: Pheidippides' two-day run in 490 BC from Marathon to Sparta (150 miles) to bring news of the Persian attack; the ride of Paul Revere, in the American War of Independence, to alert his compatriots that the British Redcoats were on the march. Jungle drums, smoke signals, yodelling have all been used over time and in different societies to communicate news faster than the human body; in recent ages, better roads, trains and boats have accelerated

---

2   Geoffrey Nunberg, 'Farewell to the Information Age', in Nunberg (ed.), *The Future of the Book*, pp. 103–38.

3   Mitchell Stephens, 'A Short History of News', Center for Media Literacy, <http://www.medialit.org/reading_room/article409.html> (accessed 1 March 2007).

word-of-mouth communication. The complexities of production and delivery processes mean that newspapers cannot, and never could, compete with the speed with which individual items of news can be delivered by direct means. Where newspapers excel is in the comprehensiveness, variety and range of their content, in the expansiveness of their comment on events and current affairs, and in their low cost, convenience and portability. It is now many decades since anyone relied upon newspapers for the football results, but sports pages remain hugely popular in all general daily and weekly newspapers, with football the most popular sport, and readers almost as eager for opinion, comment, nuance, gossip and even bias, as they are for the bare news. Though the advent of the telegraph in the nineteenth century (the first technology to convey news and information across vast distances instantaneously), and of radio and television in the twentieth century, changed news reporting, they have not yet obviated the need for newspapers.

Periodical newsbooks, the ancestor of the modern newspaper, appeared in England in the 1620s, while London newspapers became widely available throughout the country during the course of the eighteenth century. For the last 200 years, newspapers, magazines and journals have been among the most widely and regularly consumed and the most influential print objects. Over this time, newspapers have been the threshold for our adult relationship to print, the basic tool of our literacy that we all aspire to: people who never read anything else will read newspapers. It is estimated that some 500 million newspapers are sold every day worldwide, though their circulation is likely to be much higher than this, with papers passed around within the home, the workplace and other public spaces. In regions where literacy levels are low, the literate will read newspapers aloud to the illiterate. At the same time, printed news has always shared porous boundaries with other, higher literary forms: poetry, fiction and criticism have regularly found a place, and often a first articulation, in the columns of a daily or weekly paper. In the newspaper, and its allied forms the journal and periodical, distinctions between high and low culture that might operate elsewhere have conventionally broken down under the pressure of variety in voice and subject, but also in authority: a common editorial practice dating back to the eighteenth century was the collapse of the writer-reader distinction in letters and opinion pages. Newspapers can thus claim to represent the demotic reach of the printed word: we all read or, perhaps, we must now say we all used to read news.

Over the same 200-year period, the newspaper industry has been at the frontier of technological innovation. It is important to register the interconnectedness of the two phenomena – the mass appeal of newspapers and technical development – because the one fuelled the other. It was the offices of the London *Times*, not of some book-industry entrepreneur (though such existed), that installed in 1814 the first steam-driven press for commercial use. The paper's first leader of 29 November read:

Our Journal of this day presents to the public the practical result of the greatest improvement connected with printing, since the discovery of the art itself. The reader of this paragraph now holds in his hand, one of the many thousand impressions of *The Times* newspaper, which were taken off last night by a mechanical apparatus. A system of machinery almost organic has been devised and arranged, which, while it relieves the human frame of its most laborious efforts in printing, far exceeds all human powers in rapidity and dispatch. That the magnitude of the invention may be justly appreciated by its effects, we shall inform the public, that after the letters are placed by the compositors, and enclosed in what is called the form, little more remains for man to do, than to attend upon, and watch this unconscious agent in its operations. The machine is then merely supplied with paper: itself places the form, inks it, adjusts the paper to the form newly inked, stamps the sheet, and gives it forth to the hands of the attendant, at the same time withdrawing the form for a fresh coat of ink, which again itself distributes, to meet the ensuing sheet now advancing for impression; and the whole of these complicated acts is performed with such a velocity and simultaneousness of movement, that no less than eleven hundred sheets are impressed in one hour.[4]

The book trade, generally untroubled by the need to produce long high-speed print runs, lagged comfortably behind by several decades. By contrast, press production on the *Times* accelerated from 250 to 1,000 perfected sheets an hour. It is difficult to overestimate the consequences of such growth: the high-circulation newspaper and a mass-reading public together represented an explosive information alliance. A repository of current events and organ of opinions, the newspaper's regular punctuation of the working week and its centralizing overview formatted its readership, for good or ill, as a collective consciousness; both were the direct consequence of steam-power.

The last 20 years have seen similar momentous technological and distributive change, and equally momentous shifts in how we relate to news, beginning in the 1980s with the move to an almost totally electronic workflow, in which production processes – from submission of copy, editing and typesetting, to page composition – were streamlined. Though constituting a major high-cost investment, this switch was practically invisible to the readership because the final product was still a printed paper. But electronic production meant that the industry was poised to move relatively rapidly into electronic delivery of various kinds: for example, e-papers are derived from the same files as those for the printed paper. The whole point of a paper, especially a daily, is that it reacts fast to new developments; it stays ahead of the competition or its sales wither. The pursuit of the scoop, the exclusive interview, the fastest breaking news, are all aimed at outwitting rival papers, stimulating the readership and keeping circulation up, generating advertising revenue, and making

---

4   <http://infotrac.galegroup.com/itw/infomark/507/19/35915174w16/purl=rc2_ TTDA_2_mechanical+apparatus__11/29/1814> (accessed 27 May 2008).

money. If one paper implements a new feature, others soon follow. But currently the fear is that the Internet is changing reading and communication habits, and with them newspaper production and consumption, beyond all recognition; to the point where some fear newspapers as printed products may soon be a thing of the past.

In India and China, the world's fastest growing economies, the newspaper market is booming; in South Africa, too.[5] This new popularity is almost certainly owing to increasing literacy rates, as well as increasing democracy and the recent emergence of a free, or less fettered, press. Though some reports suggest the rise in Internet use in China is causing a decline in reading generally, it is not clear if this is yet affecting newspapers.[6] By contrast, the developed world has seen a slow but steady decline in printed newspaper production in the last ten years. Recent decline comes in the wake of an earlier falling off caused by television, which had a profound effect on our print relations in the second half of the twentieth century. A University of Maryland study, reported by Mitchell Stephens, found that, in the United States, 'the share of the adult population that "read a newspaper yesterday" declined from 85 per cent in 1946 to 73 per cent in 1965, and to 55 per cent in 1985'. These numbers had dropped to 39 per cent by 2002, and during the 1991 Gulf War, 'a grand total of 8.9 percent of Americans kept up with the war news primarily through newspapers'.[7]

Declining circulation is not the consequence of a diminished hunger for news but of a rapid increase in the choice of sources; in particular, online sources, and the availability of portable devices, such as mobile phones, to which news can be delivered directly. The driving factor for recent developments is the Internet: the pervasiveness of broadband connections, the increased capacity of processors, and improving quality of screens on desktop and mobile devices mean that the Internet is fast becoming the preferred news and information medium. Some of this news and information is supplied by the traditional public and commercial broadcasting and publishing organizations, which have diversified their operations and established an online presence; but the new technologies have also ushered in a huge increase in alternative providers. There is a predictable demographic division in this narrative of changing access, with younger age groups turning to the Internet for news more regularly than older. A report of June 2006 on Japanese reading habits, for instance, found that 'The Japanese are spending more time

---

5   Sebastian D'Souza, 'Fishing For The News', *Time Magazine*, 19 September 2005, <http://www.time.com/time/magazine/article/0,9171,501050926-1106460,00.html> (accessed 1 March 2007); 'South Africa: Newspapers Booming', *Editor's Weblog*, <http://www.editorsweblog.org/print_newspapers/2006/09/south_africa_newspapers_booming.php#more> (accessed 8 October 2007).

6   'More Chinese Prefer Electronic Reading', *China View*, <http://news.xinhuanet.com/english/2006-05/20/content_4574715.htm> (accessed 8 October 2007).

7   Mitchell Stephens, *A History of News* (New York and Oxford: Oxford University Press, 2007), p. 285.

scanning the Internet than reading newspapers as their way to learn news', and continued:

> The survey also showed that the older a person was, the less time he or she generally spent on the Internet, although Internet use still overwhelmed newspaper reading in all age brackets except for people in their 60s, who spent 58 minutes on newspapers and 50 minutes on the Internet [per day].[8]

These findings seem to be confirmed by our informal survey among British colleagues, which suggested that those over 35 prefer newspapers, television and radio news, while the under 35s on the whole prefer online sources. Among those who prefer broadcast news, a feeling of community remains important:

> One reason for me to prefer listening to the news on the radio or watching it on TV might be a kind of fascination to know that when I listen to a radio program, for example, that at exactly the same time hundreds of thousands of others are listening to exactly the same program. And you just don't get that with a podcast.[9]

The key to the health or otherwise of newspapers is of course economics: they are hugely profitable; many fortunes have been built in newspaper publishing over the last 200 years. They are also hugely expensive enterprises. Indeed, the cost of newsprint is so high that the cover price does not even pay for the paper on which the news is printed. Content, journalism, analysis, comment, and so on, are all funded from advertising revenues; if these revenues decline, savings must be made. Since the mid-1990s and the early days of the Web, most major national newspapers throughout the world have established a serious online presence, delivering a version of the daily paper, together with other enhancements: audio versions, blogs, premium content for subscribers. Initially, such websites acted as little more than trailers for print. The WayBackMachine, the Internet Archive's access point for archived websites,[10] has a version of the *Guardian* newspaper's website from 5 November 1996, referred to as 'a jumping off point for the *Guardian* web projects'. The interface is plain, and the content a greatly curtailed version of the paper. The *Guardian* launched its full news site, *Guardian Unlimited*, three years later, in 1999, by which time it had developed from a print 'taster' into a digital repurposing of the print object: far more extensive than its 1996 e-presence, it incorporated a 'Breaking News' facility, updated throughout the day. By 2003–04, *Guardian Unlimited* was Britain's second most visited news

---

8   'Internet Beats Newspaper as Popular News Source in Japan', *China View*, 29 June 2005, <http://news.xinhuanet.com/english/2005-06/29/content_3153348.htm> (accessed 8 October 2007).

9   Gerhard Brey, personal email communication, 8 February 2007.

10 The Internet Archive, <http://www.archive.org> (accessed 8 October 2007).

site, after the BBC. Its print newspaper, a serious, left-of-centre broadsheet, then had a circulation under 400,000, but *Guardian Unlimited* had 7.5 million unique visitors per month, 2 million of those from overseas; it now reaches 12 million readers each month. *Guardian Unlimited* won the Best Newspaper category in the 2005 and 2006 Webby Awards ('the online Oscars', according to *Time Magazine*), beating the *New York Times*, the *Washington Post*, the *Wall Street Journal* and *Variety*.[11] In June 2006, the *Guardian* became the first British newspaper to adopt a 'web-first' policy, with the news appearing on the Web before it is printed in the newspaper. Other British newspapers soon followed: the *Times* only a week later began to publish foreign news online before in print.

Online sites are highly successful, clearly achieving market penetration and user satisfaction. They are largely free to readers, and these days most do not even require registration. Revenue comes, as it long has with printed news, from advertising (with such massive hit rates, they are hugely attractive display cases), and from charging for premium services like the daily crossword. In the case of *Guardian Unlimited*, readers can also opt, for a modest fee (currently £20 per year), for an ad-free site. The impetus for creating a strong online presence for newspapers is partly visibility and partly falling print sales, especially during the working week. As Emily Bell, editor of *Guardian Unlimited*, pointed out in a 2003 interview:

> there are so many other outlets available that I think if you didn't have a Web site, those readers would go altogether. They would almost forget that you were there, because they've gone from an offline world into an online world – and once people are in the online world, then they lose the habit.[12]

In common with other newspapers, the *Guardian* and its Sunday sibling, the *Observer*, see an upturn in paper sales for weekend editions, when readers have more leisure to peruse comment, analysis, reviews and all the other supplementary materials.

> People have become used to a breaking news environment. There's a certain expectation for news during the day. You want something that moves and breathes and lives. On the weekend you want something more reflective, bigger features. I think that's reflected in big rates in Saturday sales, and a relative decline in Monday-to-Friday sales.[13]

---

11   <www.webbyawards.com/> (accessed 8 October 2007).

12   'The Guardian of the Web', interview with Emily Bell, *Online Journalism Review*, 11 September 2003, <http://www.ojr.org/ojr/business/1063229872.php> (accessed 8 October 2007).

13   Ibid.

How do we classify online versions of newspapers? They share visual features with the printed product – banner and layout – though contrary to print, they all use sanserif typefaces. But they also share visual and structural characteristics with news sites that do not have a print counterpart: BBC, CNN, Fox News, Yahoo News, for example. They are hybrids, clearly related to their parent publications, but because material is not bounded by the confines of the physical page, whether broadsheet or tabloid, stories can be longer; in some cases items are published online when space constraints dictate they do not make it into the print paper. On the other hand, if the information supplied by online news sources may be 'unlimited', only a fraction of it is visible; by contrast, a five-minute scan of the whole edition of the print version can give a good overview of what is available. Once the workflow becomes electronic and text for newspapers is marked up in some form of SGML (originally for print purposes), it can be directed down two different channels with little extra cost in terms of finance or time. The next step is a decoupling of print and online versions: they are clearly related products, share the same copy and similar design, but they are not two manifestations of the same thing. Unlike print, online news can be updated throughout the day; so it begins to be a news site, not a newspaper. Another way to think about the relationship might be to invoke the 'Stop Press' column, once a regular feature of twentieth-century newspapers. 'Stop Press' occupied the small section by convention reserved on the front page of a paper issue for very late or breaking news items. Though now discarded from print, what online papers permit is the burgeoning of 'Stop Press' into a leading characteristic of news delivery and a further refinement of the underlying principle that news is information with a time stamp.

Besides offering an online edition of a newspaper, a large number of titles now also offer 'e-papers', also called 'digital papers' or 'smart editions'. These are surrogate newspapers with all the presentational features of print, but available online for viewing or printing. Full pages are displayed in single- or double-page view, and individual features can be magnified (zoomed) for reading. All the various supplements and magazines are available as with the printed version, and a number of e-tools are provided – searching, bookmarking and 'smart' navigation. This digital paper is (largely) identical to its paper form, costs more for access to the same information and is not updated as regularly as online news; it is difficult to know what to make of e-papers. Do they represent a failure of confidence, a temporary blip in digital progress? They purposefully recouple what online delivery decouples – digital and paper characteristics – and from the technological point of view, they make little sense. But they do make limited economic sense in terms of an overseas market anxious to replicate some of the comforts of paper while avoiding the freightage costs of the real thing. Currently, British daily newspapers cost around three euros throughout Europe, and weekend newspapers up to five euros; but a one-off payment of around 2.50 euros will give 24 hours of electronic access to the last 13 issues of the *Guardian* and the last four issues of the *Observer*. Thus British e-papers are currently targeted at an expatriate rather than a home audience. The *Guardian* group, for example, states:

> Now you can read the *Guardian* and *Observer* anywhere in the world, just as we do in the UK. Page by page. Picture by picture. Exactly as it appears in print.[14]

What the e-paper claims to offer is a newspaper-reading experience as close as possible to that of a print edition from a traditional source; what it does not offer is up-to-the-minute electronic currency, as generally only one edition is available per day.

The difference between an online newspaper and an e-paper seems to be the degree to which the one publication is customized to the latitude of the online environment and the other simulates the print object. The two e-forms represent an uneasy accommodation – to the old technology, to the new and to each other. E-papers are a back-formation, *after* the development of online news sites, and represent, however bizarrely given their electronic delivery, nostalgia for paper and print. David Crow, writing in *The Business*, suggests that 'while newspaper websites are constantly improving, some customers dislike viewing content online and miss the feel and design of the printed product'.[15] With this particular print object, the familiar formula may be as valuable as the content it carries; or, as Harold Evans, a former editor of the *Sunday Times* and the *Times*, pointed out in his 1973 book *Newspaper Design*, 'the design cannot be separated from the product. The format, the typography and the printing are as integral a part of a newspaper as the words.'[16] This is a point worth dwelling on: much of any newspaper's significance or message has long been acknowledged to lie in its form; form has always played a constitutive role in structuring content and guiding the reader's interpretation. We need only think of paper size (tabloid or broadsheet), the ordering and layout of an article on the page, the mix of fount sizes, width of columns, the interposition of photographs in the text block, to realize how rich in connotation such visual signals are – far richer and far louder than the visual signals incorporated in other common print objects, like novels, for instance.[17] To confuse things further, some online newspapers now offer a print version as a kind of cross-over between the two digital formats, giving readers the chance to print off a PDF of a section, with stories updated all day. The *Guardian*, for example, announces the G24 service with the invitation 'Print your own PDF'. There are five PDFs to choose from: Top

---

14   <http://www.guardian.co.uk/digitaledition/subscribe> (accessed 8 October 2007).

15   David Crow, 'Newspapers Look to the Digital Edition in Battle Against Decline', *The Business*, 14 February 2007, <http://www.thebusinessonline.com/Document. aspx?id=C9C1342F-42DA-4D0E-B220-0583C2152C10&doc_page=1> (accessed 1 March 2007).

16   Quoted in 'Introduction', in David McKitterick (ed.), *Do We Want to Keep Our Newspapers?* (London: Office for Humanities Communication, King's College London, 2002), p. 7.

17   For a recent example, see the comments accompanying the *Guardian's* redesign in 2005 in Berliner format, <http://www.guardian.co.uk/theguardian/0,16390,1552451,00. html> (accessed 8 October 2007).

Stories, World, Media, Business and Sport. The *Daily Telegraph*, whose stated aim is the creation of a 'digital universe, without distinction between print, podcast or PDF', produced *TelegraphPM* (described as 'your multimedia afternoon newspaper') in September 2006. It was made available at 4.00pm and updated at 5.30pm, offering the reader a ten-page digest to be downloaded as a PDF, with the encouragement to 'Read it on screen or print it out to read on the way home'. This was discontinued as a daily service in January 2008.[18]

These examples would seem to indicate that, just as early printed books simulated features of manuscript copies, in moving from a print to an online world, we too are reluctant to lose functions familiar to us from the older technology, even though in this case the shift is larger, and the fit between the old and new technologies less evident. News publishers, traditionally in the vanguard of print developments, may be taking advantage of new possibilities, but they are also hedging their bets. This is particularly true when it comes to evaluating the look of a site in relation to its functionality: should online news sites look like websites or like print papers? Which will ultimately have the greater appeal to the customer? How do we assess the intermediate forms, which mimic closely the printed object on screen, in some cases even trying to reproduce the experience of analogue interaction, by offering a 3-D-like appearance of the 'original' with facilities such as page-turning? Anyone using electronic page-turning devices will soon find that they do not perform well in moving from one part of a digital text to another: false imports, intended to make us feel comfortable in the new environment, they actually impede our naturalization within it. By contrast, in the digitization of historic newspapers, a close simulacrum of the printed paper is a huge advantage to a sense of the real value of the object in its social and cultural time.

If in newspaper publishing we are currently witnessing a gradual decoupling of news from paper and print, with along the way hybrid signs of both experiment and formal nostalgia, there is an undeniable significant collateral benefit of electronic technology – aggregation. To achieve economies of scale in the digitization of news, the same underlying software is used to present, in aggregation, all the titles licensed by a single supplier. NewsPaperDirect, a key supplier, has created an integrated solution to the availability of newspapers for worldwide access. The company offers (as of April 2008) 650 newspapers from 77 countries in 37 languages, including many of the world's most-read dailies and weeklies, in the form of e-papers or printed papers through a print-on-demand service and using a browser called PressDisplay. The front page of PressDisplay can be customized in a variety of ways to operate across a number of titles or chosen subsets of titles simultaneously, allowing the user to personalize the view of any particular paper and make comparisons across a range of publications, by title, country, language or author. Several news titles can be cross-searched from one screen, and search

---

18   <http://www.pressgazette.co.uk/story.asp?storyCode=35648&sectioncode=1> and <http://blogs.pressgazette.co.uk/wire/1444> (accessed 14 April 2008).

hits from different titles can be merged and listed together in order of relevance rather than by individual title. The benefit to the reader is in comparative searching of different versions of the same news item. Since searching and the list of hits is usually free, the benefit to the papers themselves or to the aggregators is collateral in as much as it leads people to more purchasable content, the sites making their money through recoupling, that is, print on demand of individual issues. By contrast, one of the disadvantages of many individual online news offerings is the disaggregated or 'silo' approach to information, in which it is possible to burrow deep into one resource but difficult to move across to another and look at the same topic from a different perspective. (But see below the discussion on RSS feeds and personalization of news for further exploration of these issues.)

Over 500 years, the textual desires of literate societies have taken shape as print. We are now transferring what seems to us best about print into the digital realm and the online environment; at the same time we are learning to accommodate to the new things we believe the new technologies do best. There is a persistent view that technology is something that does not work yet: or, put another way, nobody recognizes as technology those devices we take for granted, like books, alphabets, wheels. Current computer and communication technologies offer storage and retrieval, searchability and interconnectedness; but the price we pay is an expensive, cumbersome and unreliable machine interposed between reader/ writer and text. Print offers portability and cheapness, as well as a seemingly 'direct' experience. There are still, and there may always be, some things that paper does best: the access mechanism of the codex book in the hands of an experienced reader, for instance, can offer faster retrieval of known information than a computer. In the case of newspapers, the page is a highly sophisticated and evolved piece of design, offering fitness of purpose as well as ease of use, and supplying its textual contents with rich associations. The screen-page assembled for paper printing does not yet work as well; on the other hand, a great deal of ingenuity and expensive software development have gone some way to produce digital solutions which are surprisingly successful for both current and historic newspapers. Where e-papers score over online papers is in their translation into something just like the day's newspaper; where online papers excel is in their currency. Online news can be updated as the day goes on and as a story breaks; it is interactive: through blogs and comment forms, readers can have their say, and engage in a dialogue with journalists and other readers. The difference in e-papers and online papers actually comes down to how each handles the logical units that make up a complex textual object like a newspaper. These logical units are articles, ads, pictures, and so on, which are mapped onto physical structures such as pages or pixels. When the page is the physical structure, this has a fixity that the pixel lacks, being an electrical phenomenon. In the case of e-papers, the fixed page composition is a delivery decision, not a physical necessity. With online papers, the logical units are delivered in ways that suit the electronic medium, though they may continue to share some design features with their paper or paper-like siblings: type design, banner, and so on. The advantage of the logical unit unbound from a page is that it can be delivered in different ways to different devices (which include paper). The reader can opt to personalize the news and have it delivered to computer screen, mobile phone, MP3 player and other handheld devices. Currently, the disadvantage of the unbound pixellated news unit is the doubtful status of the long-term reliability and preservation of its information, given the frequency with which that information is updated. What, in this new world, is the paper of record? Probably still the printed paper.

***

One type of print newspaper bucking the trend and flourishing over the last ten years is the local free commuter paper. Free dailies overall have seen an astronomic rise in circulation worldwide, increasing 43 per cent to 35 million in 2006. The largest is probably *Metro*, which began in 1995 with a single free paper in Stockholm, Sweden, and which now publishes in 100 cities in 20 countries in Europe, Asia, and North and South America.[19] In Britain, it is the fourth biggest newspaper. The key to the success of free papers is distribution method: they are given out on public transport in major cities and in city centres. Light on editorial content, heavy on entertainment and readers' stories, images and advertising, free papers are resolutely local. Aimed at a younger audience less likely to buy a daily paper, they are designed to be read and discarded during a 20 to 40-minute journey to or from work.[20] Traditional local and regional newspapers are the hardest hit by declining sales: some attribute this to the falling off in classified advertising now that many free websites exist to advertise jobs and sell goods. Interestingly, instead of hastening this decline, the advent of free papers has stimulated a resurgence of some regional titles. The *Manchester Evening News*, for example, chose to hand out papers free in the city centre while still charging for the paper in the suburbs and beyond; a tactic which resulted in a large jump in circulation, and therefore in advertising.[21] However, one commentator has suggested that paper, free or purchased, will in the future only be a lure to get readers to news websites:

> The free copy of the *Manchester Evening News* which was thrust into my hand this week ... contained in the top right-hand corner of the first of its 52 pages a box hinting at the reason for the turning-away from print journalism.

19   'CEO of Global Free-Paper Publisher Metro International Stepping Down', *Editor and Publisher*, 13 February 2007, <http://www.editorandpublisher.com/eandp/departments/business/article_display.jsp?vnu_content_id=1003545051> (accessed 1 March 2007).

20   'A Brief History of Magazine Journalism', University of Westminster, <http://www.westminsterjournalism.co.uk/Print06/freenewspapers/Origins.html> (accessed 8 October 2007).

21   'Price Matters', *Newspaper Innovation* blog, 1 February 2007, <http://www.newspaperinnovation.com/?cat=5> (accessed 8 October 2007).

'Online now:

Police have released CCTV footage of a vicious racist attack on two men in a Wigan takeaway. You can see the shocking film online now and read details on page 6. Also get our daily lunchtime video bulletin straight to your desktop – log on to manchestereveningnews.co.uk'

Perhaps the only future for printed newspapers – all of them given away – is as come-ons to persuade readers to visit a news Web site.[22]

Ten years on, the revolution seems complete: where the *Guardian* announced its 1996 website as a print-taster, the verdict on the print version of the *Manchester Evening News* is that it deputizes for its e-version. Is the free print paper, then, less rooted in print than it seems? In reality, yet another avatar of paper-less news, its materiality is diminished by its successful simulation of various electronic strategies: multiple local mirror sites, reader participation, light editorial control and super-ephemerality.

***

While strategies for decoupling and recoupling content from and to a paper vehicle still shape many of the ways in which we interact with news, there are other areas where the formal properties and the idea of paper have disappeared completely; where news is genuinely paperless. Google News currently aggregates 4,500 news sources of many different kinds in English for searching or browsing, with a front page which can be customized according to interest. Google News is also available in other languages: all the major European languages, Arabic, Hebrew, Chinese, Japanese and Korean. The news in all languages is updated continuously, computer-generated from thousands of sources. Google News groups similar stories together, displaying them according to each reader's personalized interests; links are offered to several versions of every story, permitting choice by topic and version of topic. Articles are selected and ranked by computers which evaluate, among other things, how often and on what sites a story appears online. As a result, Google claims that news stories are sorted without regard to political viewpoint or ideology. If the claim appears disingenuous – there can, after all, be no such thing as a neutral perspective on news; and the choice of sources to search itself determines a viewpoint – Google's declared unbias is particularly ironic in light of the agreement they reached in 2006 to help the communist government in China block access to websites containing politically sensitive content (references to the

---

22   Peter Hinchcliffe, 'The Relentless Decline of Paid-for Newspapers', *OhmyNews*, 17 February 2007, <http://english.ohmynews.com/articleview/article_view.asp?at_code=393125> (accessed 8 October 2007).

Tiananmen Square massacre and criticism of the politburo).[23] Only a year later, Google admitted the alliance had caused the company's reputation damage in the United States and Europe.[24]

Where Google makes a parade of its aggregated non-bias, there are highly influential paperless sites which are openly political and vehemently partisan – where news and opinion are as potent a mix as in any print journal. The Drudge Report began as an email newsletter and has, since its inception in 1994, become one of the most powerful media influences in American politics. The plain and functional website, drudgereport.com, has received an estimated five billion hits in the last twelve months and is regarded by many as the first port of call for breaking news. Matt Drudge and his army of informants trawl television and the Internet for rumours and stories which are posted as headlines on the site. Mostly, these are direct links to traditional news sites, though Drudge sometimes writes the stories himself: in 1998 he was the first to report on the Monica Lewinsky affair, and in 2008 he broke the news that Prince Harry was on the front line with troops in Afghanistan. Many of Drudge's critics, especially those on the left, 'view his reportage as biased towards conservatives, careless, malicious and frequently prone to error'; on the other side, he has been hailed (by Camille Paglia) as 'the kind of bold, entrepreneurial, free-wheeling, information-oriented outsider we need more of in this country [USA]'.[25] Whatever one's view, Drudge's importance in the American news arena is difficult to dispute.

Salon.com is an influential and successful online-only news magazine, describing itself as a 'smart tabloid'. It prides itself on its provision of original, professional-standard media content over the Internet. Started by journalists in San Francisco in 1995, it had its origins in a newspaper strike:

> When the San Francisco *Examiner* was shut for a couple of weeks in 1994 a few
> of its journalists taught themselves HTML and had a go at doing a newspaper
> with new technology. They found the experience liberating, and David Talbot,
> the *Examiner*'s arts editor, subsequently gave up his job and launched the kind
> of online paper he had always wanted to work for.[26]

---

23   Jonathan Watts, 'Backlash as Google Shores up Great Firewall of China', *Guardian Unlimited*, 25 January 2006, <http://www.guardian.co.uk/china/story/0,,1694293,00.html> (accessed 8 October 2007).

24   Jane Martinson, 'China Censorship Damaged Us, Google Founders Admit', *Guardian Unlimited*, 27 January 2007, <http://business.guardian.co.uk/davos2007/story/0,,1999994,00.html> (accessed 8 October 2007).

25   John Naughton, 'Websites that Changed the World', *Observer*, 13 August 2006, <http://observer.guardian.co.uk/review/story/0,,1843263,00.html#article_continue> (accessed 2 March 2008).

26   Ibid.

Salon attracts contributions from a wide range of well-known American writers and journalists, including Garrison Keillor and Arianna Huffington. Its name, borrowing associations from the regulated intellectual and conversational space of French Enlightenment salon society, reflects its policy of linking professional contributors with readers. To this end, Salon has established two extensive discussion board communities, available only to subscribers: Salon Table Talk and The WELL. Since 2005, comments on editorial stories are open to all readers. The publication is strong on news and opinion, and claims to feature:

> some of the most in-depth and hard-hitting political coverage found anywhere, as well as breaking news, investigative journalism and commentary, and interviews with newsmakers, politicians and pundits. The War Room is updated throughout the day with breaking news.[27]

Salon is popular and successful, but without major commercial sponsors it has always had a precarious financial basis.

Salon is a good halfway point between different modes of digital journalism and the aggregation of mainline news, each able to trace a formal connection to news or informed opinion in print, and more idiosyncratic, personal or experimental information sites, such as YouTube and MySpace or blogs, which give public presence to the private and thereby stretch or strain the category of information. There are other halfway sites, with the specific brief of reporting news and opinion outside the mainstream. One such is OhmyNews International.[28] Its tagline, 'All The News That's Fit to Share With You', consciously adapts the masthead logo of the *New York Times* ('All the News That's Fit to Print'). Founded in South Korea in 2000 'after decades of authoritarian rule had left the South Korean media deeply co-opted',[29] and initially available only in Korean, OhmyNews is 'Part blog, part professional news agency' and 'gets up to 70% of its copy from some 38,000 "citizen reporters" ... basically anyone with a story and a laptop to write it on'.[30] An English language version was launched in 2004, and OhmyNews now claims to have, besides its army of Korean reporters, 1,300 citizen reporters in over 100 countries outside Korea. It also has around 20 'featured writers', information professionals and freelancers, contributing quality content on a regular basis. OhmyNews publishes about 150 stories and gets one to one-and-a-half million

---

27   <http://www.salon.com/press/fact/> (accessed 8 October 2007).

28   *OhMyNews International*, <http://english.ohmynews.com> (accessed 8 October 2007).

29   Lev Grossman, 'Power to the People', *Time Magazine*, 17 December 2006, <http://www.time.com/time/magazine/article/0,9171,1570816-11,00.html> (accessed 8 October 2007).

30   Donald MacIntyre, 'The People's News Source', *Time Magazine*, 29 May 2005, <http://www.time.com/time/magazine/article/0,9171,1066945,00.html> (accessed 8 October 2007).

page hits a day. Articles are edited and fact-checked by professionals to filter out inaccuracies and potentially libellous claims. If a contribution is deemed extra-newsworthy, the editors give it a higher billing and a token $20 fee. OhmyNews is now one of Korea's most powerful media outlets, credited with influencing the outcome of the last Korean presidential election.[31]

As a concept, citizen journalism (sometimes also known as participatory journalism, grassroots journalism or public journalism) is difficult to define. The boundary with professional journalism can be fuzzy, but it appears to marry the roles of reader and writer in the news arena. In Korea, citizen journalism is a response to a deeply compromised professional media sector; it works less well where the mainstream product is trusted. Audience participation in mainline news media has, in the analogue world, hitherto been limited by the technology to readers', listeners' or viewers' letters, or radio and television phone-ins. On the Internet, the technical barriers and costs of making available material contributed by the public are slight, and people's desire to participate is considerable; so blogs and reader comment facilities attached to news sites are well used. This is not journalism; but once the boundaries between news and opinion, producer and consumer become less fixed, the parameters of what is and is not journalism change. A general feature of paperless news is the erosion of the paper-based notion of an expert editorial team selecting and directing news and opinion to readerships whose identities are, in some senses, group-constituted by the paper they read. This model now comes under pressure from informed users who interact with sophisticated tools and services provided by news suppliers (which may be online papers or paperless aggregated systems) to generate, and on occasion to respond to and initiate, news as a more personally or locally tailored service. The shift in the newspaper's function is potentially momentous – from mass collective identification to mass individuation – entailing a consequent shift in the status of information.

The Fort Myers News-Press in Florida, owned by Gannett, the world's largest newspaper chain and proprietors of *USA Today*, is experimenting in the redefinition of newspapers in direct response to lost readership and revenue to the Internet. Their solution is radical: 'the chain's papers are redirecting their newsrooms to focus on the Web first, paper second. Papers are slashing national and foreign coverage and beefing up "hyper-local," street-by-street news.'[32] This news is provided by mobile journalists, or mojos, out on the streets every day looking for local stories, backed up by dozens of 'reader experts' who review documents and data on local issues and produce reports. Gannett has coined the term 'crowdsourcing' to describe this kind of outsourced journalism. Fort Myers' initiative is actually a return to an earlier mode of journalism, dying out because it was too labour-intensive and

---

31 Ibid.

32 Frank Ahrens, 'A Newspaper Chain Sees Its Future, And It's Online and Hyper-Local', *Washington Post*, 4 December 2006, <http://www.washingtonpost.com/wp-dyn/content/article/2006/12/03/AR2006120301037.html> (accessed 8 October 2007).

costly; by enlisting amateur, and therefore cheaper, assistance, news publishers are effectively reinstating the local roving reporter.

The greatest costs in running a news source are editorial: serious, in-depth, investigative journalism and professional editing do not come cheap; many publications have been cutting their editorial costs as revenues decline. As Andrew Marr pointed out, in an article in which a number of media professionals gave their views on the future of news, there is a huge increase in the sources of news, but most of the actual information is recycled; there is not much more new reporting:

> Although there's an enormous amount of online news-related material, if you analyse it, very, very little is actually new fact, new information – it's almost all parasitic journalism carried out either by broadcasters or newspapers … what you have not got, obviously, is a new source of original proper journalism, because that costs money and someone has to pay for it.[33]

According to the *Economist*, the decline in 'proper' journalism is a consequence of dwindling newspaper revenues in the face of stiff competition from the newer media. Its current policy is to take a middle view on citizen journalism: it welcomes the opening up of 'the closed world of professional editors and reporters to anyone with a keyboard and an internet connection' and cites a number of cases where bloggers and citizen journalists have called attention to critical issues; but it argues that for 'hard news' reporting, as opposed to comment, their contribution is limited.[34] Citizen journalists are outside the mainstream and often untrained; but sites like OhmyNews have shown that, in combination with professional editors and writers, their contributions can be valuable. Where problems arise is when the use of non-professionals is seen by the paymasters of the mainstream media as a way to save money, or by new entrepreneurs as the way to set up a lucrative business without investing in skill. Robert Niles, editor of *Online Journalism Review*, comments scathingly:

> Perhaps this frenzy to create a 'reporterless' news publication is simply the logical extension of the disdain that many in news management have had for employing actual journalists over past decades. It's the ultimate Wall Street fantasy – a newspaper without reporters.

Niles is not averse to the use of grassroots contribution to news publications; rather, he objects to the lack of any professional journalistic or editorial leadership

---

33 Ian Burrell, 'The Future of Newspapers', *Independent*, 13 November 2006, <http://news.independent.co.uk/media/article1963543.ece> (accessed 8 October 2007).

34 'Who Killed the Newspaper?', Leader, *Economist*, 24 August 2006, <http://www.economist.com/opinion/displaystory.cfm?story_id=7830218> (accessed 8 October 2007).

in such enterprises.[35] Professional journalists themselves are concerned about the incursion of the amateur into their realm, and one can understand why: surgeons would be worried if members of the public with the skill to apply a band-aid or administer an aspirin decided they would like to carry out operations. Just because people can use a keyboard and have an opinion does not give them journalism skills; though when they carry a camera phone and are in the right place at the right time, it can make them news photographers: the terrorist attacks on the London transport system on 7 July 2005 were captured visually by hordes of bystanders on camera phones and used extensively by the media.

In a July 2005 posting on his 'Complete Tosh' blog, Neil McFarlane, head of editorial development at *Guardian Unlimited*, suggested that we stop using the term citizen journalist and instead refer to such contributions as 'citizen *storytelling*'. For McFarlane, the desired aim is not a society with '"citizen journalists" overthrowing the professionals', but an integrated ecology of news reporting in which 'countless individual stories [are] told, and then highlighted when they happen to touch on a matter of mainstream interest'.[36] For Robert Niles, this integrated ecology is actually a benefit for the mainstream, with readers and writers, professional and amateur, joined together in a news enterprise:

> 'Citizen journalism' provides professional reporters the chance to collect many more data points than they can on their own. And 'mainstream media' provide readers an established, popular distribution channel for the information we have and can collect. Not to mention a century of wisdom on sourcing, avoiding libel and narrative storytelling technique.

> And our readers don't care. They just want the most complete, accurate and engaging coverage possible. They don't know how we make the sausage, or even who makes it. They just want to eat.[37]

***

The paperless, unbounded availability of vast and diverse news sources seems like a benefit to a world constantly hungry for news; but how do we cope with the volume? If we have seen everything we can find on a topic, are we well-informed? And how much is everything? One answer to dealing with the flood is personalization: choosing only the sources or parts of sources that seem to match our interests. Either we can choose for ourselves what news we want to

---

35 Robert Niles, 'Fake Grassroots Don't Grow ...', *Online Journalism Review*, 11 January 2007, <http://www.ojr.org/ojr/stories/070112niles/> (accessed 8 October 2007).

36 Neil McFarlane, 'Let's Forget About Citizen Journalism', <http://www.completetosh.com/weblog/2005/07/lets_forget_abo.html> (accessed 8 October 2007).

37 Robert Niles, 'The Silliest, and Most Destructive, Debate in Journalism', <http://www.ojr.org/ojr/stories/070103niles/> (accessed 8 October 2007).

receive from whom, or regularly visited sites might learn our preferences from our behaviour and cater for us up front, much in the way that book sites like Amazon give us recommendations based on our past purchases. If we want to personalize our online news sources, we might set up what are called RSS feeds, permitting the user to collate and access a constantly updating stream of material from a web browser; or we might create a Google personalized page integrating various news feeds with useful tools, including calendars and calculators. RSS is the acronym for 'Really Simple Syndication', and establishing an RSS feed involves downloading a small program to a browser and then choosing the feeds. As described by the *Times*, 'It's like having a very efficient butler who cuts out the headlines of your favourite newspaper and serves them to you on a tray'.[38] This could be the answer to controlling the volume, but what do we gain and what do we lose from this kind of targeted approach? We can receive information that matches our interests closely, but where we gain in precision, we lose in range: the degree of serendipity which may save each of us from tunnel vision. The beauty of a traditional paper newspaper is the opportunity to find out about things we did not know we were interested in. The seemingly random page layout is in fact well composed, with a balance of large and small items, images and advertisements, and the opportunity for 'radial reading', described by Jerome McGann as 'the most advanced, the most difficult, and the most important form of reading because radial reading alone puts one in a position to respond actively to the text's own (often secret) discursive acts'.[39] Lateral reading across, or constantly updated reading within, a space tailored to our individual tastes does not equate to this. And yet the interesting thing is that such reader refinement or second-guessing has long characterized the kind of highly commodified text that newspapers represent in the alliances they forge between disparate items. Throughout modern history, the newspaper one read offered a shorthand expression of one's political colour, social standing and taste. Miscellaneous digests of news and opinion, newspapers have long informed (shaped) our collective and individual consciousnesses. The instant expertise, based on the tactical deployment of the telling allusion, fact or statistic, which in so many areas is a promise of the sophisticated resources of an online world, was always implied in the newspaper's model of knowledge transfer. Similarly, recent developments in e-text distribution, like Google's selling of contextual advertising space wrapped around other people's content, now extended to the marketing and distribution of e-books, is a direct development from newspaper economics. What has changed is the scale and the fine-tuning of the newspaper's functions as its economies and its implied reading culture shift from paper to screen and as its

---

38   'Times Online RSS Feeds', *Times Online*, <http://www.timesonline.co.uk/tol/audio_video/rss/> (accessed 8 October 2007).

39   Jerome J. McGann, *The Textual Condition* (Princeton: Princeton University Press, 1991), p. 122. McGann first used the phrase 'radial reading' in 'Theory of Texts', *London Review of Books*, 18 February 1988, pp. 20–21.

conceptual model sets a standard for the electronic delivery of other textual forms than those associated with the news.

Digitizing Historic Newspapers

Alongside the massive move online of current news publications, various organizations have been digitizing runs of historic papers, right back to the first issue. Some of the same developments – technical advances in processor power, bandwidth and screen quality – are driving both initiatives, and change in this area is rapid. As recently as 2001, a report on historic newspaper digitization commented 'there is still no good, cost effective means of providing the researcher with full text or connecting story lines broken by column and page breaks'.[40] Seven years on, a number of solutions with a range of functionalities exist, and a considerable volume of material has been digitized; but it is still only a tiny proportion of the potential content. Historic newspapers engage a broad audience. No other medium records every aspect of human life over the last 300 years – on a daily basis, earning for newspapers the claim that '[f]or historians of every period since the eighteenth century, they constitute surely the most important single archive'.[41] Yet the information the newspaper contains has always been considered by its creators as essentially ephemeral – important today, discarded tomorrow. This is the paradox of the newspaper or journal: as material form it supplies its content with rich associations; yet it also signals its disposability. So, it is printed with cheapness in mind, rather than survival. Its paper is flimsy, often acid and itself perilously time-stamped, and its opinion and information are immediately consumed. At the same time, the newspaper's structure has become more complex over the centuries in format and layout. As well as news, papers accrued at different stages comments, reviews, advertisements, obituaries, notices, recipes, pictures and increasing numbers of supplements, each with its own internal organization and often its distinct optical as well as literary effectiveness. The most trivial item may encode a history of forgotten opinion: a search in the British Library Newspaper Pilot[42] for the word 'cigarette' provides this appeal (from the *Weekly Dispatch* of 1 July 1917) to the British public to help keep the hospitals at the Front well provided with tobacco, for 'No wounded man ought to ask for a smoke in vain. It is our privilege to keep him supplied.'

Libraries and archives have long recognized the value of newspapers to the historic record; they are collected and stored as part of the legal deposit requirements

---

40   'Project Report: Caribbean Newspaper Imaging Project, Phase II: OCR Gateway to Indexing', University of Florida, <http://web.uflib.ufl.edu/digital/collections/cnip/eng/CNIP2report.htm> (accessed 8 October 2007).

41   Robert Tombs, 'The French Newspaper Collection at the British Library', in McKitterick (ed.), *Do We Want to Keep Our Newspapers?*, p. 59.

42   See the *British Library Newspaper Pilot* at <www.uk.olivesoftware.com>.

in most countries. But what makes historic newspapers a unique resource is what also makes them so difficult to manage: material fragility, size, variety, volume; and, as Ron Zweig argues from his work on the *Palestine Post* (published between 1932 and 1950), the same frailties that suggest digitization as their solution are also obstacles to its success:

> Newsprint ages badly ... during the war years, when there were severe material shortages in the Middle East, supplies came from different sources (possibly India) and were of lower quality. The paper for 1942 and 1943 has a strong pink hue, while the paper for the other years has aged into a yellow of various shades. In other words, the contrast between text and background on the newsprint was constantly changing.[43]

Zweig's project, one of the earliest to tackle a long run of a historic newspaper, treated no more than an 18-year span of one title, and it digitized 30,000 pages. This gives some idea of the potential scale and challenge of newspaper digitization.

Concerned for the preservation of the national record, major libraries – the Library of Congress and the British Library, for example – have been microfilming newspapers for many decades as well as, or instead of, preserving the print objects. However, microfilm is generally recognized to be a better preservation than access tool, especially when most newspapers are minimally indexed. It is possible to recover information from newspapers in collections of clippings on specific topics; agencies provide this service to government, large companies and other organizations. But extracting content from the text of newspapers without presenting all the supporting linguistic and bibliographic or material information around it – adjacent content, details of layout and typographical arrangement – is an impoverishing exercise. Newspapers are multi-voiced organs, and the single voice sounds differently inside and outside its determining context. In historical perspective, this suppressed context represents a lost resource of social, economic, political and cultural information. On the other hand, researching in non-indexed and unwieldy broadsheet-sized bound volumes of crumbling newspapers or in miles of microfilm surrogates requires diligence and dedication; and then discovery is often serendipitous. Furthermore, there is serious mounting concern about even the preservation status of microfilm: some of the earliest, from the 1950s and 1960s, is already relatively degraded.

The fate of historic newspapers became a matter of public debate in 2000 with mounting controversy in Britain and the United States over the de-accessioning by the British Library and the Library of Congress of a number of original newspaper runs, all by that time preserved on microfilm. The main protagonist in the debate was the American novelist, Nicholson Baker, who wrote an impassioned article, 'Deadline: The Author's Desperate Bid to Save America's Past', in the July

---

43   Ronald W. Zweig, 'Lessons from the *Palestine Post* Project', *Literary and Linguistic Computing*, 13 (1998), p. 92.

issue of the *New Yorker*. Baker accused the major public libraries of a massive deception over the state of historic newspaper collections; he challenged the truth of their claims that the print objects were deteriorating so fast as to be almost beyond preservation, arguing that, on the contrary, they were microfilming these collections for cynical reasons: 'Librarians have misled us: for more than fifty years, they have disparaged paper's residual strength, while remaining as "blind as lovers" (as Allen Veaner, former editor of *Microform Review*, once wrote) to the failings and infirmities of film.' It was not the microfilming *per se* that was so objectionable to Baker, but the disposal of the originals.[44]

As Richard Cox pointed out in his critique of Baker's piece, 'there are never any easy answers [in the preservation of information] and, at best, solutions may bring as many additional problems with them as what they are supposedly resolving'. In a subsequent debate in the *Times Literary Supplement*, David Pearson remarked 'critics are happy to ignore the realities of choice over the use of resources which any major library must face'; and he went on to suggest that large-scale digitization programmes might provide the answer.[45] While this would not solve the debate over the value of original objects versus surrogates, the presentation of newspapers in digital form, especially if this is enhanced by indexing (preferably generated automatically), is a great advance on microfilming; good digital archiving could represent not only a long-term preservation solution but an immense advance in making such large corpora accessible to complex searching. On the back of these cultural and political preservation anxieties, a major conference in London in 2001 brought together a group of diverse participants with interests in historic newspapers – academics, archivists, librarians and journalists – to debate the issues, and a volume of essays provided a record of the day.[46]

The critical points from this debate centred on the degree of loss to users when working with a surrogate in place of the original, versus the costs and management issues for librarians in storing and making available the unwieldy original print objects. Microfilm, for example, is described by Schuchard as a 'disabler of scholarship' and prone to 'promote error and oversight';[47] against this, the retention of all newspapers in original form is simply not possible in practice, given finite storage facilities. Digitization, if done well, would seem to offer a useful middle way; in some cases, it promises to afford better access than current

---

44   Nicholson Baker, 'Deadline: The Author's Desperate Bid to Save America's Past', *New Yorker*, 24 July 2000, passim; see also Nicholson Baker, *Double Fold: Libraries and the Assault on Paper* (New York: Random House, 2001).

45   Richard J. Cox, 'The Great Newspaper Caper: Backlash in the Digital Age', *First Monday*, 5(12), 4 December 2000, http://firstmonday.org/htbin/cgiwrap/bin/ojs/index.php/fm/article/view/822/731 (accessed 6 October 2007); David Pearson, Letter, *Times Literary Supplement*, 8 September 2000.

46   McKitterick (ed.), *Do We Want to Keep Our Newspapers?*.

47   Ronald Schuchard, 'Why I Go to Colindale', in McKitterick (ed.), *Do We Want to Keep Our Newspapers?*, p. 54.

paper archiving. For example, not only is it possible to digitize whole runs of a paper, reconstituting gaps from diverse sources, but it is also practicable for a library to gather and reunify in a virtual collection all the editions of a single day's issue. Even major copyright libraries cannot be assumed to have all paper editions of a particular daily number (the British Library keeps only the last edition printed each day).

Who is the digital newspaper's ideal reader? In the provision online of current newspapers, this is an easy question to answer: those who buy newspapers, listen to the radio and watch television; that is, everyone who wants to know what is going on now. As *New York Times* publisher Arthur Sulzberger, Jr. pointed out, 'Newspapers cannot be defined by the second word – paper. They've got to be defined by the first word – news.'[48] Current news is being delivered differently, but it is still news. By contrast, the content of historic newspapers is not news; it is history in the making. Part of the public record of society at any given time, the historic newspaper shared a passing moment with and influenced, often in profound ways, other products whose print trajectory was far different: essays, poems and fiction found a first audience in the newspaper or periodical press before being reprinted in single-author volumes; literary or other print works were reviewed in its pages or merely circulated at the same time. Historians of all kinds – political and social, labour, book and literary historians – are key beneficiaries of newspaper digitization. For them the digitized archive 'makes possible research that was inconceivable in the past':

> Changing patterns of opinion, as reflected in commentaries, editorials, and correspondence, can be traced. Also, newspapers are often the only repository of details of events that are not recorded in other sorts of records. Easy and immediate access to these sorts of information is a boon for any historian.[49]

The first English newspaper with a mass edition was William Cobbett's weekly *Political Register*, with a circulation, from 1816, in its two-penny form of 40,000 or 50,000, and perhaps as high as 70,000. Together with the metropolitan and provincial papers that its success spawned over the next few years, Cobbett's *Register* established an identifying voice, a collective view and a print resource for the radical protest of an emergently literate class, decisively shaping a public appetite for political journalism. In their time, the years when, according to social historian E.P. Thompson, a working class was decisively formed, these papers spread ideas and information to a newly defined readership. By distributing the newspaper's technology of virtual communication to a new section of the public,

48 Quoted by the World Association of Newspapers at <http://www.wan-press.org/article2824.html> (accessed 8 October 2007).
49 Zweig, 'Lessons from the *Palestine Post* Project', p. 94; and see Alison Jones, 'The Many Uses of Newspapers', 2005, <http://dlxs.richmond.edu/d/ddr/proinfo/papers.html> (accessed 8 October 2007).

society reached a new stage in its political empowerment. When we digitize a historic newspaper, we rediscover not of course its living engagement with history in its formative moment (that remains locked in history), but a world of connections and connotations lost or overlooked because they were previously inaccessible. Significantly, too, we remediate the newspaper's texts within a comparably situated modern technology, driven even in its quality-end initiatives by the same commercialized values of popular culture, often chasing the same kinds of advertising association and revenue.

Companies already geared to serving the library and academic markets with full-text content have embraced newspaper digitization as another rich source of material. Other investing organizations have financial return more squarely in mind, while individual newspapers are discovering new markets through digitizing their back copy. When the *Scotsman*'s digital archive went online in 2005, the expectation was that the greater proportion of the audience would be composed of organizations with site licences. In fact, the reverse has been true, with more of the revenue derived from individuals buying daily, weekly or monthly passes. Alistair Brown, the Managing Director of Scotsman.com, commented: 'I had one academic who had been working in the library on some aspect of Scottish history who said that he had got more done in one morning than in the previous ten years.'[50]

If generally there is little evidence of how older newspapers are used by the non-academic library community, there have been at least two useful surveys carried out in Scotland by NEWSPLAN, a UK-based project that seeks to preserve newspapers, national and local, through cataloguing and microfilming. These surveys found that:

> ... half of the users were reading titles less than 100 years old. Of those users who were seeking titles older than a hundred years, the major reasons for using the newspapers were family and local history. Users wanted to look at birth, marriage and death records. Other reasons for using the newspapers included weather reports, shipping records, information on soldiers, school board information, and gaining insight into the Scottish perspective on major historic events.[51]

Burgeoning, e-generated, interest in genealogy and family history makes this a large and lucrative audience. As Ron Zweig found in developing the *Palestine Post* project, the historical perspective offered by the newspaper appears to come free of certain kinds of bias. In a sense it is a rawer kind of history:

> Historical newspapers ... place historical events in the context of other events of the time ... and they offer a narrative that is not mediated by textbooks and

---

50   Quoted on the Olive Software website, <http://www.oliveapa.com/Default/Skins/APADemo/Client.asp?Skin=APADemo&enter=true> (accessed 8 October 2007).

51   Jones, 'The Many Uses of Newspapers', 2005, p. 26.

scholarly writing. The electronic edition makes a primary resource immediately available. … Most importantly of all, despite the fact that most newspapers had an ideological or political orientation, serious newspapers aspired to apparent objectivity.[52]

Among the challenges is how to devise a business model to provide a source of funding for the development and ongoing maintenance and preservation of the digital content and structural forms of historic papers. Different players in the digitization game – in-house newspaper archiving programmes, libraries, third-party companies, academic projects – have come up with very different plans for newspaper archives. One key issue is copyright, and the attendant intellectual property rights, moral rights and other legal issues. Rights in newspapers are highly complex; even in the case of older issues from the eighteenth and nineteenth centuries, there can be legal restrictions on digitization. For instance, rights to such formal or identifying features as trademarks or mastheads can be of very long duration, especially if the company is still in existence. Different methods of digital capture and delivery, different organizational and business models, all suggest there will continue to be little cohesiveness in the online offerings of historic newspapers.

Technical problems remain as considerable as representational choices. The simulation of a broadsheet page on screen in such a way that the user can both see the overall layout of the page and read its fine print is a challenge. Accurate text capture is difficult; though on the positive side, capture of content as image files is now relatively straightforward, with digitization from microfilm fast and cheap and offering relatively good results. It is also possible to create acceptable content files from compromised originals which can then be digitally enhanced for better readability. However, the problems users find in microfilm are likely to be taken across into the digital environment if digitization is done from film rather than paper. Creating searchable content is far more difficult than the capture of acceptable images of the content itself, given the dynamism of the newspaper page: its mixed media format, in which text, images and advertisements are juxtaposed and interspersed to accommodate maximum content in minimum space; and features or stories regularly run across widely separated pages. The complex structure which formally characterizes the design of the newspaper also changes over time and between titles; so no one solution fits all.

Early attempts at optical character recognition (OCR) failed because the quality achieved was too poor for adequate retrieval (and correction was too costly). The reasons are easy to see: OCR engines operated on linear text, not individual content objects, and OCR recognized page structure rather than the complex structures of the discrete items making up the page, with the result that

---

52 Zweig, 'Lessons from the *Palestine Post* Project', p. 94.

words were assigned to the page not the item, making retrieval imprecise.[53] Visual elements, too (pictures and fancy typography), are rarely legible in OCR. Then the large format of most newspapers makes hunting through a whole page for a hit time-consuming and frustrating, and Boolean operators are rendered useless when proximity searching is in relation to page rather than item. Some suppliers have accepted this limitation and offer searching at page level only.[54] Particular problems for OCR from microfilmed content include curved or rotated lines from tight bindings and 'noise' or garbage elements, caused by microfilm deterioration, dirt on the scanner or imperfections in the original – broken lines, scratches from overuse of the microfilm and broken characters. Manual indexing and re-keying offer more accurate results than conventional OCR, but with the volume involved they are too costly. Given the reservations of some scholarly users over the quality of microfilm, scanning from originals rather than microfilm would seem to be a better choice, but again costs of scanning from large-format originals are too high to make this affordable for most organizations, especially if colour is needed. Colour scanning of large originals entails the added difficulty of unmanageable file sizes.

Further problems attend the decision to scan and present multiple daily editions of a paper. Multiple issue is a characteristic feature of newspapers for which the kinds of solutions encountered in editing book texts are unlikely to offer any useful models. A scholarly audience may want to see all the available editions of a title; a broader audience may be satisfied with only one edition. But most projects will probably appeal to a variety of audiences; so the question has to be resolved. The Nineteenth Century Serials Edition (NCSE) project, based at Birkbeck College and King's College, London, is one of the few initiatives currently tackling the representation of multiple contemporary editions. NCSE has created a full-text digital edition of 100,000 pages of content from six diverse nineteenth-century serials to be made freely available via the Web. Aimed chiefly at an academic audience, the titles chosen represent individually significant but under-researched publications, which together suggest something of the huge diversity of the nineteenth-century reformist periodical press: the *Monthly Repository* (1806–38); *Northern Star* (1837–52); *Leader* (1850–60); *English Woman's Journal* (1858–64); *Tomahawk* (1867–70); and *Publishers' Circular* (1880–90). Recovering multiple editions has been challenging as the British Library, source of most of the material, generally filmed only one edition of any periodical.[55] By tracking down

---

53   The Hawaiian Languages Newspapers project, begun in 1997, for example, mostly presents only page images, as the originals are in too poor a state for OCR to be successful, <http://libweb.hawaii.edu/digicoll/newspapers.htm> (accessed 8 October 2007).

54   See, for instance, Cold North Wind and NewspaperARCHIVE.com, which have some tens of millions of pages online between them, and offer searching by page without segmentation into separate items, <www.coldnorthwind.com> and <http://newspaperarchive.com/> (accessed 8 October 2007).

55   Nineteenth Century Serials Edition (NCSE), <http://www.ncse.kcl.ac.uk/> (accessed 13 March 2007).

multiple editions and by publishing this diverse group as an aggregated critical resource, the NCSE electronic newspaper edition derives its principles from those that governed in the production of the originals: that is, it simulates as far as it can periodical form, instability and diversity, and it foregrounds generic features in the reproduction of content.

NCSE proposes one solution to a fundamental technical issue to which different electronic archives offer different solutions: whether to present stand-alone or fully contextualized news content. Many digitization projects assume the vital significance of the whole visual field of the page and so retain its formal features through the use of facsimile images. By divorcing content from context, you rob the material of some of the meaning it derives from its formal appearance (alongside other, different or similar content); against that, visual surrogates of complex broadsheet pages challenge the computer screen. Most online delivery of current newspapers resolves this challenge by linking full page images to searchable text. There is no reason why this cannot be regularly extended to historic papers, though in practice it is not. Accessible Archives, Inc., for example, prides itself on high quality transcription of key articles from a number of early American periodicals 'assembled into databases with a strict attention to detail allowing access to specific information with pinpoint accuracy'.[56] While accuracy is to be welcomed, there is a loss in stripping away material features (typography, layout, position) which conventionally carry considerable coded significance. For some purposes even corrupt online texts are of real use. Early sites like the Internet Library of Early Journals (ILEJ) in Britain (completed in 1999 and consisting of a core set of texts from three eighteenth- and three nineteenth-century periodicals) kept costs down by offering huge tracts of uncorrected OCR text linked to images.[57]

Major national newspapers and periodicals in Europe and America are digitizing their own back archives and creating cohesive systems within which users can search from the earliest to the most recent issue; others are separating recent online material from the archived issues digitized from paper copies. National libraries have also been driving forward programmes with a strong emphasis on local and regional, daily and weekly, general and specialist papers, as well as on the national papers of record. The British Library carried out a highly successful pilot digitization of historic newspapers[58] in 2000–01, and has since been awarded two major grants, for British Newspapers 1800–1900 and British Newspapers 1620–1900. Together these projects will make available four million pages of

---

56   Accessible Archives, Inc., <http://www.accessible.com/aboutus.htm> (accessed 8 October 2007).

57   Internet Library of Early Journals: A Digital Library of 18th and 19th Century Journals, <http://www.bodley.ox.ac.uk/ilej/> (accessed 8 October 2007).

58   *British Library Newspaper Pilot*, <www.uk.olivesoftware.com> (accessed 8 October 2007).

important national, regional and local British papers.[59] In America, the National Digital Newspaper Program (NDNP) has embarked on the large-scale digitization of historically significant newspapers published between 1836 and 1922 to be housed at the Library of Congress and made freely available via the Internet.[60] Alison Jones gives an excellent overview of many more national newspaper projects throughout the world.[61] For the academic and educational markets, ProQuest Historical Newspapers offers full-text and full-image articles for major national, mostly North American, newspapers dating back to the eighteenth century. To give an example of the scale of such projects, migrating the *New York Times* alone involved scanning, digitizing, zoning and editing over 3,400,000 pages from microfilm into digital files.[62] The British company Thompson Gale has digitized and made searchable the *Times* of London, presenting every complete page of every issue of the newspaper from 1785 to 1985,[63] and the *Guardian* launched the first tranche of its digital archive in November 2007, covering the period 1821–1990 for the *Guardian*, and 1791–1990 for its Sunday sibling, the *Observer*, with the remaining materials to follow shortly.[64] In view of costs, it is understandable that many large-scale initiatives will concentrate on major national papers; but there is a danger that smaller titles will be neglected and our perception of the reach of a demotic print culture accordingly skewed. Some projects are trying to rectify this: for instance, as part of its *Nineteenth Century in Print* initiative, the Library of Congress, in partnership with Michigan and Cornell Universities, has digitized 23 smaller North American magazines and journals, with an emphasis on those intended for a general audience; currently around 750,000 pages are available.[65]

The large-scale digitization of historic newspapers and periodicals is bringing many millions of pages of lost content within the reach of scholars, students and the general public. Only electronic technology, with its massive storage, retrieval and search functions, countering the sheer drudgery and difficulty of access to complete runs of degrading newsprint, makes research into the periodical press a serious possibility for more than a few. This of itself has the potential to transform our engagement with the print forms and communities of the past as it makes

---

59   *British Library Newspapers*, <http://www.bl.uk/collections/newspapers.html> (accessed 8 October 2007).

60   *National Digital Newspaper Program*, <http://www.loc.gov/ndnp/> (accessed 8 October 2007).

61   Jones, 'The Many Uses of Newspapers', 2005.

62   Proquest Historical Newspapers, <http://il.proquest.com/products_pq/descriptions/pq-hist-news.shtml> (accessed 8 October 2007).

63   The *Times* Digital Archive, <http://www.gale.com/servlet/ItemDetailServlet?region=9&imprint=000&titleCode=GALEN4&type=4&id=171940> (accessed 8 October 2007).

64   The *Guardian* and *Observer* Digital Archive, <http://archive.guardian.co.uk> (accessed 8 May 2008).

65   *The Nineteenth Century in Print*, Library of Congress, <http://memory.loc.gov/ammem/ndlpcoop/moahtml/snchome.html> (accessed 2 March 2007).

visible the significance of a dimension of the medium which, though known and recognized, by its scale and ephemeral identity has so far defeated extensive investigation. Renewed digital access cannot fail to make an impact on the kinds of scholarship academics undertake and to effect a reassessment of literary to other relations within our print culture. In Victorian Studies, for example, the shift is already apparent as online resources bolster fashionable cross-disciplinary research linking the arts with politics, journalism, science and technology, law and medicine, making it ever more easy to traverse print classifications by instantaneous searching of materials of whose existence, in any substantial sense, one may have almost no knowledge. There is already a considerable volume of material available, with the promise of much more to come. But there are problems in current provision which may not be addressed by increasing this volume further.

One of the benefits of online access is the ability to cross-search many different resources and organize the hits logically. In some contemporary newspaper systems and online news sources, this gives new perspectives on current events. With NewsPaperDirect, for example, it is possible to cross-search hundreds of current newspapers from all over the world instantly, and have the searches listed together. To retrieve an article which has been archived (anything earlier than the current day is archived), there is sometimes a fee to pay, but the hits are displayed with a paragraph of context free. In the case of digital historic newspapers, however, things are more complex. Libraries and archives like the British Library or the Library of Congress offer full text access to content free; newspapers themselves generally offer free historic archive searching, but paid retrieval of content; content aggregators and commercial companies require registration and payment of some kind, by subscription, licence or one-off fees. These various limitations can be explained by the different goals and strategies of the providers of digitized historic newspapers, many of which do not prioritize scholarly use. Currently, therefore, it is easy to study a particular historic newspaper or periodical diachronically, but synchronic access to a wide range of titles for one particular date or topic is impossible, and tracking information down can be time-consuming and costly. At the same time, the expanding provision of content for search and retrieval is itself likely to become a problem for the user who must sift through the ever expanding results of hits. This is a challenge in any large information space, and of course it is vital on the Web. Research into information retrieval has resulted in the development of tools for sorting large volumes of unstructured information, such as keyword extraction, automatic summarization and automatic classification; but with few exceptions developers of newspaper systems have yet to implement such tools. NCSE is one of the handful of academic projects currently pursuing this research solution.

In the new digital data stream, previously distinct spheres of print converge: on screen, despite sophisticated visualization tools, many of the physical features of the varieties of print are levelled. Cultural studies, in particular in its material guise, might be invoked here and the computer seen as the agent of its agenda to collapse high and low, or élite and popular, culture: legitimately, we might argue, since we all inhabit both spheres, however we decide to separate their effects for certain purposes. But looked at another way, it appears that digitization is offering a limited range of futures for a vast range of print objects. It is often difficult, where technology habitually masquerades as worth, to hold apart two different kinds of e-resource: on the one side, the resource which provides bodies of text that defy reprinting in conventional paper form or whose enhanced functionality in the electronic environment is widely appreciated; on the other, the resource in which technological capacity overrides its generally perceived use value. Historic newspaper collections and dictionaries undoubtedly fall into the first group, many digitized books fall into the second, while current newspapers hover somewhere in between. In the case of historic newspapers, digitization is set to recover a more resonant textual legacy, distinct from or interacting more powerfully than ever before with the products of high culture, to be mined by researchers into our past. Historic newspapers, as content and as form, are made newly visible through electronic preservation and access. Furthermore, aggregation, a principle and method that impels so much in the electronic environment, also defines the newspaper from its origins: the sheer importance to its identity (as distinct from the products of high culture) that it be seen and read in its complex alliance of textual, contextual and material connections. In an important sense, what these connections foreground in both the electronic world and the world of newsprint is the connectedness of the disparate and the unexpected. Conversely, the fragmented nature of online reading and its compelling features of disaggregation – in respect of searching and the arbitrary appearance of electronic hits – finds its historic counterpart in another feature of the newspaper: its assemblage of short text units and their invitation to short attention span.[66] At the same time, there can be no total reconnection online with the news products of the past: facsimile images may restore to wider circulation some aspects of the look of a historic newspaper, but not its smell, nor the physical challenge of its size, nor our strategies of folding and segmenting the paper for ease of reading; and certainly not the experience of newsprint on skin. Some might argue that what rubbed off physically was a vital component of the form, part of its engagement with the everyday world. What rubs off now may be the powerful appeal of chance association – the topical, immediate and disposable item. As Patrick Leary has argued: 'Fortuitous electronic connections, and the information that circulates through them, are emerging as hallmarks of humanities scholarship in the digital age.'[67] We already take for granted, thanks to search engines like Google and Yahoo, the informational assembly and function of a vast range of materials. In the online world, the preferred model for our old and new encounters with text may be the newspaper.

---

66   Compare the argument offered in Patrick Leary, 'Googling the Victorians', *Journal of Victorian Culture*, 10 (1) (Spring 2005), pp. 72–86.

67   Ibid., p. 73.

Chapter 3
The Cultural Work of Editing

Books, Texts and Work-sites

In 1959, Bruce Harkness published an important article in the major journal for textual bibliography, in which he argued the existence of what he called 'the novelistic fallacy': the fallacy being that to critics and students, dedicated to the close reading of literary works, the source of the text of a novel does not matter. Unlike play or poem, for which a well-edited and well-printed text were by then held to be the standard starting point for critical investigation, the cheap reprint of an error-strewn novel text was still widely considered good enough for all specialist purposes. According to Harkness, 'People … commit bibliographical nonsense when handed a novel.' But as he also conceded, '[a] false word in a sonnet may change a fifth of its meaning; the punctuation at the end of the "Ode on a Grecian Urn" can be considered crucial to the meaning of the whole poem; but who … can stand the prospect of collating 700 pages of Dickens to find a few dozen misplaced commas?'[1] Summarized thus, the essay's vigorous counter-argument for the importance of inspecting the print history of the texts of novels strikes an implausible note, even in the ears of the committed textual critic, its assumed reader. If by any remote possibility a general reader had found her way to the article, this passing rhetorical flourish might seem the only piece of common sense in an otherwise bewildering thesis: who, after all, cares about 'a few dozen misplaced commas'? What does it mean to say that the literature we buy, borrow and read might be in need of correction? Are we wrong to take texts on trust?

Fifty years on much has changed. Within a few years of Harkness' call for a critical revaluation of the novel (which is what his plea for accurate texts amounted to), the inauguration in 1962–63 of the Center for Editions of American Authors (CEAA; in 1976 restyled the Committee on Scholarly Editions, CSE) enshrined rigorous procedures for the editing of nineteenth-century American fiction – at this point, according to eclectic and idealist principles.[2] About the same time in Britain, Kathleen Tillotson's 1966 Oxford University Press Clarendon edition of *Oliver Twist* launched the first full critical edition of any major English novelist since R.W. Chapman's *Novels of Jane Austen* in 1923. Refining upon the principles and

---

1   Bruce Harkness, 'Bibliography and the Novelistic Fallacy', *Studies in Bibliography*, 12 (1959), pp. 60, 64.

2   The current version of the MLA CSE-approved guidelines includes advice for editing in the electronic medium and are online at <http://www.mla.org/cse_guidelines> (accessed 20 July 2007).

practice of twentieth-century textual critics like R.B. McKerrow and W.W. Greg in Britain, and Greg's disciple Fredson Bowers in the United States, such editions were designed to produce reading texts whose features were the fulfilment, as their editors argued, of authorial intention, previously betrayed by production processes and failures of transmission, and now at last deduced by expert collation of and selection from authorially sanctioned variants from as many different states of the text as their history, complex or simple, dictated. Bowers' own edition of *The Works of Stephen Crane*, completed in ten volumes between 1969 and 1975, is an excellent witness to the painstaking nature of such editorial labour. Despite local differences of approach, scholarly editors on either side of the Atlantic were united at this time in believing it might be possible to make definitive editions, accessible to specialist, student and general reader, and of such an accuracy and comprehensiveness as never to need editing again.

The faith of such later twentieth-century practitioners lay in what we might call ideal stasis: the establishment, through emendation and the eclectic compression of a range of textual states, of as stable a textual form as the inevitably corrosive laws of history and the material limits of the book form would allow. Tillotson, for example, held as a guiding principle in her work on Dickens the re-instatement of the early periodical versions of his novels, which had been subsequently heavily cropped and forfeited to the tighter demands of volume production. In these years, the CEAA guidelines for editing required a full register of variants to be presented in tabular form as a back-of-book apparatus so that the reader might reconstruct the complete textual history of a literary work and, if she wished, weigh or question at every point the reading chosen by the editor from multiple variant texts to best represent that work. In Britain, a similar concern for accessible evidentiary detail resulted in rich foot-of-page displays of variant readings. The complexity of such apparatus and procedures, already extended to the presentation of poetry and play texts, substantiated in some profound if ultimately unclear way the cultural value of the object in hand, usually a canonical literary work issued by a major academic press.

The preparation of scholarly editions of major literary works based on theories and methods derived from textual criticism has long been one of the most recondite and resonant activities in our cultural engagement with texts. Recondite, because few, even among professional academics, choose to assemble scholarly editions, and those few have over centuries invested their activity with intimidating discourses and explanations; resonant, because such editions nevertheless hold privileged status, among the slightly larger few who read and engage critically with them, and, to surprising extent, among the many who do not. Scholarly editions are iconic: that is, they function as surrogates for or representations of the works that define our heritage – the plays of Shakespeare, the poems of Milton, Wordsworth or Shelley, the novels of Charlotte Brontë or Henry James. Scholarly editions have been presented to us as those works at their most richly expressive; and we have largely assented to their claims. Hence statements of extravagant attachment to particular textual icons: like the poet Rupert Brooke's assertion in

1913 that 'the Clarendon Press books will be the only thing our evil generation may show to the cursory eyes of posterity, to prove it was not wholly bad'; or, more mundanely, the Brontë Society's endorsement of the Clarendon edition of *Wuthering Heights* as 'probably the nearest we shall ever get to what Emily Brontë had in mind'; or the description of the ongoing 50-volume Cornell University Press edition of Wordsworth's poetry as 'one of the great scholarly enterprises of our time'; or of Longman's two-volume edition of Milton's poetry as 'a very Bible of a Milton'. A particular strength of the Longman Annotated English Poets series is that it is aimed not at a few professional scholars but, in the words of its founder F.W. Bateson, writing in the 1960s, at 'university students and teachers, and the general reader'.[3] Such editions win our wide approval not solely by virtue of the completeness and enhancement they propose for great authors, but increasingly through their immense size and cost.

Editing reminds us of the monumental status of literary works; its apparatus buttresses their authority. And not only within the scholarly community: witness the high textual standards advertised in the lists of Penguin and World's Classics, or Broadview and Norton editions, all of which have a general as well as specialist readership in view. Indeed, the economics of adoption, as it is called in the publishing trade, demand that scholarly editions serve several markets over several decades, otherwise the costs involved in their commissioning and production would not be feasible. In the form such editorial labour took until the late twentieth century, there was still discernible a set of assumptions about literature and authors traceable back to the origins of vernacular textual criticism in the recovery and study of classical texts in the city states of fifteenth-century Italy. The authority that Roman republican texts bore in the emergent Italian city states generated a shared lexicon of crucial textual and legal terms which linked the well-being of the state to the well-being of its texts, interpreted as their recurrent cleansing and guaranteed freedom from error.[4] A comparable process of canon-formation through textual correction was getting underway in England in the course of the eighteenth century where it found its focus in the editing and re-editing of Shakespeare as the distinctive native English author. Throughout the twentieth century scholarly editing has regularly drawn authority from its extended cultural significance. When Jane Austen's novels were issued in uniform edition in 1923, they were widely welcomed as a national restorative in the aftermath of the First World War, linked through their public reception to the recovery of local English values. The massive Edinburgh edition of the Waverley novels, begun in the 1990s with sponsorship from the Bank of Scotland, is openly patriotic and

---

3 Most of the quotations are taken from the covers of the relevant editions. Rupert Brooke's remarks are to be found in his review of Herbert Grierson's two-volume Oxford edition of *The Poems of John Donne* (1912), in Christopher Hassall (ed.), *The Prose of Rupert Brooke* (London: Sidgwick & Jackson, 1956), p. 92.

4 See Stephanie H. Jed, *Chaste Thinking: The Rape of Lucretia and the Birth of Humanism* (Bloomington and Indianapolis: Indiana University Press, 1989).

honours Scotland's best-known novelist, Walter Scott, as a timely representative of devolved enterprise. In Australia, the ongoing Academy Editions of Australian Literature emanate from the Australian Scholarly Editions Centre, housed in the Australian Defence Force Academy. Conversely, recent critics have argued against the editorial agenda established by the CEAA in 1960s' America, linking its programme for 'textual sanitization' to contemporary policies for political and cultural segregation now under scrutiny.[5] The point should not be pressed too hard, but there is nevertheless a persistent connection between the editing of a canon of literary works and other forms of social regulation: to define a nation in terms of its writings is always a selective act (these writings and in these versions by these authors) long recognized as bound up with issues of territorial mapping and demarcation and the promotion or obliteration of the interests, rights and cultural identity of some.

Digital technology is changing how we interact with our textual heritage in its high literary forms. The expanded capacity of the computer as a text-repository appears to license certain kinds of cultural deregulation by enabling the storage of literary works as something other than composite or single-text editions within monolithically regulated systems of print. For some the new technology has prompted the recognition of the prescriptive reasoning behind such editions as no more than a function of the technological limits of the book, less desirable and less persuasive now that the computer makes other possibilities achievable: namely, multiple distinct textual witnesses assembled in a virtual archive or library of forms. Among the most ambitious and most exploitative of the new medium are scholarly editions built from series of high resolution digital images of manuscript and bibliographic artefacts, together with accurate transcriptions of their linguistic texts (the actual words and punctuation of the digitized objects) re-keyed for complex search and analysis, and any amount of supporting information on provenance, detailed descriptions of original physical structures, annotation and commentary of various kinds. In so far as electronic archives are developed in this form, we could say that they are the inheritors of the claim previously made for the eclectic scholarly print edition, of definitiveness. Where the technologies of print demanded a highly synoptic arrangement of the evidence supporting editorial intervention, the computer's display of full variant forms minimizes the need for intrusion. If in the scholarly print edition it has been technically possible to reconstruct from collation tables alternative readings and hence those textual forms suppressed in favour of the editor's chosen text, in the electronic archive full forms can be juxtaposed and displayed without any compromise of their distinct states and without any justification for editorial conflation. So, the new definitiveness is marked by a rebased authority in which the emphasis shifts from

    5   See, for example, arguments offered by Joseph Grigely, *Textualterity: Art, Theory, and Textual Criticism* (Ann Arbor: University of Michigan Press, 1995), pp. 23–7; and Benedict Anderson, *Imagined Communities: Reflections on the Origin and Spread of Nationalism* (1983; London and New York: Verso, 1991).

intervention and interpretation to evidence. Of course, principles of selection will still apply: no electronic repository, however massive, can hold everything; and in any case definitions of everything are also subjective. Despite such qualifications, many engaged in large electronic text projects celebrate their openness or facility for display as a good in itself. *The Hypermedia Archive of the Complete Writings and Pictures of Dante Gabriel Rossetti*, developed at the University of Virginia, is an elegant example of a lightly edited collection of this kind, described thus on its web page:

> When completed in 2008, the Archive will provide students and scholars with access to all of DGR's pictorial and textual works and to a large contextual corpus of materials, most drawn from the period when DGR's work first appeared and established its reputation (approximately 1848–1920), but some stretching back to the 14th-century sources of his Italian translations. All documents are encoded for structured search and analysis. The Rossetti Archive aims to include high-quality digital images of every surviving documentary state of DGR's works: all the manuscripts, proofs, and original editions, as well as the drawings, paintings, and designs of various kinds, including his collaborative photographic and craft works. These primary materials are transacted with a substantial body of editorial commentary, notes, and glosses.[6]

At the same time, the shift from book storage and delivery to electronic storage and delivery denotes more than a mere change in technology; it reconfigures the agents and activities that define our textual culture within a revision that has been underway at the level of critical thought since the 1960s. In this recalibration, the computer is both instrument and enabler, a relationship impossible and pointless to disentangle, as Raymond Williams argued at an earlier stage.[7] Until recently, books were the most privileged containers in which texts were stored, and texts (as strings of inscribed characters, words and punctuation) were the non-self-identical sign systems that together or separately constituted an author's work; the work itself being a kind of ideal collective entity or notion, the sum of all its parts, and the text gaining physical dimensions through its carrier – usually a book. Accordingly, a book held a text and a text represented a work. *Paradise Lost* or *Tess of the D'Urbervilles* or *Dubliners* are, by this way of thinking, the various books of those titles, and the multitude of different textual witnesses, however they are stored or recorded, that individually or together make up the work so named in its dispersed existence. These general assumptions have been under considerable threat from critical theory and computers. Recent arguments have chipped away at the old fiction of the author as solitary genius to show a more complex picture involving other people, a broader spectrum of institutional relations, and widening networks of production: Mary Shelley or

---

6   <http://jefferson.village.virginia.edu/rossetti/> (accessed 20 July 2007).

7   See Williams, *Marxism and Literature* p. 54 (quoted above) at pp. 5–6.

Dorothy Wordsworth copying out the poet's manuscripts; Vivienne Eliot and Ezra Pound suggesting improvements to *The Waste Land*; the publisher's editor making changes to Byron's poetry or Austen's prose; the collaborative input of compositors and press workers transforming manuscripts into print; the time and place of publication (different versions of Hardy's or Woolf's novels being prepared for a British or an American audience) and a variety of material forms (on a page of a newspaper, in an expensive quarto volume, as a serial instalment, on stage) all contributing significance.

Scholars have also dismantled the usefulness of the static concept of the work in favour of multiple versions: the quasi-independence of several versions of Wordsworth's *Prelude* and of Pope's *Rape of the Lock*. Where the single or composite text, freed by skilled intervention from the mishaps of transmission, provided what once was defended as the author's most accurate (even most intended) appearance before a readership, now the contingency of the transmission process itself determines the course of much critical discussion, implicating not only how we think about literary works and their construction but also their dissemination and reception.[8] This way of arguing has never been computer-dependent but it is computer-convergent. In the electronic archive, multiple texts of a work are less likely to be represented as its collective authorial presence than as a kind of work-site, a place where the work is under construction not by the author but by the reader or user, who manipulates its various textual forms. Paul Eggert develops this sense of a textual building-site when he writes:

> The work-site is text-construction site for the editor and expert reader; and it is the site of study of the work (of its finished textual versions and their annotation) for the first-time reader, as well as any position in between. Because the building of such textual and interpretative work-sites will be piece by piece, collaborative and ongoing, we are starting to look at a future for humanities, work-oriented research that is, if not scientific exactly, then more than *wissenschaftlich*, in the German sense, than what literary critics, historians, and others are used to.[9]

Peter Shillingsburg raises the stakes further when he redefines electronic editions as 'knowledge sites'.[10] In both cases, the emphasis is on the contingency and provisional status of what is constructed (and by whom) within the new technology.

---

8   Interestingly, much of the recent thinking along these lines derives from Book History, a field of study linked to cultural studies and social history, and concerned with the key role print has played in our culture, as well as with the book as material object. For a useful conspectus, see the essays collected in *The Book History Reader*, David Finkelstein and Alistair McCleery (eds) (London: Routledge, 2002).

9   Eggert, 'Text-encoding, Theories of the Text, and the "Work-Site"', p. 433.

10   Peter L. Shillingsburg, *From Gutenberg to Google: Electronic Representations of Literary Texts* (Cambridge: Cambridge University Press, 2006), especially pp. 80–125.

The old book-bound author–editor alliance has been firmly replaced by an editor–reader partnership, brokered by the computer.

Where economies of scale in print-based editing led to procedures for minimizing the relevance of different physical forms of a literary work, for conflating textual versions and for banishing notions of social agency, now by contrast, the computer's display of text as the changing sum of its reproductive conditions can seem a primary rationale within the digital collection. 'How to read 58 texts at once' is the epigraph introducing *The Miller's Tale on CD-ROM*, edited by Peter Robinson in 2004 as the third in the series of single-tale editions prepared by the innovative *Canterbury Tales Project*. The edition contains a full set of materials for the study of the tale in all extant fifteenth-century witnesses: that is, 54 manuscript and four print incunable versions. There are digital images of every page, full transcriptions linked to full collations and a spelling database. The in-house-designed Anastasia interface offers access to all manuscript readings and images, and to all variant readings at each word; a 'variant map' shows how they are distributed across the families of witnesses. Specialized searches permit retrieval of variants according to selective distribution: for instance, all readings found in the Hengwrt manuscript but not in the Ellesmere manuscript. As an example of computational power in the service of speculative Chaucerian textual criticism, this is an impressive resource. Yet the sheer size of a single-tale edition thus defined, coupled with non-interoperable CD-ROM delivery, means that each tale is amputated from the larger creative grouping in which Chaucer placed it, making searches across tales impossible and incapacitating any understanding of larger issues of design. To push Eggert's description further, this editorial model is more laboratory than work-site: the reader, or more likely experimental editor, is invited to prod, manipulate and inspect textual variants under conditions of extreme cultural isolation. Here 58 witnesses to one tale take precedence over the 23 tales that constitute the authored work that we know by the name of *The Canterbury Tales*.[11]

In what might strike us at first as a strange kind of reasoning, the computer has become a modeller of displaced materiality. Where in the past the physical limits of the book were used to support an editorial theory of textual idealism, the spatial liberation proposed by electronic storage and dissemination persuades at least some of us that the computer gives access to the historical versions of texts as real things; and that digital facsimiles are faithful or trustworthy equivalents of originals. The digital image, with its exaggerated verisimilitude, has recently come to be seen as balancing or redressing the intimidating analytic or database function of encoded text. In the words of Martha Nell Smith, executive editor of the *Dickinson Electronic Archives*, 'the ability to provide artefacts for direct examination (rather than relying on scholarly hearsay)' is a present 'boon' that alters both the general

---

11   See <http://www.canterburytalesproject.org/> (accessed 20 July 2007). A 'Multitext Edition' of *The Canterbury Tales* is also forthcoming and will allow some comparison across the whole text of the *Tales*, but across eight rather than 58 witnesses.

perception of the usefulness of computation to the humanities and our expectations of editions.[12] The electronic paradigm focuses on the advantages of the size of the computer's storage capacity, the speed of electronic collation and searching across variant forms, the accessibility of high quality digital images of unique or rare documents, the active participation of readers in making editorial choices; above all, the advantages of creating a collection that does not need to privilege as authoritative one particular text or document or one particular perspective on the evidence. It would seem that the case for electronic editions is made; except that it is not yet clear who wants them or what general needs they will fulfil.

Bruce Harkness began his attack on the 'novelistic fallacy' by adapting one of the most instantly recognizable and most travestied sentences in English Literature, rendered thus in his version: 'It is a truth universally acknowledged, that a critic intent upon analysis and interpretation, must be in want of a good text.' The formal parody of moralistic discourse implied in Jane Austen's famous opening to *Pride and Prejudice* ('It is a truth universally acknowledged, that a single man in possession of a good fortune, must be in want of a wife') derives its full, sly impact from the tension between the sentence's apparent grammatical architecture and its contrary semantics: the wealthy single man may be the sentence's grammatical subject but his fortune makes him the object or prey, in effect, of its predicate. The humour lies in the easy inversion of subject and object ('single man', 'wife') as the real limits of the 'universal truth' of the aphorism hit home, supported by the ambiguous agency of the phrases 'in possession of', 'in want of'. A less richly coded version would be: single women are always on the look out for rich husbands. By contrast to such subtlety, Harkness's repurposed Austenian wit risks exposing the flaw in his whole thesis: that good interpretation requires good texts. On the contrary, and perverse though it may seem, the literary critic and the textual critic have traditionally led separate lives. Literary criticism, in all shapes, has regularly flaunted its power to determine the text through reading, while at the other extreme textual criticism as editing has as regularly claimed the critical neutrality of its curatorship. Harkness too subscribes to the idea that the text of a literary work can be fixed with certainty and that this fixed object will validate (or invalidate) in point of detail and in general terms the critical activity performed upon it; that, in some sense, the texts of literary works are not themselves the products of critical thought but its basis. Hence, the editor's assumption that good interpretation depends on good texts; but what do good texts depend on if not good interpretation?

Unlike the case to be made for newspapers, where the cultural implications of the transfer from print to electronic forms can be accommodated relatively easily within abiding populist and commercial aims, electronic technology challenges many of the principles by which our high literary heritage has long been curated

---

12   Martha Nell Smith, 'Electronic Scholarly Editing', in Susan Schreibman, Ray Siemens and John Unsworth (eds), *A Companion to Digital Humanities* (Oxford: Blackwell, 2004), p. 309.

and disseminated. By its very existence, electronic technology, like the codex before it, redefines previous understanding of how knowledge and information are organized and, to use a potent word, how they are legitimated. Electronic technology and humanities computing, through which many of its features and procedures are carried to scholars in the arts, provide at the very least a way of organizing that brings its own inflections to what is organized, inflections that are as ideologically and economically defining and defined as the procedures supporting book technology. Where books, and advances in print technology over the centuries, disseminated expert knowledge to an ever widening readership, computerized text proposes a diffusion of the very concept of expertise itself. In other words, the technology is not what it once seemed back in the 1980s: simply a matter of technical support and services, whether locally or globally provided. Nor is it what it still appears to be to many practitioners in the early twenty-first century: a totally mimetic space unshaped by the constraints of its own medium.[13] In consequence, its uses need to develop in terms of a reflective understanding of our responsibilities and practices, and through a continuous critical assessment of the powers and limits of the technology.[14]

In an important, sceptical book published in 1999, *The Internet: A Philosophical Inquiry*, Gordon Graham draws on arguments from political and moral philosophy to examine the place of electronic technology in human culture. The challenge he set himself was to steer clear of the unformulated rhetoric of despair and celebration in which so much of its history, implications and future is still couched. Accordingly, one of the concepts he scrutinizes most closely is 'the ideology of technology'. Why, in Graham's view, the ideology of technology can appear irresistible is down to two powerful and unexamined assumptions that tend to hold sway at any given moment: the first is the belief that technology is not self-serving but is developed in response to demands or desires that lie outside it; and the second is the belief that technology is 'neutral' and 'does not influence or determine' the ends it 'merely serves'. Refining his inquiry, he posits what he labels 'some relatively simple facts', the first of which is that 'technological advances are, in a sense, self-undermining and this inevitably lends them a measure of transience'. For this reason, he argues, we need to distinguish between two kinds of change: between the 'new' and the 'merely novel'; and, granted a truly transformative technology, between change that enables us to do better those things we have always done, and change that brings into being new purposes and values. The hard question, the question worth asking of any new technology, is 'whether the new things it

---

13   This is the thesis of the controversial essay by Mats Dahlström, 'How Reproductive is a Scholarly Edition?' *Literary and Linguistic Computing*, 19 (2004), pp. 17–33.

14   In a recent essay, Ron Van den Branden and Edward Vanhoutte argue the need for a matching reconceptualization of text editing in light of the generative and modelling properties of electronic technology. See 'Through the Reading Glass: Generating an Editorial Microcosm through Experimental Modelling', *Literary and Linguistic Computing*, forthcoming.

enables us to do make for a better world'.[15] In formulating such questions, Graham builds on an earlier critique of 'technopoly' by Neil Postman, who suggested that we should always ask of any new technology the following question: what is the problem to which it is a solution? Postman defined technopoly as 'a state of culture'. He continued:

> It is also a state of mind. It consists in the deification of technology, which means that the culture seeks its authorization in technology, finds its satisfactions in technology, and takes its orders from technology. This requires the development of a new kind of social order, and of necessity leads to the rapid dissolution of much that is associated with traditional beliefs. Those who feel most comfortable in Technopoly are those who are convinced that technical progress is humanity's superhuman achievement and the instrument by which our most profound dilemmas may be solved. They also believe that information is an unmixed blessing, which through its continued and uncontrolled production and dissemination offers increased freedom, creativity, and peace of mind. The fact that information does none of these things – but quite the opposite – seems to change few opinions, for unwavering beliefs are an inevitable product of the structure of Technopoly. In particular, Technopoly flourishes when the defenses against information break down.[16]

Refining Postman's and Graham's philosophical inquiry to one privileged category of information, we might reasonably ask: what use do we have as professional and general readers of literature for powerful electronic scholarly editions or archives? Will our uses of texts as mediated by the new technology serve any pre-existent ends or will they transform the way we think about texts; and if so, is this transformation desirable? Will it make for a better world or, more modestly, will it change our relationship to our textual heritage for the better? If it is the case, as it seems to be, that as literary critics we do not care greatly for the status of the texts of the literary works we examine, are we likely to care more when offered a menu of texts to choose from or to collate for ourselves (and possibly even create as new eclectic forms) within an electronic repository? The advantage of the fixed printed scholarly edition was the passive reliance it enjoined. If as critical readers we rarely dip into the apparatus of the print edition to question a textual emendation, will we wish to use the computer tools that urge us to investigate text as complex or at least multiple processes of composition, production and dissemination? And if we do, how will the results from this searching of the data be brought into reasonable conversation with anything worth saying? Is large-scale electronic editing as currently conceived anything more than the revenge of the textual critic?

15   Graham, *The Internet: A Philosophical Inquiry*, pp. 9–17.
16   Neil Postman, *Technopoly: The Surrender of Culture to Technology* (New York: Vintage Books, 1993), pp. 71–2.

Although electronic editions of literary texts have been under development since the late 1980s, these are still topical questions, because despite much talking up of their importance, it is arguable how worthwhile they as yet appear beyond the circle of experts who assemble them. The *Canterbury Tales Project* began in 1989, and so far four single-tale CDs have been published, with several more promised; but this is a product aimed at a highly specialist market – of prospective editors? – who, at present rates of development, may have to wait an exceedingly long time for the full set. Discrete tales are offered as the sum of their multiple textual disintegrations; as the algorithmic expression of variance; as data to be mined. Ironically, though, the scholar's freedom to interpret minutiae in these microscopic work-sites is ultimately entailed to the specific approach to editing that the whole project and its integrated software, masterminded by Peter Robinson, have been constructed to serve, an approach developed according to methods of cladistic analysis which are at best highly idiosyncratic. Ultimately, it would be difficult to find a more coercive editorial model.[17] The leading advocate of electronic text, Jerome McGann, editor of the *Rossetti Archive*, has long been committed to the belief that the philological methods displayed in scholarly editing are not preliminary to the work of literary analysis but crucial critical acts that should engage us all; for him, the advantage of the computer space lies in the possibilities for dissolving some of the outside/inside distinctions that inform textual display within book technology, with its prepared reading text and intimidating synoptic apparatus. Where texts are assembled in 'decentred' or open hypertextual electronic systems, the authority of no particular document need dominate and the reader is free to construct authority provisionally and on the fly without regard for artificial divisions of expertise enjoined by traditional paper-based scholarly editions. Not only is there the suggestion that the electronic archive is a potential leveller of textual forms (all texts being equal according to the underlying 'social theory of texts', or 'absolute' in hypertextual terms) but also of interpretational choices. As McGann explains it:

> In a hypertext, each document (or part of a document) can therefore be connected to every other document (or document part) in any way one chooses to define a connection. Relationships do not have to be organized in terms of a measure or standard ... From a scholarly editor's point of view, this structure means that every text or even every portion of a text ... has an absolute value within the structure as a whole unless its absolute character is specifically modified.

> *The Rossetti Archive* imagines an organization of its texts, pictures, and other documents in this kind of noncentralized form. So when one goes to read a

---

17   See the compelling critique of Robinson's method by Ralph Hanna, 'The Application of Thought to Textual Criticism in All Modes, with Apologies to A.E. Housman', *Studies in Bibliography*, 53 (2000), pp. 163–72.

potential work, no documentary state of the work is privileged over the others. All options are presented for the reader's choice.[18]

This is an argument worth pondering for several reasons: not only are order and hierarchy, of the most rigid kind, essential to the electronic encoding of information (for more on which, see the next section of this chapter), but the choice of material to constitute 'everything' in the archive is also perspectival, the fulfilment of some arbitrary definition, and the user interface that organizes and delivers the materials is also designed according to someone's (an editor's) preferences.

Beyond that, even supposing we suspend disbelief and accept the illusion of 'open' technology, what might this multiplicity of unprioritized textual forms mean for the kinds of critical activity we engage in within the academy and for the already strained link between general reading and professional critical analysis? Endorsing and extending McGann's boldly optimistic vision of a 'radiant textuality', Robinson objects that as yet we have barely reached beyond the model of print technology in our thinking about electronic scholarly editions. The real challenge will be what he calls 'fluid, co-operative and distributed editions' made and maintained 'by a community of scholars and readers working together'. He foresees 'a new kind of scholarly product', where readers will use powerful computer programs, drawn from evolutionary biology, to construct the history of the text, from its many textual forms, as a record of agreements and disagreements; he further imagines the edition as a collaborative space, refashioned by readers functioning as new editors far beyond initial publication.[19]

Over the last 40 years, theories of various kinds have wrapped our professional writing about literature in terminology so abstruse and exclusive as to be capable of communicating with and persuading only those few within its immediate range. In particular, we have lost confidence in forms of criticism that invite shared value judgements about good or great literature or that create broad (rather than narrowly patrolled) areas of agreement. Most of all, we in the academy have lost sight of reading as pleasure. In short, we have lost the common ground we once shared with general readers. It is quite likely that any wide investment in complex electronic archives of the kinds built and imagined by McGann, Robinson and others will exacerbate this professional disengagement, concealing it under a scientific façade of busy manipulation, interrogation and complex searching. Not only is it possible that shifting between multiple electronic versions will freeze our critical capacities as readers, redirecting them towards a wilderness of locally

---

18   McGann, *Radiant Textuality: Literature after the World Wide Web*, pp. 25, 73–4, and passim.

19   Peter Robinson, 'Where We Are With Electronic Scholarly Editions, and Where We Want To Be', *Jahrbuchs fur Computerphilogie*, 5 (2003), pp. 126–46; also at <http://computerphilologie.uni-muenchen.de/jg03/robinson.html> (accessed 20 July 2007). See note 17 above for a strong criticism of Robinson's application of biological cladistics to manuscript traditions.

variable and meaningfully inert features; but that, at an extreme, each user will choose, expertly or ineptly, her own variant text to prove her own critical point (everyone her own editor), a direct route to silencing critical dialogue and the shared life of our discipline.[20] It does not follow that, because the stablized text of traditional scholarly editing provoked diverse interpretations and engaged debate around its composite form, a decentred or unstable text will lead to anything richer or more persuasive than solipsistic self-communing. On the contrary, procedures that restrain individual impulse in certain areas and insist upon a measure of conformity may be essential; real debate depends on real consensus. Similarly, the editor's exercise of a proper expertise may be more liberating for more readers than seemingly total freedom of choice. To borrow Postman's words, it may be that the editor, someone with expertise and skill born of long training and specialized knowledge employed responsibly, is one of our necessary 'defenses' against information. This is a line of argument we will return to in other information contexts in later chapters.

Extending Graham's inquiry further, we might ask whether a technology that exposes deficiencies in another technology, and then itself supplies them, automatically qualifies as a superior technology. It is almost a mantra in technopoly that the book is a woefully inadequate technology. But it is possible that this 'deficient' technology does things the superior technology cannot, among which will be those advantages that only come through limitation. Most obvious among the advantages of limited access to textual variance may be an emphasis on evaluation over quantification, selective insight over information. One of the temptations that regularly overcame the professional textual critic in the course of the twentieth century was an exaggerated reliance on technical proficiency and the false security of system over the results it might generate and the necessarily subjective element in textual decision. A good example of this is to be found in W.W. Greg's 1927 study, *The Calculus of Variants*, in which he used algebraic formulae to weigh the material evidence of change or variance in the transmission of literary texts and thus to generate some kind of predictive scheme for calculating levels of deviance from an ideal norm. Greg's stemmatic theory may have been accurate and effective within limits (notable among which are its failure to account for cross-contamination and conflation in transmission), but its thoroughly abstracted

---

20 Cf. Fredson Bowers' defence of the work of the scholarly editor as follows: 'It is an anomaly for an editor proposing to establish a text to expect wiser heads to carry forward and then to apply the basic bibliographical examination of the document on which the very details of the establishment should have rested. "Every reader his own bibliographer" is an absurdity.' 'Principles and Practice in the Editing of Early Dramatic Texts', in Fredson Bowers, *Textual and Literary Criticism: The Sandars Lectures in Bibliography 1957–8* (Cambridge: Cambridge University Press, 1966), p. 146. Against this line of reasoning, see Edward Vanhoutte, 'Every Reader his Own Bibliographer – an Absurdity?', in Marilyn Deegan and Kathryn Sutherland (eds), *Text Editing, Print and the Digital World* (Aldershot: Ashgate, 2009).

model proved ultimately unhelpful and it has been employed rarely by editors. In determining the value of significant readings, something less systematized and less thoroughly substitutive for its literary original is probably always necessary. What appears to be the situation with complex electronic editions is that a pseudo-scientific model of complete reproductive and algorithmic power is currently persuading some editors that they are not engaging in subjective and partial activities. The rigorous functionality of analytic processing and the high quality of image-oriented hypertextual models both foster this illusion. And because much of the operation of the hardware and software through which chosen materials are mediated is beyond their understanding, assemblers assume its outcomes are unconstrained or in some meaningful sense 'true', as opposed to derivative. Hence, Martha Nell Smith's reduction of the proof provided by the synoptic, print editor to 'scholarly hearsay' in contrast to the 'artefacts' for 'direct examination' available in the electronic archive. This is, in effect, a demotion of the expert human processor in favour of an alliance between the mechanical and the uninformed.

***

If as readers and users we have not yet made the kind of large commitment envisaged by Robinson and McGann to massive, multiple-witness archives of single works made up of facsimile and re-keyed texts and powerful batteries of tools, we have found other ways to link high culture and technology. The Internet is home to modest electronic editions of various kinds and varying standards; some exploit hypertextual forms and experiment with multi-media, interactive interfaces and multiply divided screens; some use the relaxation of spatial constraints to group together different texts or works by different authors or to revive the fortunes of neglected works and writers; and some, just like discarded or out-of-print book editions, gather figurative ether dust, wheeling like decommissioned satellites in space, accidentally visited in our Google searching. Many such editions exploit little more of the electronic potential than the freedom to place material on the Internet without prior submission to the regulatory authority of publishing house or editorial board; something that brings further problems for assessing the status or value of electronic products. By and large, however, despite hyper-mediation, most digital texts are still serving as surrogates for print. We continue to use them in much the same way as we use collections of books. Searching facilities speed up some processes; online access makes it easier to find a particular book; and it exposes us to a wider range of material. But our reading habits are largely unchanged. There is some shared agreement that certain texts challenge reprinting in conventional paper form, and it is worth pausing on these because their case for electronic representation is easily made. There are, for example, texts whose enhanced functionality within an electronic environment is quickly appreciated: old runs of newspapers and dictionaries, both the kind of text objects whose main use is non-sequential reading, fall into this category. So too do texts which never had or which defy a bookish dimension and linear display: Greek and Latin inscriptions on stone or the dynamic and discontinuous pages of writers' working documents and manuscripts. Not only can high resolution images of holograph papers be digitized and stored, they can be linked to transcriptions encoded to represent the page's temporal dimensions – its time-stamped layers of erasure and insertions. Among major work currently in progress we might include here experimental displays and transcriptions of the manuscripts and notebooks of Ludwig Wittgenstein and Emily Dickinson.[21]

To those enthusiasts who regularly invoke the limitations of book technology, the added value digitization brings to such projects is overwhelming. This is the thesis of McGann's influential essay 'The Rationale of Hypertext'.[22] But adherents rarely note what is at least as obvious and compelling: that for every literary work that resists or frets at its bookishness, there are hundreds that insist upon it; that assume the book as a vital component of their make up and meaning. In these everyday cases, and in the words of Geoffrey Nunberg, 'it is precisely because these [electronic] technologies transcend the material limitations of the book that they will have trouble assuming its role ... A book doesn't simply contain the inscription of a text, it *is* the inscription.'[23] For example, bibliographic accommodation, being situated within the confines of a book, is an integral feature of the narratives of most nineteenth-century novels. The feel and weight of the book's volume and its metonymic properties as a stand-in for the individual life are knit into our classic novels: 'my readers,' writes Jane Austen, 'will see in the tell-tale compression of the pages before them, that we are all hastening together to perfect felicity.'[24] Print, too, can give a fair simulation of 'this drop of ink at the end of my pen' with which George Eliot begins to write *Adam Bede*. First generation digital texts display equivalent poetic allegiances to the formal properties of electronic storage and transmission, as William Gibson's *Agrippa* and Michael Joyce's *afternoon* demonstrate. Yet, interestingly, despite claims and counter-claims, currently the biggest beneficiaries of computerization are not complexly constellated scholarly editions or born-digital text objects, but out-of-print or simply old books. In the arts and humanities, the computer is most readily used as a platform for accessing the artefacts of other media – especially book objects – rather than for textual deformation (whether as liberation from

---

21 See the Bergen Electronic Edition of Wittgenstein's *Nachlass*, <http://wab.aksis.uib. no/wab_BEE.page>, and the *Dickinson Electronic Archives*, <http://www.emilydickinson. org/> (accessed 1 August 2007).

22 Jerome J. McGann, 'The Rationale of Hypertext', in Sutherland (ed.), *Electronic Text: Investigations in Method and Theory*, pp. 19–46; reprinted in *Radiant Textuality*, pp. 53–74.

23 Nunberg, 'The Places of Books in the Age of Electronic Reproduction', p. 18.

24 Jane Austen, *Northanger Abbey*, vol. 2, ch. 16 (ch. 31).

linearity or any other constraint imposed by its bookish container) or complex editing or any other new construction.[25]

Electronic libraries or large text corpora that function as accessible copies of or sequels to their print counterparts are changing the way scholars, teachers and students work far more quickly and persuasively than experimental multiple -witness editions. Among the earliest models are the digital library of classical Greek literature, the *Thesaurus Linguae Graecae (TLG)*, founded as long ago as 1972, and the Brown University Women Writers Project (WWP), a textbase of women's writings in English from c.1330 to 1830.[26] The WWP began in 1988 under the direction of a group of scholars concerned to make visible and available the diverse tradition of women's writings which, despite growing critical interest, were still not finding their way into bookshops and classrooms. The gender and cultural politics underlying the WWP are radical in the challenge offered to the conventional limits of canonical (in-print) literature and the conjunction proposed between marginalized or neglected representations of knowledge and new technology. Thanks to the WWP's pioneering work in rekeying and encoding, texts can be searched by word and phrase across the whole collection, and this translates into a powerful demonstration of consolidation – the potential to be seen and read together, as a group. Nevertheless, its provision of customized anthologies for teaching and research and its nostalgically configured screen display of rekeyed texts in old typefaces both suggest that the WWP is geared to the loving resurrection and circulation of print objects.

This is a model which has made a huge impact on the way we use new technology to engage with large tracts of otherwise inaccessible literary and historical materials. Either, as in the case of the WWP, texts are rekeyed and supplied with deep markup for searching, or page images of a particular book copy are digitized and presented with simple metadata and tools. Texts in *Early English Books Online (EEBO)*, the remediated microfilm collection which began digitization in 1998 and went online in 2003, have a complex genesis: as copies of the microfilm copies of particular book copies; that is, as second generation surrogates. Despite such mediation, *EEBO* is still essentially a means to access an old medium, the printed book. From the user's point of view, the principles behind many such text corpora are not obvious: are they edited or non-edited, accurate or inaccurate representations of book objects? In addition, there is much overlap and repetition in provision across collections. How many among their daily users understand the status of or distinctions between the texts provided by *EEBO* and those in the rekeyed *EEBO*-TCP (Text Creation Partnership)? Or between texts in *Eighteenth-Century Collections Online (ECCO)*, Chadwyck-Healy's *Literature Online (LION)* database, and Google Book Search? In fact, we might say that, as

---

25   For a defence of the usefulness of electronic deformation of literary text, see McGann, *Radiant Textuality*, pp. 105–35.

26   <http://www.tlg.uci.edu/>, and <http://www.wwp.brown.edu/> (accessed 26 July 2007).

in the print world, where the reader needs to exercise some judgement (whether of an economic or critical kind) in deciding among multiple copies and different texts of the same work, so in the electronic world.

Much of the thinking that underlies the practices of text editing, whether in book or electronic forms, responds to the problem of how parts represent totalities. As a container, the book imposes limits of space that compel particular solutions, among which has traditionally been a highly selective representation of evidence as a unitary, shaped whole. By contrast, the reproductive potential of the computer is regularly used to enhance materiality, to store and display massive digital facsimile and transcription archives, clusters of documents, amenable to all manner of searching, display and organization, and as platforms for preparing multiple different outputs, among which might be the highly selective representation of evidence as a unitary, shaped whole; that is, as a print edition. Most electronic text collections now combine sophisticated analytic and representational functions. Indeed, the potential of the computer as visualization tool has probably overtaken its statistical and 'computational' uses for many humanists. Not so long ago, the intelligent prediction was that powerful electronic editions would use encoding to create models of the text's structure, algorithmic expressions of textual variance that would reorder the words, align them with other versions, lemmatize them, and so forth. While that is still the case, the computer's capacity for remediation currently seduces us as, thanks to advances in imaging, it appears to deliver to our desks representations that engage us like the real thing – or even better. Digital imaging is now of a very high quality; but as a surrogate of a manuscript or printed page or book illustration, all that the image simulates of the old medium are its visual properties and even these it alters or enhances – by cropping and scale distortion, by reducing colour and patina, by erasing blemishes, by powerful magnification, ultraviolet light, digital flattening and making 'improvements' of various kinds. As Diana Kichuk notes, from her careful study of *EEBO* and in an argument that challenges the naïve faith in replicability of many exponents of digital image archives (witness Martha Nell Smith above):

> Claims for an identical relationship between a digital facsimile and its original, and the transparency of the user-resource experience, ignore the myriad transformations that occur when producing a facsimile in another medium. The process of remediation lowers a digital veil of varying opacity between the scholar and the original work. The scholar, gazing through that veil, seduced by the transformations wrought by remediation, suspends disbelief in order to advance the study of the text. Successful remediation depends on the witting and unwitting complicity of the viewer.[27]

---

27   Diana Kichuk, 'Metamorphosis: Remediation in *Early English Books Online* (*EEBO*)', *Literary and Linguistic Computing*, 22 (2007), pp. 296–7.

So where exactly are we in the digital provision for our textual heritage? If digital means have come to prominence in many areas of our intellectual lives over the last three decades, they still largely serve print culture. That is not surprising nor is it cause for concern: even after a hundred years of vision and sound recording, much of our cultural archive is print, however we now choose to store and deliver it. The print we read, as books, is now the product of digital inscription, storage and processing in a close collaboration of writers, typesetters and publishers. We turn on our computers to read print off screen, to experience some of the physical properties of old books, and to download book texts. For the scholar at work on the paper-based edition, the goal remains a finished product at the point of delivery: a volume in which text and apparatus are mutually enlightening, and sufficient – ideally, for several purposes and markets over several decades. But as Julia Flanders, director of the WWP, recently remarked, 'we are at an incunabular stage in the emergence of electronic editions'. For Flanders the chief obstacles to their more sophisticated adoption are 'the granularization of online resources and the lack of cross-collection analysis functions'.[28] That is the pitfall and the challenge to the future from the technophile's perspective: images need to be sharper, more like the real thing, and resources need to be interoperable and bigger. As in the print world, different electronic projects present materials differently; images are captured in different formats, texts are encoded to different standards, and intellectual property issues pose further restrictions to integrated searching across collections. Experiments in constructing Virtual Research Environments (VREs) will make it possible over the next few years to set single complex databases within a shared electronic infrastructure, transforming the scholar's workspace by incorporating a wide range of resources, tools and techniques. VREs will link images of artefacts to diverse text corpora, to dictionaries and to online journals, bringing together research data of different types and from widely dispersed locations to enable more detailed intensive research and to create effective online collaboration sites. We continue to chase completeness: but the interactive, multi-authoring possibilities of this electronic model will set humanities research on a different course from its traditional book-bound systems of individual enterprise.

This will not be the only model for the future. We are in a transitional stage as far as electronic technology is concerned. In consequence, both print and electronic editorial methods are in flux; not only is it not clear what scholars and students will want from each (or in what hybrid combination) in the next 20 or 30 years, it is also unclear what kind of financial or publishing infrastructure will support major electronic editions. So far, they have been underwritten by large grants, usually from non-commercial agencies with little or no requirement that costs are recovered; in the case of the Arts and Humanities Research Council (the British government funding agency) it is a stipulation that electronic projects are

---

28   Julia Flanders, 'Renaissance Women, Text Encoding, and the Digital Humanities: An Interview', 8 February 2007, <http://www.academiccommons.org/library/julia-flanders> (accessed 26 July 2007).

made freely available on the Web. Other electronic editions are effectively funded through the university salaries of academic staff employing their research time. The models so far available for production and dissemination suggest that, where resources are not made freely available, they will be licensed to institutions for bulk fees or accessed through Web subscriptions. This is the situation at the moment and it effectively means that readers or users without institutional affiliation are cut off from many specialist resources. In any case, and unlike the book which is complete at the point of sale and does not obviously deteriorate or need upgrading to remain readable, these electronic editions will require ongoing maintenance and preservation just to keep them available. If, unlike print, they are also open-ended and collaborative work-sites rather than static closed electronic objects, such issues loom even larger; and there is the attendant challenge of whether material is put on the Web in such a way that it can be appropriated, augmented and reshaped indefinitely, and if so whether it is also archived at regular intervals to preserve particular states.

Arguing from his obstacle-strewn first-hand experience of developing an electronic edition of the Renaissance dramatist Thomas Middleton's *Collected Works*, Gary Taylor early noted how the prohibitive costs of digital edition building were likely to lead to an even more restricted representation than currently exists of our textual heritage:

> Changes in textual practices have always created narrow gates, through which texts have to pass if they are to remain legible. The change from uncial to miniscule script, the great vowel shift, the invention of print – these mutations of the media of representation transformed textual practices so radically that texts which were not translated into the new medium almost always perished, because they had become unintelligible to the textual classes. The change from print to digital technology has been correctly perceived as another such life-or-death gate. Unfortunately it is not a single gate, but a succession of gates, with shorter and shorter intervals between them.[29]

This would be a particularly ironic outcome of our new electronic textuality – a dwindling corpus of well-edited texts alongside a massive explosion in textual reproduction. But it could easily happen if we privilege certain complex and large-scale models of digital scholarly editing; and if we do not, we risk demoting our literary heritage to the status of all other texts. And there is another worry, that electronic storage coupled to print-on-demand technology may permit publishers to keep twentieth-century authors in copyright more or less indefinitely. If so, will this restrict the formation of integrated electronic collections of post-1900 works? Might our digital scholarship be more and more focussed on the past and less and

---

29   Gary Taylor, 'c:\wp\file.txt 05:41 10-07-98', in Andrew Murphy (ed.), *The Renaissance Text: Theory, Editing, Textuality* (Manchester: Manchester University Press, 2000), p. 48.

less engaged with those literary works that shaped the recent present? The *Willa Cather Archive* currently announces its partial state with the words 'copyright law forbids digitally republishing her post-1922 works'.[30] The presumption is that publishers and scholars will reach new arrangements over intellectual property issues as both groups discover further benefits in digitization. But as yet this is unclear, and just as current copyright law means that few twentieth-century authors are served by scholarly editions, so modern writers have a smaller electronic presence than Victorian or earlier. This further skews our textual heritage.

By contrast, major commercial initiatives like Google Books are creating massive open libraries from what were previously, for all practical purposes, research collections accessible to the scholarly few: millions of out-of-copyright books, regardless of the estimated worth or value of their contents, from the Bodleian Library, the University of Michigan, Stanford, Harvard and New York Public Libraries, among others. How pervasive and persuasive will this model be in providing access to virtually all public domain materials? How might its relatively simple immersive environment affect the closed models for archiving within hypermedia editions proposed by scholarly editors like McGann and Robinson? After all, if most of what we need is available free through Google, who will pay heavy subscription costs? Currently there is much to recommend a hybrid model of editing, in which texts are assembled and archived in sophisticated electronic repositories, maintained by academic and publishing-house partnerships, and from these repositories reading editions (customized for different markets) are printed; the repository further serving the expert or inquisitive few who wish to examine variant texts for specific purposes. The *Cambridge Edition of the Works of Ben Jonson* and the *Cambridge Editon of the Works of Jonathan Swift* both adopt aspects of this design. As David Gants, a member of the Jonson editorial team, describes it, the edition is:

> two complementary but materially distinct projects that together attempt to participate in the continuing editorial dialogue: a six-volume traditional edition that will be published in print form, and a networked electronic edition that, while initially released simultaneously with the print edition, will continue to develop dynamically on its own as scholarship and technology advance.[31]

In the future we will also see an intensive merging of different media – print, audio, visual, movie clips – within the digital space, and as a consequence a

---

30   <http://cather.unl.edu/about.html> (accessed 26 July 2007).

31   David Gants, 'Drama Case Study: The Cambridge Edition of the Works of Ben Jonson', in Lou Burnard, Katherine O'Brien O'Keefe and John Unsworth (eds), *Electronic Textual Editing* (New York: Modern Language Association of America, 2006), p. 123; and see Linda Bree and James McLaverty, 'The Cambridge Edition of the Works of Jonathan Swift and the Future of the Scholarly Edition', in Deegan and Sutherland (eds), *Text Editing, Print and the Digital World.*

blurring of editing into other kinds of remaking or adaptation as we discover further combinations for text objects and text processes.

Information and Noise: Text Encoding

In the electronic environment, the real work of editing, as the modelling of the relationship of a text to its parts or of a group of texts to one another, has shifted from the literary editor to the encoder. In a sense such encoding provides some of the mediating functions represented in book production by a range of publishing- and printing-house practices – copy-editing, formatting, text composition, setting in type and printing – all of which impose interpretative values, and over all of which the literary editor has conventionally had little control. But because in the electronic environment text has to be constructed from a more fundamental level, its composition and decomposition (that is, the units from which it is built or into which it can be divided for tagging and searching) are the subject of more rigorous critical debate than need impinge on editorial activity in book form. What this means in practice is that the computer as an inscription technology redistributes the range of specialist activities that contribute to textual production in book form and at the same time raises the interpretative stakes: either scholarly editors must also become text encoders or they must hand over this expertise to others, and with consequences. There is an implicit tension between encoding and editing; interestingly, encoders have taken over many of the claims to neutrality that used to buttress editorial work. It is the activity of the text encoder that provides the most persuasive (because the most powerful) model for the edition of the electronic era, for it is the activity of the text encoder that determines how the text will appear and how it can be searched and interpreted. Should it concern us that few literary scholars who will use and even assemble electronic editions will be their own encoders or will understand the rigorous theorizing about what text is that lies behind various encoding models?

But first, a caution about the term 'code'. Alphabets, including the set of letters employed in the Roman alphabet, are codes or systems of symbols just as much as Morse code, deaf-and-dumb signing, or the zeros and ones of all digital technologies. As Florian Cramer points out, because the alphabet is a code, this fact of itself makes literature (alphabetically encoded) 'a privileged symbolic form in digital information systems'. Unlike sounds and images, which 'are not code by themselves', literature (as linguistic text) can, it appears, be translated into zeros and ones 'without information loss'.[32] Hence the basic technology that can guarantee the printed book as a derivative of digital storage. Put another way, the new medium contains the possibility of the old within it. At the same time, we must be careful to distinguish between technical and epistemological uses of the

---

32   Florian Cramer, 'Digital Code and Literary Text', *BeeHive Archive*, 4 (2001), p. 2; and at <http://beehive.temporalimage.com/archive/43arc.html> (accessed 2 August 2007).

term 'information' within the digital medium: between electronic impulses which encode a kind of transmissional noise, part of the digital architecture, which is called digital information (as in the term Information Technology), and information in the conventional sense of useful knowledge, which may be produced or carried by informational noise. Currently, there is much confusion of the two; hence the unexplored assumptions that by virtue of computers we exist in an Information Age, and that this equates with living in an informed society. Hand-printed books also conventionally carried information or transmissional noise about their physical make up, in the form of press marks and signatures, which are distinct from that other kind of information encoded in the printed text itself. In the Information Age, however, there is simply more transmissional noise, and more code.

Some History

Scholars have been creating electronic texts for as long as there have been machines to read them, realizing early on that the calculating power of computers could be used effectively for processing textual data, for producing concordances and word lists, and for making comparisons between different versions. In the late 1940s, Father Roberto Busa, a Thomas Aquinas scholar, entered texts laboriously into machines on punched cards in order to construct huge lexical and morphological databases. Over the next four decades, the scholarly world produced ever more electronic texts in ever more languages. Some were by-products of scholarship: a work or manuscript keyed into the computer for analysis or editing in the process of preparing a conventional print publication; some were end-products: corpora of texts for analysis shared by many scholars, such as the *TLG* or the Brown Corpus of Modern English.

Work on large-scale corpora such as these brought with it a new concept: the idea that text created for one purpose might be profitably reused for quite different purposes not envisaged by its original creators. In order to facilitate this reuse, texts were collected by a number of institutions into archives and e-text collections. In textual scholarship, however, the concept of reuse was problematic: most texts available for collection were created by individuals for whom an electronic text was rarely an end in itself, but part of the scholarly process akin to the production of a typescript to be sent to a publisher. But the computer came with a new facility, storage; and so process also became product, and means became end. In editing especially, scholars welcomed the opportunity to transcribe using a computer, and then alter, correct, refine and even share texts without having to retype successive versions from scratch, possibly introducing new errors. Once a text was available in electronic form, much laborious work of checking, collating and indexing could be carried out with the aid of the computer; but, initially, the final product was still no more than a printed edition, albeit one easier to produce for both editor and publisher. This meant that at this stage the only guidelines an editor had for the production of text were those supplied by publishers, and concerned with issues of house-style and *mise-en-page* rather than internal logical structures. In using computerized analysis programs there were other guidelines to follow, though these were not usually concerned with the output of the text itself, but with processing the text for some specific purpose: collation, indexing, and so on. Any product from these programs was generally discarded when the results of the various analyses were obtained. Furthermore, given that early e-text was not produced for public consumption, much of it was inaccurate, incomplete or filled with idiosyncratic markup systems containing extraneous characters and symbols invented by its creators to mark some specific features of interest. The creation and character of such texts were often documented only sketchily, with little information about provenance, date or underlying editions from which they were derived; in some cases, texts were not documented at all. This meant that vast tracts of text deposited with organizations such as the Oxford Text Archive were not in practice reusable. Some system(s) of standardization in capture, markup and description were clearly needed.

Text Encoding Initiative

The Text Encoding Initiative (TEI) was established in 1987 as a scholarly endeavour to address the problems of the production and reuse of electronic text; the key problem being how texts were *encoded* for a variety of analyses, for exchange and transmission between different hardware and software platforms, and for long-term survival. Many in the publishing industry, which had gone over to computerized typesetting relatively early and faced similar challenges, were busy adopting a standard language for text encoding: the Standard Generalized Markup Language (SGML). The TEI provided a much-needed forum for the discussion of key issues around the production and use of electronic text, as well as a network for dissemination of guidelines and good practice in encoding. The TEI recommendations and guidelines, based initially on SGML, and more recently upon Extensible Markup Language (XML), have been largely adopted by the humanities community, and few projects creating electronic text today would use any other system without having compelling reasons to do so. However, the TEI is not without problems and critics, of which more later.

The TEI has been an intensive intellectual enterprise, engaging the interest and commitment of many scholars and technical specialists over 20 years. In the course of the discussions which resulted in their guidelines and recommendations, the underlying nature of text and its relationship to any physical manifestations of any one instance of a text have been hotly debated. An early feature was a 'positivist confidence' that, in a text, 'anything and everything of intellectual significance can be encoded, the TEI encourag[ing] the belief that everything can be interpreted: that tagging can indeed exhaust meaning'.[33] In order to define texts and develop

---

33   Peter Robinson, 'Ma(r)king the Electronic Text: How, Why and For Whom?', in Joe Bray, Miriam Handley and Anne C. Henry (eds), *Ma(r)king the Text: The Presentation of Meaning on the Literary Page* (Aldershot: Ashgate, 2000), p. 310.

some guidelines about how to deal with them in an electronic environment, some universal principles deemed to be true for all texts needed to be discovered; and some frameworks based upon these principles, able to support structures and schemas for the description and encoding of texts, needed to be developed. This description and encoding is achieved through the use of metadata and markup.

Metadata

Metadata, as a term, is much used in the description and definitions of digital objects. The simplest explanation in general use is that metadata is 'data about data'; that is, metadata is data that describes another data object. But 'all metadata is, in fact, data. Whether or not particular information functions as data or metadata is a matter of context or perspective, and what is metadata to one person or application can be data to another.'[34] So a review of a book published in a newspaper is metadata, and the book itself is data. In another context, the review may itself be data, and have metadata attached to it.

Metadata is usually external to the object being described, and in the world of textual objects in digital form, it has a number of different functions. Of course, as concept and principle of classification, metadata has a long history of use in the non-networked environment: bibliographic information about a text and a library catalogue are both forms of metadata. Generally, three types of metadata are distinguished in the recording of digital objects: administrative metadata, structural metadata, and descriptive or intellectual metadata. Administrative metadata is used to describe certain characteristics of digital objects which relate to the management of those objects over time: file formats, date of creation and other physical features. This need not concern us further here. Structural metadata describes the structure and relationships of a set of digital objects. If digital surrogates are derived from complex analogue objects (books or journals, for example), then the relationship of the components one to another has to be captured in the metadata if a true representation of that object is to be preserved in the digital format. For instance, if we take the example of a book digitized as a facsimile, we immediately have two objects which will need to be described in the structural metadata: the original and the digital version, and of course the relationship between them. These may then fit into two different hierarchies. The original may be part of a library or collection, and catalogued as such. That collection could itself be regarded as an object to which structural metadata will be attached ('collection level description' is the term applied to this); and the digitized book may be part of a digital collection which is different from the collection from which the analogue object was derived, and therefore will have a different collection level description. If we concentrate now on the description of the digital object (but keep in mind that it will have many properties of the original

---

    34   R. Wendler, <http://hul.harvard.edu/ldi/html/metadata.html> (accessed 8 March 2007).

if the digitization has been carried out in such a way as faithfully to represent the appearance of the original), we may want to record how the digital files fit together in order that the parts of the surrogate book can be presented to the user in the correct arrangement. This description will relate of course to the physical make up of the original, and have a direct relationship to a traditional codicological description, with the addition of some information about where the digital files are stored. A structural map of the object is therefore created, in which all the physical parts that make up the original, and their digital surrogates, are related to each other. Once the structure of the object is expressed in this way, the user has all the information needed to locate it in its collection, understand its provenance (in its original physical collection), and be able to view and use it as a single object with its structural parts in the right relation to each other. But this does not reveal everything that needs to be known about the structure of the object; for it also has a logical structure that may need to be represented, and this logical structure, in terms of formal description, may not cohere easily with the physical structure described by the structural metadata. This logical structure is often rendered in markup: that is, tags are inserted *into* the document to identify titles, headings, tables of content, paragraphs, lines and other features. The third type, descriptive or intellectual metadata, is used to account for the content of a digital object, as distinct from its format, provenance or structure. Descriptive metadata, too, is usually expressed as markup, which can be either internal to the object, or external, in the form of offset or stand-off markup.

Markup

Textual markup is sometimes defined as those features of a text extraneous to its content but necessary to make it make sense. All linguistic text contains markup, even the very simplest. Some would argue that the *scripto continua* of ancient manuscripts and inscriptions, being devoid of punctuation or spaces, does not contain markup, but even this has letter shapes, line endings and other features that could be regarded as extraneous to the textual symbols themselves. In the area of digital text, markup is generally used to refer to features that can be explicitly tagged for some purpose. Markup therefore describes an ontology – it tells us what something *is* – and also a function – it tells us what something *does*. In typesetting terms, markup was originally used to describe how something should be printed – how something *looks*. Markup that defines how a text might appear on a printed page (or on a computer screen for that matter) is *presentational*, while that which defines what something is or what it does is *descriptive*. The advantage of using descriptive rather than presentational markup is that it is a richer way of identifying and understanding textual features, and this translates well into the digital environment. For instance, if we come across a word or a phrase in italics in a text, in presentational markup that is all the information we have about the word or phrase. Even though italics may be used to render many different textual features, we have no way of knowing what they are from the presentational information. If, on the other hand, we identify something as a personal name, a town, a foreign word, then we can render these in italics, but we will also always have an underlying representation of what these things actually are, as well as how they appear. And if we decide later that an entity should be rendered in some different way, if it has been identified and marked up ontologically, one small command is all that is needed to change all instances.

Markup can be used to identify structural features internal to a text (paragraphs, lines, sentences) and also features which are not structural, but are part of the text's intellectual content; so markup can be linguistic, literary, historical, and so on. We need to be aware that there are some highly problematic issues in the application of markup and metadata to textual objects at any finer level of granularity than the page of the physical/digital object, and these lead to considerations and definitions of what a text actually is. As McGann reminds us: 'Most important to realize ... is that digital markup schemes do not easily – perhaps do not even naturally – map to the markup that pervades paper-based texts.'[35]

Markup, the TEI and the OHCO (Ordered Hierarchy of Content Objects) View of Text

Descriptive markup has proved to be a powerful tool in the world of digital texts. As Allen Renear observes:

> That the descriptive markup approach had so many advantages, and so many different kinds of advantages, seemed to some people to suggest that it was not simply a handy way of working with text, but that it was rather in some sense deeply, profoundly, correct ...[36]

It early led Renear and some of his colleagues to the view that somehow descriptive markup represents 'what text really is'; that 'the concepts of descriptive markup entail a model of text, and that model is more or less right'.[37] This model proposes that text can be defined as an 'Ordered Hierarchy of Content Objects (OHCO), and descriptive markup works as well as it does because it identifies that hierarchy and makes it explicit and available for systematic processing'. In practice this means that textual features must always be identified descriptively (what they are) rather than presentationally (how they look). Renear further describes the OHCO view of text thus:

---

35   Jerome J. McGann, 'Marking Texts of Many Dimensions', in Schreibman, Siemens and Unsworth (eds), *A Companion to Digital Humanities*, p. 199.

36   Allen H. Renear, 'Text Encoding', in Schreibman, Siemens and Unsworth (eds), *A Companion to Digital Humanities*, p. 224.

37   S-J. DeRose, David Durand, E. Mylonas and Allen Renear, 'What Is Text, Really?', *Journal of Computing in Higher Education*, 1 (1990). Reprinted in the ACM/SIGDOC *Journal of Computer Documentation*, 21 (1997), pp. 1–24.

The model in question postulates that text consists of objects of a certain sort, structured in a certain way. The nature of the objects is best suggested by example and contrast. They are chapters, sections, paragraphs, titles, extracts, equations, examples, acts, scenes, stage directions, stanzas, (verse) lines, and so on. But they are not things like pages, columns, (typographical) lines, font shifts, vertical spacing, horizontal spacing, and so on. The objects indicated by descriptive markup have an intrinsic direct connection with the intellectual content of the text; they are the underlying 'logical' objects, components that get their identity directly from their role in carrying out and organizing communicative intention. The structural arrangement of these 'content objects' seems to be hierarchical – they nest in one another without overlap. Finally, they obviously also have a linear order as well: if a section contains three paragraphs, the first paragraph precedes the second, which in turn precedes the third.[38]

The OHCO model has been a powerful influence on the development of the TEI and TEI encoding because it is a model of text that renders it processable by computers. As an underlying theory of text, OHCO takes a view of text as a narrowly linguistic object abstracted from a physical container with a hierarchical structure that can be clearly understood and described: it supposes some kind of Platonic ideal of the text, a pure form that underlies actual representations.[39] This works for some texts, and in particular it works for texts which are born digital and newly developed according to the OHCO principles. But it does not work so well for book texts because it represents an a-rhetorical view of text and because, in conversion to electronic formats, texts retain necessary traces of their previous physical origins. McGann cites the example of poetic texts, which fall outside the OHCO model; John Lavagnino finds support in Randall McLeod's brilliant analysis of headings and layout in George Herbert's 'Easter-wings'; and Robinson points to medieval manuscripts as examples of textual forms tightly bound to their containers and in consequence not easily rendered in the model. A key issue here, pertinent to the reservations of McGann and Robinson, is that sometimes a textual object has a presentational (or bibliographic) feature that resists easy description, and must be somehow encoded as it is. Robinson gives as examples certain decorative features of manuscripts which are non-textual and therefore difficult to encode in any kind of symbolic representation, but which are nonetheless part of the meaning of the object and therefore (possibly) of the text.[40] The obstacles to rendering the visual aspects of text are both subjective and contextual; in challenging the rigidity of the underlying linguistic model, visual text, like audial text, also raises the possibility, rejected by OHCO, that there can be no pure representation of any textual form. As Lavagnino remarks:

---

38   Renear, 'Text Encoding', p. 224.

39   See Renear's further thoughts on this in 'Out of Praxis: Three (Meta)Theories of Textuality', in Sutherland (ed.), *Electronic Text*, pp. 107–26.

40   Robinson, 'Ma(r)king the Electronic Text', p. 312.

There is less room in a digital edition for evading interpretive questions by printing something with an ambiguous appearance ... To use the TEI approach you need to believe in transcription. It is impossible for a transcription to reproduce the original object; it is always a selection of features from that object: the words but not their size on the page or the depth of the chisel marks, major changes in type style but not variations in the ink's darkness from page to page over time. Features that seem essential for a particular transcription can be encoded; what's impossible is notating everything. And it may be that the creation of a digital description of a feature has little value for analysis: what you really want may just be the opportunity to see an image of the original, if the limitations of digital images are less damaging in your case than the limitations of transcription. A transcription might be regarded more as an index of words in page images than as a reasonable working representation of the text in works intended as mixtures of words and images and in very complex draft manuscripts where the sequence of text or inscription is difficult to make out.[41]

The debate about text as an OHCO begs an important question: is it actually possible to formulate a theory about textual structure that works for all texts, in all languages, in all time-frames? And is it possible to mark up everything that might be deemed significant about a text? When we are reasoning from a particular text, can we reason about text generally? Is it necessary to mark up everything in a text, and for whom and for what purpose is the text being marked up? Some of the arguments and structures that still prevail in the world of electronic text and markup were developed when computers were used for the symbolic representation of data, not for visual representation. In consequence, they assumed that all information about the structure and content of a text had to be expressed symbolically because the user would not be able to see the text itself. But now, huge advances in imaging technologies have made it possible to create digital facsimiles that obviate much of the need to describe problematic features, especially if you believe that description is necessarily interpretation. This is what Renear labels the 'antirealist' view of text, which, rejecting pure representation, argues that texts are 'in some sense the products of the theories and analytical tools we deploy when we transcribe, edit, analyze, or encode them'.[42]

Further debate around electronic text markup addresses the issue of whether it should be embedded in a text or external to it, and related by some system of pointers. The advantage of embedding markup is that it is then always part of the text and travels with it through various transmissions and transmutations; the disadvantage is that it can become cumbersome if the text is marked up for

---

41   John Lavagnino, 'When Not to Use TEI', in Burnard, O'Brien O'Keefe and Unsworth (eds), *Electronic Textual Editing*, p. 338; and see Random Cloud, 'Fiat Flux', in Randall McLeod (ed.), *Crisis in Editing: Texts of the English Renaissance* (New York: AMS Press, Inc., 1994), pp. 61–172.

42   Renear, 'Out of Praxis', p. 122.

multiple different purposes. The TEI proposes that markup be embedded, but other projects are experimenting with offset or stand-off markup. One of the problems that has plagued the TEI community, and continues to plague it, is that of overlapping hierarchies. If text is an OHCO, then the hierarchies are presumed to nest within each other, to have a logical sequence, and not to overlap. But this is not 'how text really is', to paraphrase Renear *et al*. Any text that has, or has had, a physical manifestation will have overlapping hierarchies, as paragraphs wrap over pages and sentences wrap over lines, and so on. The editor/encoder has to come to terms with some way of representing this physicality as well as the logic of the text. Further, literary texts are potentially the most ambiguated and overlapping of all, requiring sets of descriptions that challenge discrete categorization at many points. For example, not just paragraphs that wrap over pages, but descriptions that explicitly relate text objects from different perspectives: a poem can be analyzed metrically and as sentences; a novel can be examined bibliographically (pages, gatherings, volumes) and as narrative development (paragraphs, chapters). Established technical terms like 'enjambement' (where a sentence may continue across a stanza) cover something of this inherent characteristic of literature.

The advocates of offset markup stored in separate files suggest that adopting this approach will solve the problems of the complexity of embedded markup and of overlapping hierarchies, since separate descriptions can co-exist side-by-side, providing different perspectives on the same text. However, the whole point of reusability is that electronic texts should be available over time to different people for different purposes. The danger with offset markup is that the base text and the markup files may gradually drift apart, rendering the relationship between the two meaningless. Dekhtyar and Iacob, in defining markup structures for a number of editing projects at the ARCHway project at the University of Kentucky, have proposed the use of offset markup in a series of concurrent documents that allow the editor to deal with various editorial tasks separately, and to distinguish the various logical hierarchies so that no one view of a working document contains overlapping hierarchies.[43] As they point out: 'Our principle of task separation allows the editor not to worry about concurrent markup representation during markup creation stages.'[44] A database stores the different strands of markup; then, when required, an 'ultimate' XML version can be created with all markup embedded in the document. The underlying document is still maintained separate from the markup, and the markup still exists in the database, with the 'ultimate' document produced for some specific purpose such as publication. As the database

---

43   Reported in K. Kiernan, J.W. Jaromczyk, A. Dekhtyar, *et al*., 'The ARCHway Project: Architecture for Research in Computing for Humanities through Research, Teaching, and Learning', *Literary and Linguistic Computing*, 20 (Suppl. 1) (2005), pp. 69–88. See also A. Dekhtyar and I.E. Iacob, 'A Framework for Management of Concurrent XML Markup', *Data and Knowledge Engineering*, 52 (2), pp. 185–215.

44   'The ARCHway Project', p. 84.

will store all changes, the danger of the base document and markup drifting apart is minimized.

A similar approach is taken to offsetting markup, specifically in the preparation of editions, by the Australian Scholarly Editions Centre.[45] Known as Just-in-Time-Markup (JITM), this technique also incorporates a powerful system of authentication to ensure the integrity of the underlying document. In JITM, a base transcription file is prepared containing only the most minimal structural information. Other markup is stored in any number of external files, which can be merged with the base transcription to create a particular 'perspective' on the text. This is a transient view, and as many perspectives can be created as the user wishes. Before the base file is merged, its integrity is checked by the JITM system. As Paul Eggert suggests:

> The practical effect of this authentication is that JITM allows a base transcription
> file to be annotated or augmented with analytical or structural markup, in parallel
> and continuously, while retaining its textual integrity.[46]

Two models, then, one in its enclosure within the document file replicating some aspects of the printed book, and the other suggesting an evolving series of encoded performances. In the view of the iconoclastic Ted Nelson, embedded markup's claim to contain everything you could want translates into the dismal reality of the 'T.V. dinner', where '"What else could you possibly want?" means "It's not on the menu"'.[47] By contrast, JITM's promise depends to some extent on what you cook for yourself. Either way, a computational model of text relates to a textual object only to the degree that a computer language relates to the text's own system of symbols, which, in linguistic terms, is itself a code that offers only a selection of features from spoken language. In other words, the computer language, like the novel's representation of conversation, say, is a useful tool or heuristic that helps us understand more about how computers, language and texts might work at the highest level of abstraction, but that fails, as it must, when confronted with real-world objects of any complexity. In the end, the computer, much like the book, trades in imaginary and interpretative replacements.

---

45   See Eggert, 'Text-encoding, Theories of the Text, and the "Work-Site"', pp. 425–35; and Phillip Berrie, 'A New Technique for Authenticating Content in Evolving Marked-up Documents', *Literary and Linguistic Computing*, 22 (2007), pp. 17–25.

46   Eggert, 'Text-encoding, Theories of the Text, and the "Work-Site"', p. 431.

47   Theodore H. Nelson, 'XML.com: Embedded Markup Considered Harmful', 2 October 1997 <http://www.xml.com/pub/a/w3j/s3.nelson.html> (accessed 1 August 2007).

Chapter 4
New Modes of Publishing

The publishing industry has always been ready to embrace new technologies in the pursuit of better, cheaper and faster production of its wares, as we discuss in relation to newspapers in Chapter 2. The great achievement of Gutenberg and other early experimenters around 1450 in reproducing texts by mechanical means was not initially so much an intellectual and technological advance as a huge commercial leap into mass production 300 years before the industrial revolution. On the contrary, we know that by the fifteenth century scriptoria had achieved a quality (if not a faithfulness) of reproduction that excelled that of the earliest printed books. Print, to put it simply, was just another way of making, of writing, books. But printing was successful for other immediate reasons: it lowered the costs of reproduction and massively increased the speed of duplication. It made copying (in large numbers) easier and cheaper; it did not require new methods of reading or the reinvention of book design. Books had hitherto been hand-copied manuscripts, chiefly made to order on a sell-before-you-produce model; what Gutenberg introduced was the produce-before-you-sell model that largely remains in place today, though digital technology looks set to change this in some areas. Alongside the Bible, some of Gutenberg's earliest mass-market products were indulgences, distributed by the Church to raise revenues. Indulgences, documents promising the remission, after absolution, of the temporal punishment due to sins, were a lucrative industry in the Middle Ages. Printing provided the Church with a ready solution for what was otherwise a labour-intensive bureaucratic procedure (writing thousands of identical letters by hand); in its turn, the market in indulgences provided printing, a venture with high capital costs, with a valuable and reliable cash injection, paid by the Church, as well as with important official approval. Few of these printed indulgences survive, but some 143,000 print copies of one particular indulgence were thought to have been produced by the end of the fifteenth century.[1]

Developments in the new technology, in other words, arrived at a time that was ripe for them, with products (Bibles and indulgences), an avid market and

---

1   See the statistics for pre-1501 printing in England, when it is estimated that approximately 20 per cent of Latin print production consisted of indulgences and bulls, in 'Introduction' to *The Cambridge History of the Book in Britain*, vol. 3, 1400–1557, Lotte Hellinga and J.B. Trapp (eds) (Cambridge: Cambridge University Press, 1999), pp. 17–18; and Paul Needham, *The Printer and the Pardoner: An Unrecorded Indulgence Printed by William Caxton for the Hospital of St Mary Rounceval, Charing Cross* (Washington: Library of Congress, 1986).

a rich revenue stream already in place. Ironically, too, and within decades, print proved as catastrophic for the Church as it had been propitious, when in their turn the trade in indulgences became one of the main targets of Martin Luther's reforming zeal. Luther's attacks, supported by a campaign of posters and flysheets, were also made effective through the power of the press. Yet it is equally true that in the fifteenth century, as now, there was no total or simple shift from one technology to another and no simple binary divide: scribal publication and print co-existed throughout Europe for some 200 years, into the seventeenth century. The continuity was sustained and invigorated by various kinds of hybridization: manuscript bolstering print, print books finished off by hand. In some areas, for example the religious writings of learned women, a vigorous practice of manuscript copying and circulation persisted into the eighteenth century.[2] Even now we cannot say that print has abolished manuscript. And despite our current cultural fixation, it is rarely ever one thing or the other: manuscript or print; print or digital. Paradoxically, the present scholarly emphasis upon massive online resources like *Early English Books Online (EEBO)* and *Eighteenth-Century Collections Online (ECCO)* is set to exaggerate the exclusive importance of print-based tools as they represent the past, occluding the enduring significance of the production and circulation of knowledge and ideas in manuscript. Then, again, how long will it be before students and scholars forget that the facsimile texts assembled in *EEBO* were once books with paper, board and leather bindings?

The printed codex book as physical object has not changed dramatically since Gutenberg. It has, over the centuries, acquired more wrappers and more navigation tools, in the form of material layers and organizational pointers protecting the text from or attaching it to the outside world. In the earliest printed books (before 1500) a plain unmarked sheet was wrapped around the text to keep it clean. This sheet soon acquired a short title, which was at first an aid to the printer, binder and bookseller in storing stock and later a means of advertising contents. Books were at this stage bought unbound; so the title page was a temporary covering. Only in the course of the sixteenth century did it become more elaborately designed and integrated with the text, eventually requiring a further protective wrapper of its own – first blank and later (around 1700) with a half title, which in its turn acquired a blank leaf cover. In the twentieth century dust jackets provided a paper protection, not now for the text, but for the book itself. Title pages, page numbering, catchwords, running headlines, contents pages and indexes all developed at various times, dependently upon and independently of manuscript practices, and providing either

---

2   David McKitterick, *Print, Manuscript and the Search for Order 1450–1830* (Cambridge: Cambridge University Press, 2003), pp. 47–52, makes the point forcefully. See also Harold Love, *The Culture and Commerce of Texts: Scribal Publication in Seventeenth-Century England* (1993; reissued by Amherst: University of Massachusetts Press, 1998); and recent work on the female manuscript tradition in, for example, George L. Justice and Nathan Tinker (eds), *Women's Writing and the Circulation of Ideas: Manuscript Publication in England, 1550–1800* (Cambridge: Cambridge University Press, 2002).

a scaffold around the text or tools to search it.[3] But the book's basic structure has remained much the same.

However, if the book is much the same, the production process, six centuries on, is quite different: digital technology is firmly embedded in all aspects of printing and publishing. With few exceptions, usually in the field of fine printing, every printed object now produced will almost certainly derive from an electronic text or file of some kind, and the workflow, from author or originator, through the editorial process, to printer, is now almost entirely electronic. As with the adoption of a digital workflow in the newspaper industry, technological changes (not all of them related to digital technologies) have been largely invisible to the consumer of print, except as they have enabled lower costs or improved products: the paperback book, for example, can be produced relatively cheaply because advances in adhesives technology permit binding with glues that are tough, durable and flexible. However, the rise of the Internet and the ubiquity of the means to access text electronically have led in the last ten years to the questioning of the place of the printed codex book in intellectual life and in culture generally, and to considerable debate about its potential replacement by other forms. Are we, as many have speculated, moving 'beyond the book'?

A recent volume on the future of the book asks the question, 'what is a book?' – something to which we all thought we knew the answer. But for its editors, Bill Cope and Angus Phillips, this now appears a valid line of enquiry:

> A book is no longer a physical thing. A book is what a book does. And what does a book do? A book is a structured rendition of text and possibly also images … a book … does not have to be printed … A book is not a product, it is an information architecture.[4]

This definition of a book as 'not a product' is itself problematic, since products are what publishers have traditionally sold, and selling 'information architectures' is a different and more difficult proposition from selling products, especially in a world which believes that information available in digital form should be free. We are prepared, it seems, to pay for the containers of information (books, journals, CDs or DVDs) but not for the information itself if we can download it without charge from the Internet. Exactly what distinguishes a book as 'an information architecture'? Which aspects of a book's materiality and functioning come into view when we uncouple it from its physical carrier? And granted the redefinition, what does it mean for those who commission, produce, store and sell books?

The early 1990s witnessed intense speculation about the future of the book, with predictions that the age of print was coming to an end. At that time many

---

3   Philip Gaskell, *A New Introduction to Bibliography* (Oxford: Clarendon Press, 1972), pp. 52–3.

4   Bill Cope and Angus Phillips (eds), *The Future of the Book in the Digital Age* (Oxford: Chandos Publishing, 2006), pp. 7–8.

publishers embarked upon experimental and expensive methods of production and delivery of multimedia objects, expecting the returns would be commensurate with the investment. The effect so far on the publishing industry, on academia and on the general reading public has been less than predicted. Fifteen years on, printed books are alive and well; and though book reading as popular entertainment shows some degree of decline, this is in large part owing to competition from other entertainment media (TV, cinema, electronic games, the Internet, and so on) rather than to the wholesale conversion of books to other forms. Print remains resilient, with the number of new titles published in Britain and the United States growing year on year. As the Mexican writer Gabriel Zaid has wittily remarked:

> Books are published at such a rapid rate that they make us exponentially more ignorant. If a person read a book a day, he would be neglecting to read four thousand others, published the same day. In other words, the books he didn't read would pile up four thousand times faster than his knowledge.[5]

And we must not forget that the reading and writing of text are both increasing rapidly with widespread use of email, text messaging, chat rooms, blogs and other forms of electronic literate communication. As the recent examples of *Julie and Julia: My Year of Cooking Dangerously* and *Baghdad Burning: Girl Blog from Iraq* demonstrate, the ultimate endorsement of the successful blog is currently its remediation as a printed book.[6]

Of course, over this same period some types of books have been almost entirely replaced by other media. John Pickering, writing in 1996 about hypermedia, defined certain kinds of books as 'tool-like texts':

> reference works, textbooks, manuals and lists. These are the tools and general *habitus* of literate culture. In the more specialized arena of the humanities, dictionaries, concordances, materials for language teaching, catalogues and the like are powerfully amplified by being transformed into hypermedia.[7]

These books, he predicted, would be reconfigured by digital technologies, while books that offer 'a narrative or critical argument will not be enhanced. Linearity, for

---

5   Gabriel Zaid, *So Many Books: Reading and Publishing in an Age of Abundance* (Philadelphia, PA: Paul Dry Books, 2003), p. 22.

6   Julie Powell, *Julie and Julia: My Year of Cooking Dangerously* (London: Penguin Books, 2005); the writer known as Riverbend began her weblog in August 2003, and it subsequently appeared as *Baghdad Burning: Girl Blog from Iraq* (New York: Feminist Press, 2005), with a sequel *Baghdad Burning II* (2006).

7   John Pickering, 'Hypermedia: When Will They Feel Natural?', in Warren Chernaik, Marilyn Deegan and Andrew Gibson (eds), *Beyond the Book: Theory, Culture and the Politics of Cyberspace* (Oxford: Office for Humanities Communication Publications, 1996), p. 52.

all that it may seem old fashioned, is a property of narrative and of consciousness, of Bergson's *durée*.'[8] More than a decade later, Pickering's predictions seem to have been prescient; it is indeed on practical, tool-like texts that the digital has had the greatest impact, while reflective, narrative works of developed and complex thought continue to circulate preferentially in printed codex form. Large-scale reference works may not have disappeared in print form, but they have been effectively replaced by online or CD and DVD versions. The book format served reference works like dictionaries, encyclopaedias or atlases relatively well, and the printed page could be composed with a sophistication and elegance of design that allowed straightforward retrieval of complex information according to the organizing principles of the producers. But the electronic medium serves such works better because, among its material functions, it permits, unlike the material functions of the book, the reshaping of information according to the immediate needs of the user: that is, for instant and focussed retrieval. A reference work is a database, not a narrative or an argument, and it performs better in an electronic environment. Take, for instance, online mapping sites or GPS (global positioning system) technologies that can pinpoint a location in an instant or create a complex driving route over hundreds, even thousands, of miles, work out the costs of fuels and tolls and suggest hotels and restaurants along the way. With paper dictionaries or encyclopaedias, retrieval can only be by headword or main entry; in structured electronic form, retrieval can be effected via any field or sub-field, or even by full-text searching, and the information can be kept constantly up-to-date.

One size no longer fits all. An academic journal, the *Encyclopaedia Britannica*, *Moby Dick*, a volume of verse or an edition of *King Lear* were all books (or, to be more precise, their texts were fitted to book containers) under the old dispensation. But if, as Cope and Phillips suggest, a book now is 'what a book does', then the physical limits of the container no longer signify or best serve the internal architectonics of the text. What seems a huge benefit for resources such as maps may be a potential problem for scholarly works where stability of reference is more important than currency of information. (We discuss this further in Chapter 6.) Where texts imply such different structures, purposes and audiences, we need to consider very carefully what it means to uncouple them from their traditional physical manifestation and present them in a new material form. For if a book is indeed 'what a book does', we must now begin to find ways to distinguish among the many relationships a book can have with the text it contains – some of which are more essentially bookish than others.

Journal Publishing

The changes wrought in academic journal publishing by digital technology have been profound and far-reaching; they parallel to some degree the changes

---

8   Ibid., p. 54.

in newspaper publication discussed in Chapter 2. Almost every journal now has an online version, and some journals are no longer available in print. Here the advantages of electronic dissemination are considerable for both publisher and scholar. For the publisher, printing costs can be saved and the production workflow streamlined, with the result that articles can be published faster. For the author, articles can be submitted online and tracked through the whole editorial process; proofs are easier to check as the submitted original is used for typesetting. Many publishers offer a 'publish-ahead-of-print' facility, making articles available online as soon as they have been through the editorial process, effectively circumventing the usual delay caused by assignment to a specific issue. Articles are compiled into issues only when enough have accrued to make this feasible. For author and reader, rapid publishing is a benefit, especially in subject areas like physics and medicine, where debate and research can be fast moving.

Because of the ways in which scholars have always used journal literature, little is lost and much is gained in the move to online delivery. By convention, journals are largely accessed in libraries rather than through personal subscription. Individual articles are the focus of attention, and more rarely whole issues; and since the advent of the photocopier, most scholars produce their own copies of significant articles to read, annotate and file. Little value is accorded to the material container; it is the information that is vital. In the online world, the ability to search metadata, abstracts and full text, to link from footnote references to the complete item cited, to download metadata directly, and to print off an article from the desktop, allows scholars to do better what they have always done. Increasing standardization in the structuring and encoding of online journals also means that scholars can cross-search many titles from different publishers, limited only by the subscription list of their institution or research library. But if the speed of transformation effected in our reading habits suggests the low priority of physical form, it is nevertheless noteworthy that most conventional print journals which have gone online, either instead of or in tandem with their printed version, have maintained the design, style and pagination of the original, generally using the ubiquitous portable document format (PDF), though some also have a plainer HTML version for faster downloading. When the PDF is printed, the article looks exactly like a photocopy from a print original. This familiarity is no doubt one of the contributory factors in the easy adoption of electronic journals in the scholarly world.

The great benefits derived from electronic journal publication call into question the necessity for a print version at all. If scholars can have what they always had and more, why print? One of the critical issues we discuss later is the long-term preservation of digital content, a problem currently vexing libraries and governments the world over. Apart from acid paper, print artefacts are stable and, if kept under the right conditions, have a long shelf life; far longer, some still argue, than digital formats. Accordingly, many libraries continue to acquire and bind print journals for preservation purposes. There are other instabilities associated with electronic forms: for example, changes in business and pricing models may result in loss of purchased electronic content when a subscription is cancelled. In the print world, the information object is bought and remains the property of the buyer; in the electronic world, the information may only be rented for a regular subscription, with the supply turned off when the subscription is cancelled. This is particularly the case when the digital files do not reside in the institution but are accessed by users from the publisher or other supplier. Where the new modes of journal publishing mean that information is not bounded by the pages or covers of the physical object but linked to other articles, images, sound files, datasets and various kinds of multimedia content, issues of long-term preservation are even more acute. In this case, supposing the article itself survives, what of its linked referents? The writer and/or publisher of the article may be responsible for maintaining long-term access to both digital and print versions, but they cannot be responsible for the links, which degrade rapidly over time. A book is what a book does; and one of the things a book has done very well over the centuries is protect our investment in the knowledge it contains. By contrast, electronic systems are still grappling with this issue.

There are other challenges to face. Since electronic information, unlike print, can be reproduced many times over at only marginal cost, publishers have established new kinds of deals in which institutions are encouraged to buy bundles of titles rather than individual journals. Libraries are thus faced with a wide range of purchase choices, even in relation to one title: it may be available in print only, digital only, print plus digital or as part of a larger digital bundle. We also see the rise of third-party companies who will aggregate journals from a number of publishers, an initiative comparable to such services as NewsPaperDirect, discussed in Chapter 2. Aggregation is a critical advantage of the digital format: it affords not just competitive pricing but scholarly benefits in the form of searches across a whole library of journals. Ovid, for example, offers access to 1,200 journals, over 500 books and more than 200 databases in science and medicine, and it claims some 13 million users worldwide;[9] TDNet e-Resource Manager gives access to 100,000 unique journal titles.[10] Bundling and aggregation of titles appear to hold out the enticing advantages of an instant and complete library of expert information; but it is not without problems for institutions which may be forced to take as part of a larger collection less popular journals with little appeal to their patrons. Each title may be cheaper than if purchased separately, but bundling may send up general costs.

The model, like the problem, is not really new: with the growth of a mass readership in the late eighteenth and early nineteenth centuries, print became increasingly subject to aggressive business practices in commissioning and marketing, among which were the wholesale trade in libraries, compiled, in calculated quantities, from various categories of book (travel, poetry, novels,

---

9   Ovid, <http://www.ovid.com/site/index.jsp?top=1> (accessed 23 May 2007).
10 TDNet e-Resource Manager, <http://www.tdnet.com/default.asp> (accessed 23 May 2007).

history,and so on). In some cases, library owners were also book publishers and printers, like William Lane of the Minerva Press and Library, Leadenhall Street, London. Lane, a shrewd businessman, shifted in the 1770s from trading poultry to books. Controlling both production and distribution, he had grasped that in an under-capitalized industry, fiction was a lucrative product for which the fashion-conscious and pleasure-seeking would pay highly; but that being an essentially ephemeral commodity, profits lay in circulation figures rather than sales. Bundled collections, like Lane's, ranging from a hundred to ten thousand volumes, were sold or rented to shopkeepers eager to extend their trade from haberdashery and tobacco into books. Since at this time the purchase price per volume for new works was prohibitively high for most individual readers, wholesalers and retailers made their money through complexly layered subscription systems. Steadily penetrating to the remotest towns through the later eighteenth century, by 1801 there were estimated to be a thousand circulating rental libraries in England.[11] A few decades later, in the Victorian period, Mudie's Select Library, owned 50 per cent by a publishers' consortium, not only monopolized the novel rental market but also effectively influenced the form's generic bounds (its style, format and subject), as well as its readership. What, it appears, eventually broke Mudie's stranglehold was the sheer difficulty of storage.[12]

In some instances, the changing relationship between content and container in academic journals is encouraging publishers to add value by creating portals for articles and augmenting these with other materials: contextualizing essays, teaching guides, editorial commentary, links to books published on the same topics and various kinds of meta-information. A good example is Blackwells' range of Compass portals in the humanities, with portals for history, literature, philosophy and religion currently available.[13] At the same time, these new relationships are creating new revenue streams and bringing into being new commercial organizations: not just aggregators, but indexing and citation services and metadata harvesting services. Many authors now find that the appearance of their work online, coupled with cross-journal searching, leads to higher visibility, increased citation and greater communication with other scholars. The benefits for researchers in poorer countries are also considerable: if the production of high quality content is still as expensive as ever it was, its dissemination is not, and material can be spread more widely at little extra cost to the publisher. For example, the World Health Organization has pioneered an initiative to distribute electronically biomedical and health literature to

---

11   *Monthly Magazine*, 11 (1801), p. 238.

12   See Peter Garside, James Raven and Rainer Schöwerling (eds), *The English Novel 1770–1829: A Bibliographical Survey of Prose Fiction Published in the British Isles*, 2 vols (Oxford: Oxford University Press, 2000), I, pp. 84–6 and II, pp. 18–19; and St Clair, *The Reading Nation in the Romantic Period*, p. 241.

13   See Blackwell Synergy, <http://www.blackwell-synergy.com/> (accessed 23 May 2007).

developing countries, with more than 3,750 journal titles currently available in 113 countries.[14] Most publishers now apply a sliding scale of costs, following World Bank recommendations, with poorer countries receiving free access to many journals. Such initiatives are only of value if scholars have ready access to electronic information, but there are now few academic institutions in the world where there is no online access at all.

The new modes of production and dissemination, and the new possibilities these have spawned, have in turn had significant consequences for the relationship between scholars, publishers and institutions. In the old ecology of journal publishing, the scholar worked for an institution which paid a salary. S/he would write an article for publication, the publisher would publish it without payment to the author and the institution would purchase the journal from the publisher. The rights in the material were generally owned jointly by the author and the publisher, but the author's subsequent use of the material was restricted. This model has worked well in the print world: the publisher made money, the author earned prestige, tenure and promotion, and the institution paid (in state-funded educational institutions, the public purse actually paid). The more prestigious the publisher, the more benefit to the author, and the more willing an institution to invest in intellectual capital. No better model could be envisaged; since only large organizations could sustain the expensive production chain of publishing, self- or in-house institutional publishing was rarely an option. This partnership is beginning to break down under the digital dispensation, as the wisdom is questioned of signing over the rights in the exploitation of scholarly products to commercial interests who then charge high (and rising) costs for their journals, thereby greatly restricting access to the results of publicly funded research. Some attribute rising costs to a more aggressive commercial model within academic publishing over the last 30 years, as a restricted number of large publishers buy out smaller enterprises or attract journals from professional societies and then ratchet up prices. Surveying this trend, the Scholarly Communication website established by the University of Illinois at Urbana-Champaign offers the telling example that, 'for the cost of a year's subscription to the *Journal of Applied Polymer Science*, you could get a well-equipped new Toyota Corolla'.[15] A Toyota Corolla costs many thousands of dollars.

Currently, the academic world is examining carefully a number of new strategies that might enable research to be shared more equitably. One approach has been to establish non-commercial means of academic publication with online journals freely accessible without subscription. This model has a number of problems. First of all, scholars fear (with some justification) that appointments' boards and tenure and promotions' committees will not recognize the worth of such electronic

---

14   Health InterNetwork Access to Research Initiative (HINARI), <http://www.who.int/hinari/en/> (accessed 28 May 2007).

15   Scholarly Communication, <http://www.library.uiuc.edu/scholcomm/issues.htm> (accessed 28 May 2007).

publications; in consequence, and especially in the humanities, they have been reluctant to publish in new online journals. Further, establishing and running a professional, peer-reviewed journal, even one without a print component, is not cost-free: most online journals, like print, have so far been supported by professional institutions or grant bodies; so though they are free to users, they are paid for by someone. On the plus side, one advantage is that journals appealing only to niche markets become viable; and, in turn, this broadens the research base and its dissemination. The Directory of Open Access journals, for instance, offers access to free, full-text, peer-reviewed scholarly journals in all subjects and languages. There are currently 2,697 journals in the directory (with 805 searchable at article level), providing a total of 134,007 articles. Among the more specialized journals available is the *Journal of Dagaare Studies*, produced in English by the University of Hong Kong, and publishing articles only on the Dagaare peoples of West Africa.[16] No commercial publisher could support a journal with so narrow a range; for scholars in smaller disciplines, such publication venues are invaluable.

Non-commercial, online journals are not the only means of providing wider, cost-free (to the reader) access to research. Another development is the move towards 'self-archiving' combined with open access. The model for this is a long-standing pre-print and archiving service established by the international physics community in 1991 at the Los Alamos High Energy Physics Laboratory. Now situated at Cornell University Library, ArXiv.org is a fully automated electronic archive and distribution server for research papers. Publications in physics are time-critical and traditional print journals were not processing articles quickly enough; hence a community-based archive which allows scholars to mount papers awaiting publication ('pre-prints') for viewing by other scholars; upon publication, the published article replaces its pre-print version. ArXiv has been highly successful as a model, spawning a number of similar initiatives promoting 'open access' to scholarly publication: that is, free online access to the latest articles.

'Open access' is not a new form of publishing, but a new contract between author, publisher and institution which involves a shift in the cost model and in the assignment of rights. In Britain, the EPrints for Digital Repositories service at the University of Southampton defines open access thus: 'Open Access (OA) is free, immediate, permanent online access to the full text of research articles for anyone, webwide.' EPrints suggest there are two methods of open access: one where journals (and therefore publishers) themselves provide open access to articles (the 'golden' road); and one where authors provide open access to their published articles, by making their own e-prints free for all (the 'green' road of self-archiving). Self-archiving is not self-publishing, nor is it online publishing without peer review; it is a way of making research more widely available, with

---

16   Directory of Open Access Journals (DOAJ), <http://www.doaj.org/> (accessed 24 May 2007).

fewer barriers to access.[17] Self-archiving is not a matter of putting material on a personal website, but of depositing research publications in secure and accessible archives which will manage the metadata, disseminate information about the research and preserve the publications for the long term. This, current wisdom suggests, is best done by academic institutions creating secure e-print archives or repositories. For the author, the proper management of the metadata is crucial, as this is the way the work will be found and cited by other scholars. An international standard has been developed and widely adopted by institutions, the Open Archives Initiative (OAI) Protocol for Metadata Harvesting (OAIPMH), which ensures that, if an item is placed in an OAI-compliant archive, it can be exposed as widely as possible to search engines. Scholars do not need to know anything about this standard: they merely fill in a form and upload a copy of the publication; the archiving and metadata management are done behind the scenes. In order to promote open access, a number of funding agencies are insisting that the outputs of grant-funded research be made available in this way as quickly as is feasible. At the same time, they acknowledge that this is likely to be implemented in different ways and on different time-scales across the range of academic disciplines. All Research Councils in the UK, for example, have mandated that:

> From 1 October 2005, subject to copyright and licensing arrangements, a copy of any published journal articles or conference proceedings resulting from Research Council funded research should be deposited in an appropriate e-print repository (either institutional or subject-based) wherever such a repository is available to the award-holder. Deposit should take place at the earliest opportunity, wherever possible at or around the time of publication.[18]

The UK Research Councils have also accepted that such a policy is likely to incur costs to authors. Accordingly, they are prepared for these to be added to the overall costs of grant-funded research.

The financial and management implications of this policy are considerable and have provoked intense debate between publishers, funding agencies, institutions and scholars. Many publishers allow self-archiving without any charge if the archiving takes place after a period of time has elapsed (usually one to two years after publication), and most publishers also allow pre-prints to be placed in repositories before publication.[19] If authors want full open access (the 'golden' route), this can

---

17   EPrints for Digital Repositories, <http://www.eprints.org/openaccess/> (accessed 24 May 2007).

18   Research Councils UK (RCUK), <http://www.rcuk.ac.uk/research/outputs/access/2005.htm> (accessed 24 May 2007).

19   A pre-print is usually defined as an un-refereed author version of an article, that is, a version without the value added in the editorial process.

be offered for a fee payable by the author to cover the editorial costs.[20] Initially, this move from a 'reader pays' to an 'author pays' model seems counter-intuitive: why would authors wish to publish in a journal that charges them for the privilege? In the humanities, and by contrast with science and medicine, there has been almost no uptake in this form of open access. Humanities scholarship is generally not grant-supported, and it is rarely time-critical. Consequently, the advantages of making research results freely available immediately, rather than one or two years later, are not sufficient to persuade academics or their institutions to pay. In large-scale, grant-funded science and medicine projects, however, the amounts needed to finance open-access publication are negligible as a proportion of the overall costs of the work, and the benefits of immediate access and publication are great. Many science and medicine journals are adopting the model eagerly. One key advantage to emerge from these new modes of access is that works are cited more quickly and more frequently. Stephen Harnad reports that self-archiving has been shown to increase citation between 50 and as much as 250 per cent, though only 15 per cent of authors are currently adopting the practice. Ninety-five per cent of authors are reported to be willing to self-archive, but apparently only if required to do so by their research funders or their institutions.[21]

Book Publishing

In Chapter 1 we reflected upon the widely predicted death of the book, *circa* 1990, to be killed off by the rise of electronic technologies and the hypermedia inventions they supported. These would be capable of displaying and manipulating complex interactive fictions and, it was argued, of freeing our minds and our textual resources from the restricting shackles of linearity and the sequencing of pages – the constraints of the book as container. Towards the end of the 1990s, another technology emerged, again to the fanfare that it signalled the demise of print: the e-book. E-books are not experimental or complex hypermedia productions; they are electronic versions of conventional books made available for reading on screen, designed and paginated to simulate very closely their printed sibling, though usually with some additional functionality. E-book software has been produced for a range of devices: e-books can be accessed on general-purpose equipment like computers, PDAs or mobile phones, or they can be read on dedicated readers,

---

20   For Oxford University Press and Cambridge University Press, this fee is currently £1,500 (though Oxford has a discounted rate for authors at institutions subscribing to the journal). Both Oxford and Cambridge are still experimenting with these models. At Oxford, for example, some journals have become fully open access, and in others authors are given the option to make individual articles available under open access, thus incurring the fee.

21   Stephen Harnad, 'Publish or Perish – Self-Archive to Flourish: The Green Route to Open Access', *Ercim News online edition*, 64, January 2006, <http://www.ercim.org/publication/Ercim_News/enw64/harnad.html> (accessed 14 September 2007).

the first of which began to appear in the late 1990s. But, with rare exceptions, the revolution has not happened;[22] more books are being published and printed in conventional physical formats than ever before. This is in sharp contrast to developments in the music industry, where the iPod and other portable devices have had an enormous impact on the music we listen to, share and purchase. The slow uptake of electronic books may seem surprising, given the runaway success of music players and digital cameras, but there are a number of reasons for this; among them usability, costs and rights' management.

In literate societies, book reading is ubiquitous. For most people it represents a comfortable and familiar process in which we generally forget the instrument delivering the information and entertainment to us, and concentrate on the content. We can be transported and absorbed by a book; we can reflect deeply upon it. Books do not come with manuals telling us how to use them or with chargers, CDs of software or content to load up. Books are self-explanatory and self-describing, and we use them unself-consciously. When reading is mediated by current electronic technology, that depth of immersion is more difficult; especially so when we use a multi-purpose device which makes itself obtrusive by signalling that an appointment is due or an email has arrived. This is not to suggest that electronic technology is not immersive: multiplayer games, MUDs, MOOs and chat rooms all attract users into a deep engagement; but this is a far different experience from reading a textual narrative. These electronic spaces may be entertaining, stimulating or provocative, but they are not reflective. For sustained reading, the book does not yet seem to have been bettered. The fact that some of the new generation of e-book readers associate improved reading experience with screen technology that simulates the appearance and feel of a book suggests that any real advance is premised on a capacity for imitating what books already do. If a book is what a book does, then an e-book, it would seem, is only as successful as its capacity to simulate many of the physical properties of bookishness.

---

22   Though e-books have not taken off in the wider book market, they have been adopted with some success in education. The e-book provider NetLibrary, for example, has 100,000 e-book and audio-book titles which it supplies to 14,000 libraries worldwide. These are, it claims, 'best-selling titles from the world's leading publishers' which represent 'a comprehensive collection of frontlist, newly published content that never stops growing. And there are even more types of content coming – in more formats, subjects and languages.' NetLibrary, <http://www.oclc.org/netlibrary/default.htm> (accessed 5 September 2007). There are two key drivers for the success of NetLibrary: it has adopted a pricing and licensing model that publishers can work with; and it is a part of OCLC, the world's largest library corporation, which means that it has a ready-made market. In educational institutions, NetLibrary titles are available alongside other online sources, such as electronic journals, and are often catalogued in the main library catalogue. Their delivery mechanisms function much like those for electronic journals, their contents are accessed in similar ways, and they do not require dedicated e-book readers. Through NetLibrary, popular textbooks can be made available to many students simultaneously: they are never out on loan.

The arguments in favour of dedicated electronic readers are that many e-books can be loaded onto a device which is itself no larger or heavier than a single book, and that a variety of supplementary features can be added: search and retrieval, annotation or dictionary look-up. Described thus, electronic readers are the sci-fi dream of many books in one. The e-books themselves can be directly downloaded from the Internet; so access to content is relatively straightforward. Early e-book reading devices were aimed at a commercial market for which publishers began to make available e-versions of newly published titles sold through online outlets, often by major bookstore chains alongside hardback, paperback and audio versions of the same title. At this stage, dedicated readers simulated books as closely as possible, but came with a hefty price tag. The Everybook Reader, released in 1999, was described as 'the world's first "true" electronic book ... the only two-screen, facing portrait-page electronic book system'.[23] It sold for $1,600, and was aimed at publishers in medicine and the sciences. Cheaper devices, like the Gemstar, aimed more squarely at the general reading public, were selling at the time for around $300, with a more 'book-like' version sporting a leather cover for around $700. They have proved limited in their appeal, partly because of the high cost of both reader and content. Where e-books have been successful, it is generally when they are supplied in formats for use on a PDA or desktop/laptop computer. Though many e-books were, and still are, available online free, these tend to be out-of-copyright works, or highly illegal pirate copies of in-copyright titles, with current publications in e-book format selling for around the same cost as a hardback book.

Format itself has always been an issue: different devices run different software and it is rarely possible that e-books bought for one reader can be read on another. For example, the e-book supplier eBookMall has books in ten different formats and lists eleven devices from which they can be read.[24] Rights' management imposes further limitations, and it is ironic that electronic information, hailed as democratizing and transformative, is bound more tightly by legal restrictions than a printed book. Once a printed book is bought, it is owned by the purchaser who can give it away, resell it or loan it many times over. A commercial e-book can often only be read on the machine to which it was first downloaded, or at best on a limited number of other machines; and it cannot be resold or loaned unless the machine is sold or loaned with it. The restrictive rights' environment also affects copyright deposit libraries, who are not only required to sign a contract for digital materials generally tighter than any covering print, but such contracts can prevent usages under the conventional 'fair dealing' arrangement. Formerly such

23   *BiblioTech Review: Information Technology for Libraries*, in an e-book update of February 2000, <http://www.biblio-tech.com/BTR900/February_2000/e-book_update. html> (accessed 29 May 2007).

24   eBookMall, <http://www.ebookmall.com/> (accessed 29 May 2007).

arrangements would have allowed copying for archiving purposes or reformatting for use by the visually impaired.[25]

Not only has an e-book culture so far shown no sign of developing, in a number of environments dedicated readers once tried have been abandoned. In 2000 the Richmond Public Library in British Columbia, Canada, piloted the delivery of e-books to its patrons, initially with some success: e-book readers were pre-loaded with 13 popular titles and issued as though they were books. At the time of the experiment, the library reported as follows:

> The Ebook is just one more way to provide improved service to our customers and offer them access to the world of knowledge, information and entertainment. The important thing for the library is to connect people with books, reading and learning, in whatever format. Traditional books will always be around. The future will likely be a mix of new technology and traditional materials and services. One advantage of having Ebooks is that customers have access to more books than will fit on the actual library shelves. They are also terrific for people who travel and don't want to carry a bunch of books with them.[26]

However, success was short-lived and the use of the readers soon dropped off. Richmond Library now dismisses them as a cumbersome and inconvenient fad. Charles McGrath, writing in the *New York Times* at the end of 2006, summed up this generation of dedicated readers thus:

> About a decade ago, some publishers were predicting that books would soon be a thing of the past, and that we would all be reading downloadable texts on portable hand-held screens. Wishful thinking, it turns out. The book is still with us ... while the various book-replacement devices available back then have mostly been dumped on the recycling heap. They were too hard to read, people complained, and also too heavy, guzzling so much battery power that they quickly grew hot in the hand.[27]

A second wave of technology has brought a number of new dedicated devices onto the market. These have greatly improved screens which reflect rather than transmit light (known as 'electrophoretic'). They are mostly black and white and with a matt appearance, making the reading experience even more like that of

---

25 'Library warns of "more restrictive" DRMs', British Library 2006 Press Release, <http://www.bl.uk/news/2006/pressrelease20060607.html> (accessed 4 June 2007).

26 Marilyn Deegan and Simon Tanner, *Digital Futures: Strategies for the Information Age* (London: Library Association Publishing, 2002), p. 79.

27 Charles McGrath, 'Can't Judge an E-Book by Its Screen? Well, Maybe You Can', *New York Times*, 24 November 2006, <http://www.nytimes.com/2006/11/24/books/24eboo.html?pagewanted=1&ei=5070&en=a0561d20ee96036e&ex=1181102400> (accessed 4 June 2007).

reading paper; and some versions use rollable screens that can fit into a pocket but be rolled out to page-size. Amazon's device, Kindle, launched in November 2007, is the size of a paperback and much thinner. (The name Kindle apparently denotes the aim to 'kindle' the love of reading.) The Kindle has built-in wireless capacity, using mobile phone technology, which allows material to be downloaded without cables or other computers. With an almost limitless list of titles available for sale from its online bookshop (currently around 90,000, each downloadable in 30 seconds) and a capacity to hold around 200 titles at a time, the assumption at Amazon is that Kindle, and its like, will now finally replace the book.

Initial reception of this new generation of readers from Amazon, Sony and Epson has been mixed. Kindle's screen is small (only six inches diagonally), and since an aspect of its bookishness is flip-page technology, then with the screen set to a large type size (which is what most readers now prefer) you have to turn the page very frequently indeed. McGrath is disconcerted by the typeface used in the new Sony Reader (a version of the inelegant Courier), and, while the screen does look much like paper, the combination of typeface and layout is exactly the same for every text displayed:

> every book looks exactly the same. On my machine, for example, there is nothing whatsoever to distinguish a page of 'Portrait of a Lady' from a page of 'After Hours', by Jodi Lynn Copeland, in which people have hot, un-Jamesian sex first and then get to know each other afterward.[28]

The objection is a serious one: among the things a book does (and does well) is conjure an aesthetic effect through the relationship it creates between typography, page design and text; we scarcely notice, until it is lost, the associations contributed by a particular typeface to the pleasures or significance of a text. It could be argued that the e-book reader will come into its own as a means of carrying round bulky essential documents and books to take on journeys, or for loading up work materials. But without a screen big enough to lend itself to split functionality, even this aspect of its storage capacity is seriously compromised.

It remains to be seen whether electronic reading devices will succeed in changing our relationship with books, frequently described in this context by technophiles as the last defence of the analogue. For the moment, it is worth comparing the runaway success of portable digital music players with the relative failure of e-book readers. One reason often given for the poor uptake of readers is cost: current entrants into the market are retailing at around $200–400 in the United States and up to 650 euros in Europe. Charlie Stross, commenting early in 2007, asserted:

---

28   Ibid., and see reviews of Amazon's Kindle in the *Independent* and the *Times*, 20 November 2007.

> Expecting people to cough up $200 for a reader so that they can then pay $25 for new novels to read on it – as opposed to buying the novels for $25 (less discount) in hardcover and having the cultural artefact – is, well, it's just bogus.[29]

However, listeners will pay this amount for a music player, and for music downloads. Where does the difference lie? First of all, music devices have a simpler and more familiar interface than reading devices, while broadcast or recorded music has almost always needed complex electronic equipment on which to play it; and this has rarely come cheap. Further, music has been available in digital formats for more than 20 years, since the advent of the compact disc. For anyone with a CD collection and a computer, recording music for transfer to a player is straightforward – and much simpler than recording cassette tapes. Digital music devices accordingly represent a simplification in copying, sharing and listening to music. With e-books, on the other hand, the readers are exponentially more complex than the device they aim to replace, and currently emerging technologies for reading do not seem to be changing this. It is also more difficult and more expensive to get the textual content into the readers: one could conceivably upload an entire personal music collection, but would one scan a comparable book collection? Crucially, too, in this respect, the difference between analogue and digital recordings of a piece of music cannot easily be perceived by the listener; even though they derive from distinct underlying representations, both are output as sound. By contrast, the difference in underlying representations of text – analogue or digital – produces a reading experience which is profoundly altered. This gives us some confidence in proposing that a digital reading device can *never* give the same experience as reading a book. The book itself is part of the reading experience, much as the instrument on which a tune is played; a music device, however, is not part of the experience of listening in quite the same way. The intimacy we have developed and take for granted with books leads to some curious lapses in our accounting for the technology, as for instance when the aesthetician Elaine Scarry, writing in *Dreaming by the Book*, dismisses in such lingeringly physical terms the relevance of paper, ink and type to the reading effect.[30] Then there are other physical limitations and psychological factors to take into account. Music can be listened to in situations where reading is impossible: while driving, walking, running. This is one reason among others why radio did not die out with the advent of television; even with portable televisions, it is rarely possible to watch on the move. People are prepared to carry round an entire music collection in case they have a sudden urge to hear Puccini or Stevie Wonder; but to be accompanied by a whole library in case of a sudden need for *War and Peace* is less plausible. As yet, and perhaps finally, the technology does not present itself as an elegant

---

29   Charlie Stross, 'Why the Commercial Ebook Market is Broken', *Charlie's Diary* (Blog), 27 March 2007, <http://www.antipope.org/charlie/blog-static/2007/03/why_the_commercial_ebook_marke.html> (accessed 4 June 2007).

30   Scarry, *Dreaming by the Book*, p. 5, quoted at p. 4 above.

solution to any problem we confront as readers. For most reading purposes, books continue to be what physical book containers do, as experiments in developing the e-book reader paradoxically acknowledge, with each generation moving closer in appearance to book-likeness and further from computer-likeness.

***

If the general appeal of e-books and e-book readers remains in doubt, there has been nonetheless a revolution in publishing caused by electronic book production. The paradox is that its impact has been greatest on conventional printed books. Through a new printing model – print-on-demand – and through new business models made possible by Internet marketing and distribution, electronic production has reinvigorated print.

The economics of book production, where publishers operate with the produce-before-you-sell paradigm, have in the past favoured large houses which make most of their profits selling long runs of a small number of titles, offsetting losses on short runs of other, riskier works. Most books sell in short runs and make only modest profits; and most authors either have other income possibilities or live on very little. A widely quoted report of 1998 on the British book market drawn up by the business consultants KPMG suggested that only 3 per cent of titles accounted for 50 per cent of the volume of retail sales.[31] At one extreme, university presses, rarely answerable to shareholders, have traditionally been able to offer short runs of specialist titles likely to sell only a few hundred copies, mainly to libraries, by attaching high cover prices; by contrast, trade publishers are in the business of making money. Up to a certain point in the publishing chain, the overall costs of producing a book will be the same, whether it is to sell in the hundreds or hundreds of thousands. Editorial work, copy-editing, design, typesetting, and so on, are the same for niche market and for highly popular books. It is printing costs, paper, the size of the initial print run, the overall marketing strategies and the rate at which the book sells that will dictate publishers' profits. In the end, the economics of book production are inevitably driven by technology: what the printing press did in creating the mass market was make the unit costs of each book ever lower, but only if large numbers of the same book are printed at one time. And this calculation only results in a profit for the publisher if the majority of the books printed are then sold. What this means is that in order to manage risks, publishers will be more likely to publish books which appeal to the widest possible readership; they will be reluctant to take chances on unknown authors or experimental writings. This is good business sense, but it may be less good for literate culture.

The business model goes to the heart of the dilemma, as some have always seen it, of print. On the one hand, books have been represented through history as

---

31   Reported in Christopher Kular, 'The Venues for Vanity: Methods and Means for Self-Published Books', in Cope and Phillips (eds), *The Future of the Book in the Digital Age*, p. 58.

our chief means of acquiring knowledge, wisdom and, at times, even virtue; on the other, the mass economies of print have over the centuries led to accusations that the press brings knowledge within the reach of those unsuited to appreciate it or, even worse, that it dilutes the standard and narrows the choice of what is printed to achieve maximum communication and sales. Charles Knight, Victorian pioneer of cheap useful books for the masses, chose the life of the early English printer William Caxton as the subject for the first in his series of *Weekly Volumes*, issued on a subscription basis through his book club. Romantically, if inaccurately, he linked Caxton with knowledge for everyone, arguing:

> The process of printing, compared with that of writing, is a cheap process as ordinarily conducted; but the condition of cheapness is this, – that a sufficient number of copies of any particular book may be reckoned upon as saleable, so as to render the proportion of the first expense upon a single copy inconsiderable. If it were required even at the present time to print a single copy, or even three or four copies only, of any literary work, the cost of printing would be greater than the cost of transcribing. It is when hundreds, and especially thousands, of the same work are demanded, that the great value of the printing-press in making knowledge cheap is particularly shown.[32]

For Knight, himself a publisher, the ability to make thousands of copies of the same work is the key to the diffusion of knowledge. By contrast and only a few decades before Knight, writers suspicious of the link between technology and literature were expressing themselves uneasy at recent developments in printing and the promiscuous circulation of cheap books and periodicals. For both Wordsworth and Godwin, the reader of print (as opposed to the restricted audience of the manuscript writer or public speaker) was unknown and uncontrollable, a dangerously unintended consumer. How can you be sure that a book, the object of mass production, will convey its text, the product of artistic and intellectual discernment and discrimination, in the right way to the most suitable reader? Around the same time, Hugh Murray, in his treatise *Morality of Fiction* (1805), argued for a correlation between printing, the downward spread of literacy, and the alarming proliferation of pulp fiction:

> The origin of this mode of writing is easily accounted for. The invention of printing, and consequent diffusion of books, has given birth to a multitude of readers, who seek only amusement, and wish to find it without trouble or thought.[33]

---

32   Charles Knight, *William Caxton, the First English Printer: A Biography* (London: Charles Knight and Co., 1844), p. 135.

33   H[ugh] Murray, *Morality of Fiction; or, An Inquiry into the Tendency of Fictitious Narratives, with Observations on Some of the Most Eminent* (Edinburgh: A. Constable and Co. and J. Anderson; London: Longman, Hurst, Rees and Orme, 1805) p. 40; and see

From the publisher's point of view, the moral danger implied by the proliferation of print and mere bookmaking scarcely exists. As Knight makes clear, their problem lies in the manufacturing model itself. The difficulty besetting the produce-before-you-sell model is estimating the market for any one book and printing the right number of copies. This is next to impossible unless the author is well known and likely to sell large numbers, or unless the book has some additional high-profile promotion beyond what the publishers can afford to provide. If today a book is reviewed widely and well in the national press, taken up by celebrity book clubs (*Richard and Judy* in Britain, *Oprah* in America) or is a film or television spin-off, then its sales can with reason be predicted to be high. At the end of 2007, for example, Elizabeth Gaskell's *Cranford*, first published as a series of sketches between 1851 and 1853, was in the British paperback bestseller listings, purely as a consequence of a popular television dramatization. It would be interesting to know how many purchasers read it to the end. There are exceptions, of course: some books sell well purely through word of mouth; for example, Louis de Bernières's *Captain Corelli's Mandolin* or John Grisham's first novel, *The Firm*, described thus by Otto Penzler:

> Publishers also take chances because publishing isn't an exact science; you don't know which books will be the big winners. A few years ago Doubleday published a legal thriller, gave the author a $25,000 advance, and did a first print run of 25,000 copies. How did *The Firm* go from 25,000 copies to more than a million? Doubleday did not advertise the book. They did nothing special. Grisham didn't tour. It was word-of-mouth.[34]

But this is the old world of print. Now new developments in print production are set to change the publishing industry dramatically, and to fuel the rise of new kinds of niche and self-publication models.

What we can begin to think of as traditional printing (as distinct from the new digital model) has undergone vast change in more than 500 years: through movable type, to the Linotype or, in Britain, more commonly Monotype, that inaugurated mechanical typesetting at the end of the nineteenth century (popularly known in the trade as hot metal), on to offset lithography and the short reign of phototypesetting. But even today, almost all methods suffer from the same limitation: at the end of the typesetting process a fixed image of some kind (nowadays a film) has to be produced which is then the image carrier for the process of printing. Multiple pages are printed on a sheet at a single time: from two pages per forme in the earliest books through to 32 pages or many more at the end of the twentieth century.

William Godwin, *Thoughts on Man, His Nature, Productions, and Discoveries* (London: Effingham Wilson, 1831), pp. 251–2.

34   Otto Penzler, 'The Economics of Publishing', talk delivered at a meeting of Mystery Writers of America, New England, April 1999. Available at <http://www.mysterywriters. org/pages/resources/library/economics.htm> (accessed 4 June 2007).

But there is a maximum number that can be printed per sheet of paper, and so the image carrier has to be changed regularly. The sheets have to be cut down mechanically into units for bundling and gathering or prepared as single leaves for adhesive binding. There are high pre-press costs, high printing costs, and since books are heavy and bulky, there are high storage, transportation and distribution costs. Digital printing changes all that: digital printing machines can print all the pages of a book in sequence, just like a desktop printer; and since there is no intervening image carrier, printing is direct, which cuts set-up time dramatically. This means that the unit cost of printing a book is the same whatever the print run, even if it is a run of one copy; and if an error is discovered after typesetting, it can be corrected instantly. The consequence is lower pre-press costs, lower printing costs, lower storage costs (since smaller runs can be printed at need), and there is less risk of space-greedy unsold stock.

Machines are now available equipped to handle the whole book production workflow – from printing to collation, trimming and binding the finished product – with little human intervention. Jason Epstein, former editorial director of Random House, described one in action in January 2005:

> we watched a machine, about two-and-a-half meters long and half as high, receive a digital file, adjust itself to the dimensions of the desired book, and transmit the file to a duplex printer. The printed pages were then gathered and bound within a cover produced by a separate, four-color printer. The entire automatic process took about two minutes. The bound, 256-page book was next conveyed to a trimmer and finished, all without an operator. It was a transcendent moment.[35]

If we set alongside Epstein's wonder at the speed of automation the record of an earlier production model that his account both echoes and displaces, we begin to register just how fundamental and sudden has been the change. By the eighteenth century, dictionaries and encyclopaedias, the vast knowledge databases of their age, like those famously compiled by D'Alembert and Diderot in France and Ephraim Chambers and William Smellie in Britain, sought to systematize and summarize descriptions of the practical and mechanical arts for a public fascinated by techniques and processes, the workings of which were beyond their competence. They did so in the context of emerging models of production that relied on diversified skills and collaborative procedures. As now, it was a period of dizzying development and information explosion. But, contrary to now, mechanization ran alongside what were seen to be the economic benefits of a widespread division of labour which represented society to itself as a network of interdependent activities. Hence, this widely referenced definition, from a German economic lexicon of 1753, of the book:

---

35   Jason Epstein, 'The Future of Books', *Technology Review*, January 2005, <http://www.technologyreview.com/Infotech/14064/page3/> (accessed 8 June 2007).

BOOK, either numerous sheets of white paper that have been stitched together in such a way that they can be filled with writing; or, a highly useful and convenient instrument constructed of printed sheets variously bound in cardboard, paper, vellum, leather, etc. for presenting the truth to another in such a way that it can be conveniently read and recognized. Many people work on this ware before it is complete and becomes an actual book in this sense. The scholar and the writer, the papermaker, the type founder, the typesetter, and the printer, the proofreader, the publisher, the book-binder, sometimes even the gilder and the brass-worker, etc. Thus many mouths are fed by this branch of manufacture.[36]

By contrast, what Epstein's panoptic description of the new book production makes abundantly clear is the potential for much of the process to operate without subdivided labour. What is truly remarkable about this is that, though relations within the printing and publishing industry, and between authors, printers, publishers and readers, have changed in various ways over the centuries and in association with technological developments and shifts in demand and consumption, nevertheless until almost the end of the nineteenth century, typesetting (after paper, the major production cost) was done much as it had been since the beginnings of printing in the mid-fifteenth century. And even after its mechanization, around 1900, it was still based on the method of letterpress printing used by Gutenberg and Caxton, remaining both labour-intensive and strictly regulated until almost the end of the twentieth century. Hot-metal composition still made sense for many books into the 1980s, while the roles of copy-editor, designer, compositor or typesetter and proofreader continued separate. Only in the last 25 years have these distinct skills largely disappeared from commercial production in response to a range of developments: the availability of standard software for desktop use and professional publishing applications; the reusability of keyboarded data; and the globalization of print production. With digital technology, the tools used by author, publisher and printer have converged with startling speed. Disturbingly, the intensive industry of the large hot-metal composing room (the inheritor of much of the workflow of Caxton and Gutenberg's printing house) now resolves itself into two possible models: the small-scale, localized operation described by Epstein; or, at the other extreme, the globalized reality by which data-capture, text-processing, printing and binding each takes place on different continents. Globalization of production marks the end of an older model of specialism and subdivided labour that fuelled the economic development of industrializing nations from the later eighteenth century, just as surely as Epstein's single-site model of near total automation. What it also finally severs is the link between a nation and its books as objects of physical as well as intellectual manufacture, in which is invested some of the pride

---

36   Georg Heinrich Zinck, *Allgemeines Oeconomisches Lexicon*, 3rd edn (Leipzig, 1753), col. 442. Quoted in Martha Woodmansee, *The Author, Art, and the Market: Rereading the History of Aesthetics* (New York: Columbia University Press, 1994), p. 48.

that it feels for its own literary heritage. As recently as 1951, Seán Jennett, writing in *The Making of Books*, made this confident declaration:

> Division of labour began very early in the history of the industry, and is to-day practically complete. The average compositor can no more do the work of the pressman than the pressman can do that of the compositor; and even if he could the regulations of one of the strongest trade unions in the country forbid him to do so. He must be one or the other and he cannot be both together.[37]

But compare Jennett's remarks with these from John Trevitt in his revisions to S.H. Steinberg's classic study of the relations between printing and civilization, *Five Hundred Years of Printing*. Originally published in 1955, Steinberg's treatise required by 1996 the following major adjustment:

> What was a connected sequence of interdependent activities carried out under one roof has become a set of discrete functions each of which may be performed anywhere in the world.[38]

Espresso Book Machines, as they are called, like the prototype described by Epstein, would seem on the face of it to alleviate some of Wordsworth and Godwin's anxieties. If the publisher's greatest fear is a huge printing bill and low or slow early sales, the experimental or highbrow author's fear is the loss of exclusive and targeted readerships, the sympathetic audience of insiders, and the swamping of an innovative literate culture by unchallenging mass products. In taking possession of an Espresso in November 2007 (one of just four in the world, it was then claimed), the University of Alberta bookstore argued that it would revive the fortunes of local publishing – Alberta books for Alberta people – stemming the drift away from a rooted, independent product and shoring up the strong regional commitment represented by many small popular and academic presses. Jerome Martin, of Edmonton-based Spotted Cow Press, described plans for an event at which local poet Joyce Harries would launch her new collection and watch it as it came off the press; and he commented tellingly: 'It's just a wonderful machine to watch run. It's so organic.'[39] The potential to stimulate print in the preservation of local knowledge as just that, local, challenges the inevitability of the counter-argument for global networks. For long print runs, it is currently still cheaper to use conventional printing presses which, once set up, can print hundreds of thousands

---

37 Seán Jennett, *The Making of Books* (1951; reprinted London: Faber & Faber, 1956), p. 94.

38 S.H. Steinberg, *Five Hundred Years of Printing* (1955), edited and revised by John Trevitt (London: British Library, 1996), p. 239.

39 Jeff Holubitsky, 'U. of A. Pioneers Micro-publishing', *Edmonton Journal*, 3 November 2007, <http://www.canada.com/edmontonjournal/news/story.html?id=5f1d48f5-ab3b-464e-b280-c77ebe10e300&k=90514#> (accessed 18 December 2007).

of pages an hour; but for small runs, digital printing makes economic sense. There may be some trade-off in quality: books printed digitally are sometimes inferior in appearance. But with many titles, this is unlikely to matter; and recent history has proved that readers quickly adapt to such lowering of production standards, as the unjustified, typewriter-quality text blocks and generally poor page design of some academic presses from the 1980s (Croom Helm, for example) attest. What machines like the Espresso contest is not the survival of the physical book but of the production and supply chain that have by convention delivered it.

If the unit cost of book production is the same regardless of run-length, it is a small step to printing individual copies as they are ordered – print-on-demand – which, as Manfred Breede points out, allows publishers to return once more to the sell-before-you-produce model that predated print.[40] Like the medieval copyist, the digital machine can produce a single complete copy, reversing the economies of 500 years of press production. Print-on-demand has been adopted by a number of publishers – Oxford University Press among them – to keep current a long back-list of titles and to publish niche titles more economically.[41] In response to the technology, Random House has launched a new series called 'Lost Classics': 'now you can have a brand new paperback printed when you want it'. They claim to offer titles that otherwise the reader would have to hunt down in second-hand bookshops, and 'when [each title] arrives it will be as good as new – because that is exactly what it will be ...'[42] Printing and delivery take a week from order, which is only a few days longer than ordering an in-print book from an online source.

While the availability through print-on-demand of out-of-print or hard-to-find books is good for the publisher and for the reader, it nevertheless appears a worrying development from the author's point of view. Simon & Schuster, one of the largest publishers in America, has recently been in dispute with the American Authors' Guild (established in 1912) over the reversion of rights when a work goes out of print. The company has invested heavily in digital technologies which will allow them to make books available in a wider variety of formats, including print-on-demand, e-books, digital downloadable audio, online page views, and so on. Their goal is to keep books in print longer; with no extensive printing or warehousing costs and minimal costs for storage of digital files, books need never

---

40   Manfred Breede, 'Plus ça Change ... Print-on-Demand Reverts Book Publishing to its Pre-Industrial Beginnings', in Cope and Phillips (eds), *The Future of the Book in the Digital Age*, pp. 27–45.

41   Oxford University Press Print-on-Demand, <http://www.oup.co.uk/booksellers/pod/> (accessed 8 June 2007).

42   Books at Random, <http://www.randomhouse.co.uk/pod/> (accessed 8 June 2007). The economics of this service, however, do not always as yet add up. To take one example from their list: Josephine Tey's crime novel, *The Man in the Queue*, first published in 1929 and costing £7.99 from Random House. The same edition (Arrow, 2002) of this title is also on sale as a regular paperback at Amazon.co.uk for £6.39, and a quick search of the second-hand online bookseller ABE Books reveals many second-hand copies from as little as $1 (£0.51).

be out of print, even when no printed copies actually exist. This means that the rights to a title may never revert back to the author. Accordingly, Simon & Schuster drew up a new author contract permitting the company to consider a book to be in print, and under its exclusive control, so long as it continues to be available in any form, regardless of physical copy. As the Authors' Guild pointed out: 'With the new contract language, the publisher would be able to stop printing a book and prevent the author from publishing it with any other house.'[43]

This makes authors nervous, and with good reason. Under the new digital dispensation, the publisher could refuse to promote a book actively, but at the same time prevent the author from making it available through some other agreement. Such has been the level of protest from the Authors' Guild that Simon & Schuster have agreed to modify their definition of an in-print book. They more recently express themselves willing to consider the reversion of rights if sales fall below a certain threshold and to negotiate a 'revenue-based threshold' to determine whether a book is in-print.[44] This may be a substantial concession, but it still raises troubling issues, to do with how income on books will be measured and in relation to whose interests (to the publisher's or the author's or even the reader's?). Roughly since 1774, when the case of Donaldson v. Becket made bookselling history in Britain by its successful challenge to monopolistic printing practices, publishers' exclusive privileges have been tempered or broken and eventually, if rather more slowly, authors' rights have been established. By the same competitive processes, readers' access to affordable, often reprinted, works has been guaranteed. The new relationships that digital technology brokers (between text and print; text and matter; text and publisher/author/reader) are encouraging us to discover as shifting and malleable some of the agreements that, after more than 200 years, we have come to see as immutable.

***

Print-on-demand requires hefty machinery to process an entire book, machinery which in turn requires massive capital investment; significant through-put is therefore essential to make economic sense. This through-put can take a variety of forms: from multiple copies of the same work or single/small-run copies of diverse works. It matters little in digital printing, whose economies are totally different from the multiple duplications of traditional production. Publishers do not make this investment; rather, third party organizations do, selling capacity to publishers large and small. In response to the shift we are beginning to see new kinds of publishing companies, the outgrowth of print-on-demand and the Internet, and they are predicted to cause some upheavals in the industry. According to Sam Jordison:

---

43   Authors' Guild press release, 17 May 2007, <http://www.authorsguild.org/news/05_17_07.htm> (accessed 18 June 2007).

44   Apology, Movement from Simon & Schuster, 1 June 2007, the Authors' Guild, <http://www.authorsguild.org/> (accessed 18 June 2007).

> Leading the charge is Heidi James, the 33-year-old owner and sole employee of Social Disease, a new kind of publishing company. It does most of its marketing and talent scouting on the internet and relies on new print on demand technology to keep its costs sufficiently low to ensure that, even if it can't compete with the publishing behemoths, it won't be crushed by them anytime soon either.[45]

In addition to micro-publishers like Social Disease, whose stated aim 'is to publish extraordinary literature regardless of its pedigree or "niche" in the market or indeed lack of',[46] authors can choose to go it alone completely and publish for themselves, using online publishing sites such as Lulu, Trafford, BookSurge (an Amazon company) or iUniverse.[47] Lulu is probably the best known, describing itself as 'the Web's premier independent publishing marketplace for digital do-it-yourselfers'. With Lulu, simple instructions guide the author through the uploading and formatting of content. When the digital files have been made ready for printing, the book is 'published' and listed on the Lulu website. The author chooses the final price, and can then advertise the volume's availability. Lulu charges nothing for production, but takes a 20 per cent commission on all sales; so if there are no sales, there are no charges. The entire process is risk-free, and commission rates to the author are actually higher than with a commercial publisher, because the costs are so much lower and the author sets the price.

Self-publishing is a development of what was formerly called 'vanity publishing', where the publisher would publish anything at all as long as the author paid 100 per cent of the costs and in practice took all the risks. As a business model, self-publishing using conventional publishing technologies has always held a fatal flaw: once the author has paid the upfront costs, the publisher has made money and has little incentive to promote the book. Self-published books are rarely reviewed, and publishers take little interest in marketing them; this devolves to the author. In the print-before-selling paradigm, this meant that the author could be, and often was, left with many expensive unsold copies. In the nineteenth century, a version of this model had some commercial success, and it was not uncommon for professional authors to publish 'on commission' or at their own expense. Such writers could expect in return more control of their work, since they held onto its copyright, and possibly even greater profits. Jane Austen, for example, chose to publish all her novels, apart from *Pride and Prejudice*, in this way. Lewis Carroll, Edgar Allan Poe and Rudyard Kipling all did so at various times, and the practice was not viewed negatively, though as William St Clair has remarked, describing the early nineteenth century, the bargain could still be risky: 'most books published on commission had fulfilled their commercial purpose simply by being manufactured,

---

45   Sam Jordison, 'Literature for the MySpace Generation', *Guardian*, 7 February 2007, <http://books.guardian.co.uk/departments/generalfiction/story/0,,2007744,00.html> (accessed 8 June 2007).

46   <http://socialdisease.wordpress.com/> (accessed 18 December 2007).

47   Lulu, self-publishing website, <http://www.lulu.com/> (accessed 8 June 2007).

and there was no need for them to be promoted or sold, let alone read.'[48] Now the situation is different once again; the Internet cannot be bettered as a marketing tool, capable of refinement and exquisite customization, especially when social networking sites like MySpace can be used for free promotion.

A business case can perhaps be made for self-publishing and self-promotion, but can a good intellectual case? In the traditionally accepted publishing paradigm, a book is a product created by an author in partnership with a range of expert services whose function it is to make a saleable item and a valuable cultural artefact. These two aspects of publishing do not always cohere: bad books can be skilfully edited and sell well; critically acclaimed books can sell badly. But value (however we choose to define it) is added through this chain of literary agents, specialist readers, editors and publishers. The book that emerges from this process can be very different from that initially submitted by the author; in some cases, it may have been substantially revised. Value is also added by means of the publisher's imprint, implying as it may a reputation for quality and reliability, while the publisher's marketing and promotion services have conventionally represented an author's best hope of being read. The author wishing to self-publish has to forgo all these services, or she has to find them in some other way. New kinds of companies are emerging, such as Raider Publishing ('a publisher founded by writers for writers')[49] iUniverse.[50] iUniverse aims to provide 'supported self-publishing' and is, it claims, the only company to offer editorial services comparable to those of traditional publishers. These are comprehensive, ranging from straightforward copy-editing, through fact checking and research, to 'developmental editing', which is a complete professional edit providing extensive suggestions for revisions. iUniverse even offers ghostwriting, marketing and promotional packages, and a distribution network. Services are paid for by the author and range, in price and extent, from modest to highly interventionist. One of the features distinguishing iUniverse from a traditional publishing house is its commitment to publish regardless of an unfavourable assessment, so long as the author can afford its services. Social Disease, on the other hand, was set up to solicit the kinds of books that are so experimental they might only have a small market. As James explains:

> I realised that I really hate the homogeneity of the publishing world where it's next to impossible to get genuinely interesting work published. The big publishing houses would have you believe that there isn't a market for new and

---

48   St Clair, *The Reading Nation in the Romantic Period*, p. 167.

49   Raider Publishing International, <http://www.raiderpublishing.com/>; (accessed 8 June 2007).

50   iUniverse: The New Face of Publishing, <http://www.iuniverse.com/> (accessed 12 June 2008).

exciting work that takes a few risks and makes a demand on its readers, but that's bollocks. Absolute bollocks.[51]

The economics of the new publishing mean that James can afford to take the risk of soliciting work that might appeal only to a small market. Digital workflows and print-on-demand, and marketing via MySpace and other Internet outlets, keep the costs low. James' declared motive is not money, but a desire 'to nurture new talent, promote new writing, give writers a platform and at the same time offer the public choices that big publishers can't or won't'.[52]

Niche publishing and self-publishing are bucking a trend over the last 20 years for hefty conglomerates to swallow up small enterprises that catered to specialist audiences. It has been all too easy for the large company to discard the principles and practices of its smaller dependents in favour of blockbusters, thereby limiting reader choice. Interestingly, the market for niche products is surprisingly large in total: we said above that 3 per cent of titles represent 50 per cent of the retail sales in publishing, but the 97 per cent of titles that makes up the other 50 per cent still adds up to a massive market, though a highly fragmented one. Further, the market for books is not inelastic in the same way as the market for many other consumer products. One can only buy and use a small number of digital cameras or mobile phones; so once the market is saturated, new, 'improved' models are needed if there are to be further sales. The book market does not work in the same way. As Chris Anderson points out in *The Long Tail*, his recent study of the economics of choice in a digital world, the decentralization of publishing and the low costs of marketing may create unexpected demands for an ever wider range of books:

> The theory of the Long Tail can be boiled down to this: our culture and economy are increasingly shifting away from a focus on a relatively small number of hits (mainstream products and markets) at the head of the demand curve, and moving toward a huge number of niches in the tail. In an era without the constraints of physical shelf space and other bottlenecks of distribution, narrowly targeted goods and services can be as economically attractive as mainstream fare … the true shape of demand is revealed only when consumers are offered infinite choice.[53]

However, infinite choice is a dangerous promise, because it offers much but delivers little of quality: infinite choice is what we have on the Internet, and in consequence the world is awash with disinformation, misinformation, pornography, exhibitionism and rehashed gossip posing as serious news or even knowledge. Infinite choice is really no choice at all, given that a world of infinite possibilities

---

51   Quoted in Jordison, 'Literature for the MySpace Generation'.
52   Ibid.
53   Chris Anderson, *The Long Tail* (London: Random House Business Books, 2006), p. 52.

must necessarily lack expert evaluation and pre-selection, both functions of conventional publishing. As Andrew Keen points out, in Anderson's market of infinite choice:

> the real challenge ... is finding what to read, listen to, or watch ... The one resource that is challenged all the more by this long tail of amateur content is our time – the most limited and precious resource of all.[54]

Despite the acknowledged conservatism of the industry in general, publishers have always been resourceful and creative in the relationships they have brokered with authors and readers; and the long hegemony of print contains within it comparable shifts in manufacturing and the harnessing of new technologies to similar economic and cultural effect. From the early nineteenth century, for example, the iron hand press (and later printing by steam), machine-made paper, ready-made bindings and stereotyping all accelerated the production and consumption of books and magazines. Reprints of out-of-copyright works benefited most from the cheapening effects of a variety of linked and fortuitously connected innovations. This in turn led to the first large-scale marketing of collections of classic or canonical poetry and fiction and to a vogue for abridgements, anthologies, serializations and adaptations, all forms that did much to close the gap between an educated and a mass readership.[55] Currently, new technologies are generating a range of experimental partnerships between publishers, authors and readers, some of which will prove more durable than others, while even others will appear and evolve or perish. The book itself may continue to look much the same but it will reach us, with or without a conventional publisher's imprint, and by a variety of routes, of which some will declare themselves and some will not. The digitization of the production workflow will lead to new hybridizations, among which a self-published work will look much like a work published through a traditional publishing house. Dedicated electronic readers also look set to become more (not less) book-like. Not the death of the book, then, but its rebirth in paper (with print-on-demand) and electronic forms and its bookish features triumphantly maintained.

As far as academic publishing is concerned, changes brought about by digital technologies have not resulted in an overall decline in quality, because peer review and scholarly reputation matter above all else, and the checks and balances on academic writing are still fairly stringent: publishers, writers, reviewers and readers still honour the compact that maintains quality. At the same time, here,

---

54   Andrew Keen, *The Cult of the Amateur: How Today's Internet is Killing Our Culture and Assaulting Our Economy* (London and Boston: Nicholas Brealey Publishing, 2007), p. 32.

55   Kathryn Sutherland, '"Events ... Have Made Us a World of Readers": Reader Relations 1780–1830', in David B. Pirie (ed.), *The Romantic Period* (Harmondsworth: Penguin Books, 1994), pp. 1–48; and St Clair, *The Reading Nation in the Romantic Period*, pp. 122–39.

if anywhere, there are pressures on the book as physical object. Despite some serious issues over long-term preservation, the future for scholarly journals looks set to be electronic; and this is likely to be the case for academic monographs too: books which, like journals, are searched rather than read sequentially from cover to cover, and whose organization and modes of argument benefit from a permeable relationship with other written voices, in the form of other books and journals. With PDF technology, even the electronic product will retain some parity of display with the printed page, and of course the possibility of conversion into paper form. In the non-academic sphere, choice is valuable, variety is to be welcomed and experimentation in writing is to be encouraged. These desirables need to be balanced by maintenance of quality and respect for expertise – in writing, publishing, reviewing and criticism – in the pursuit of excellence, much as at any time in the past.

Chapter 5
The Universal Library

> The library in the digital age is in a state of flux, which is indistinguishable
> from a state of crisis – not only for institutions but for the books they contain,
> preserve and propagate, a crisis for the culture of letters whose roots are firmly
> planted in the library. The universal library pretended to answer the question
> 'What belongs in a library?' And yet in a world that seems to make ever more
> room for information, this question retains its ancient force.

Thus writes Matthew Battles in his quirky and personal meditation, *Library: An
Unquiet History*. Battles goes on to detail the many challenges to modern libraries,
which include lack of funds and lack of space, and which result in the deaccessioning
or removal to remote storage of vast tracts of materials.[1] Libraries are indeed in
crisis, and we pose another fundamental question in this chapter: in the digital age,
what is a library? Bill Cope and Angus Phillips suggested that, in this new era, a
book is what book does.[2] Can we in turn suggest that a library too is more aptly
defined as what a library does? If this is allowed, then the next question must be
'what does a library do'? Throughout history, libraries have been created to fulfil
particular functions: initially to reflect the interests, greed, acquisitive powers or
humane learning of private readers and collectors; later, as institutions for storing
and circulating books as a statement of munificence or civic pride and as a public
and social good. Over centuries, they have developed sophisticated and economic
methods of maintaining, preserving and making books accessible. When we think
of libraries, we tend to think of physical mass: of collection and storage. We would
argue that recent changes in the way the contents of books are produced, stored
and displayed, as digital bits and pixels rather than ink and paper, do not do away
with the need for libraries: scholars and the wider public need what libraries do
more than ever. Texts, written inscriptions, book-like documents, information,
knowledge – how we designate the contents of libraries is itself a matter of history
and of cultural value. For the moment, let us stick with books and texts as the
most neutral. We still need the conventional functions of libraries to make sense
of books and texts.[3]

---

1 Matthew Battles, *Library: An Unquiet History* (London: Vintage, 2004), p. 212.
2 Cope and Phillips (eds), *The Future of the Book in the Digital Age*, pp. 7–8.
3 We refer to 'books' and 'texts' throughout this chapter, in the full knowledge that
libraries hold many other types of materials.

A Brief History of Libraries

Change in the way books and texts are produced, stored and displayed accelerates exponentially; at the same time the amount of textual matter also increases exponentially. Systems of writing and storage media have been in existence in the Middle East and the Western world for around six millennia (possibly longer in China and the Far East); we are now in the sixth century of printing from movable type and in the sixth decade of electronic text. According to the estimate of Kevin Kelly, 'senior maverick' at *Wired* magazine:

> From the days of Sumerian clay tablets till now, humans have 'published' at least
> 32 million books, 750 million articles and essays, 25 million songs, 500 million
> images, 500,000 movies, 3 million videos, TV shows and short films and 100
> billion public Web pages.[4]

These figures undoubtedly woefully underestimate the number of books printed, never mind texts in other forms. But it is impossible to arrive at accurate publication figures (however we construe 'publication'), and no one actually knows either how many book titles or how many book copies are extant worldwide. The ready blurring of titles and manifestations in talk of millions itself points to part of the problem. Another is that so much is irrecoverable: most of what has been written and much of what was published in the history of the world has been destroyed. If we include manuscript as well as print, then what is recoverable is less by so much more than what is lost. Physical texts and their containers may appear durable, especially in the light of digital media, but most have proved ephemeral. This is as true of total works as of individual copies or exemplars.[5] OCLC's WorldCat, a database of integrated catalogues of 25,000 libraries around the world, lists 32 million unique catalogue records for items that may exist in multiple copies, and it is presumably Kelly's authority. But this figure does not (and could not) represent every book still available, never mind every book ever published. WorldCat's records are derived from amalgamating cataloguing effort, but there are libraries, in Africa, say, that do not yet have computerized catalogues of their own collections. A much quoted figure, but one nevertheless to be treated with extreme caution, argues that as early as the end of the fifteenth century (only 50 years after the arrival of printing in the West), 'at least 35,000 editions had been produced, amounting, at the lowest estimate, to 15 or 20 million copies'.[6] The Library of Congress in Washington, DC, currently the world's largest library,

---

4   Kevin Kelly, 'Scan This Book!', *New York Times*, 14 May 2006, <http://www.nytimes. com/2006/05/14/magazine/14publishing.html?_r=1&oref=slogin> (accessed 1 October 2007).

5   See, for example, R.M. Wilson, *The Lost Literature of Medieval England* (1952; 2nd edn, London: Methuen, 1970).

6   Febvre and Martin, *The Coming of the Book* (London: Verso, 1997), p. 186. See the sceptical dismantling of the basis for these figures in Joseph A. Dane, *The Myth of Print*

holds more than 20 million book copies among its 130 million items. Jean-Noël Jeanneney posits a far higher figure for unique items: 'since the time of Gutenberg, the books produced by the human race (and I am speaking only of those printed in the West) amount to more than one hundred million.'[7]

If, regardless of caveats, we take a mid-point between 32 million and 100 million and estimate 60 million extant printed books worldwide, that might give us a page count of something in the region of 15 to 20 billion pages. The case is no easier with manuscript, because it is difficult to define a manuscript. In its broadest sense, it is anything handwritten, but in the narrower sense of manuscript books, which were produced in large numbers both before and after the advent of printing, there are probably of the order of 60 to 200 million known and significant manuscripts held and catalogued in libraries and archives, large and small, around the world. In any case, the distinction between manuscript and print for these purposes is an artificial one. In India alone, where printing replaced manuscript production only in the nineteenth century, there are estimated to be 30 million manuscripts scattered nationwide.[8]

Written artefacts have survived for centuries, some indeed for millennia: there are Egyptian papyri that date back 4,000 years, and clay tablets and stone inscriptions even older. Many written records owe their continuing existence to libraries and collectors, and to the durability of the materials on which they are inscribed. Some, paradoxically, remain through more haphazard means: the carbonized papyrus scrolls, buried at Herculaneum when Vesuvius erupted in 79 AD and discovered in the mid-eighteenth century, comprise the only extensive library of texts from the classical world. As Battles points out, this library survived because it was buried under hot ash and fortuitously protected from other ravages.[9] In support of inactive preservation, he also cites the materials discovered in the geniza of the Cairo synagogue in 1890: 'books, letters and sundry papers piled up, mingled and mouldered for a thousand years', some of them of huge significance, like the fragment of the Hebrew text Ecclesiasticus, lost for centuries. In the Jewish tradition religious books cannot be discarded or destroyed when they are worn out because of the sanctity of their words; and so, though they are not actively conserved, they are placed in a geniza, a graveyard for dead books. Hidden from view, the materials in the Cairo geniza were also hidden from other forms of interference (among which Battles lists handling by readers, theft and authorized

Culture: Essays on Evidence, Textuality, and Bibliographical Method (Toronto: University of Toronto Press, 2003), pp. 32–56.

7   Jean-Noël Jeanneney, *Google and the Myth of Universal Knowledge: A View from Europe*, trans. Teresa Lavender Fagan (Chicago and London: The University of Chicago Press, 2006), p. 5.

8   Omar Khalidi, 'Islamic Manuscript Collections in India: An Overview', paper given at The First Islamic Manuscript Conference held in Cambridge in 2005. Abstract available at <http://www.islamicmanuscript.org/resources/2005Conference.html>.

9   Battles, *Library: An Unquiet History*, p. 55.

curation), and in consequence, like the Herculaneum papayri, 'they fared better over their long incarceration than books do in even the most conservation-minded libraries'.[10]

For the policed storage and conservation of written materials, private and public libraries existed in many ancient civilizations throughout Egypt, Mesopotamia, Syria, Asia Minor, Greece and the Roman Empire. The earliest development of writing systems is generally attributed to the Sumerians, who also stored and classified their written documents: clay tablets which preserved business records, hymns, prayers and incantations.[11] Libraries in Mesopotamia, known from the third millennium BC, reached their height in the seventh century BC, during the reign of Ashurbanipal II, who ordered the collection and organization of clay tablets on multiple topics in many languages. At its height, his library at Ninevah held some 25,000 tablets, of which an astonishing 20,000 survive in the British Museum in London. These were excavated by the Museum in the nineteenth and twentieth centuries, and are being ordered and interpreted by an international team of scholars, who, with the Museum, are creating a new and up-to-date catalogue.[12]

The idea of a universal library with the express function of collecting all the world's knowledge in one place is generally supposed to be classical Greek in origin, with the famous library at Alexandria as its prototype. Founded in the third century BC, the library was an adjunct to the museum, both of which were under the patronage of the royal family of the Ptolemies. At that period Alexandria was centre of the papyrus industry and so centre of the book trade. The number of books in the library at its height is estimated in different accounts to have been between 500,000 and 700,000, figures held to represent some 30 and 70 per cent of all books then in existence.[13] This formidable collection was amassed through edict: any book entering the city was borrowed or confiscated and copied in pursuit of a monopoly on knowledge. Legend has it that the library was eventually destroyed by fire, this destruction being ascribed variously to Julius Caesar (in 48 BC); to Theophilus, Patriarch of Alexandria (in c. 391 AD); and to Caliph Omar (in c. 640 AD), among others. Alexandria as the site of the first universal library and tales of its inevitable destruction have acquired such mythic status in Western intellectual life that it is difficult to disentangle fact from fantasy. The great library and a flourishing tradition of scholarship are not in doubt, but we need to apply caution to some others of the 'facts'. First of all, what do the numbers quoted above mean? They almost certainly refer to scrolls, given that the golden period of the library's

---

10   Battles, *Library: An Unquiet History*, pp. 194–6.

11   Fred Lerner, *The Story of Libraries: From the Invention of Writing to the Computer Age* (New York: Continuum, 1998), p.14.

12   British Museum Research Projects, Ashurbanipal Library Phase 1, <http://www.britishmuseum.org/research/research_projects/ashurbanipal_library_phase_1.aspx> (accessed 1 October 2007).

13   Kevin Kelly, 'Scan This Book!'

existence was pre-codex. Uwe Jochum, using the lower figure of 500,000 scrolls as estimated by the Byzantine scholar Johannes Tzetzes in the twelfth century, calculates these would equate to 20,000 modern books:

> I think we can shed some light on this question by asking how many modern books 500,000 papyrus scrolls would be. This is easy to calculate: the 24 cantos of the Homeric Odyssey required 24 papyrus scrolls, and today those 24 cantos can be printed in a single small volume. If we divide the figure of 500,000 scrolls by 24, this comes out to be slightly more than 20,000 modern books ... The megale bibliotheke [great library] with its 500,000 papyrus scrolls was therefore much smaller than one might have imagined.[14]

Jochum further casts doubt upon the 'universality' of the library, which in his view served most closely the research interests of the attached scholars, largely preoccupied with 'Greek culture as it had been implanted in Egypt'.[15] Opinion is also divided about the true fate of the library; in reality many factors probably accounted for its gradual disappearance over time rather than cataclysmically, with the books 'mouldering slowly through the centuries as people grew indifferent or even hostile to their contents'.[16] The drama of a conflagration is a potent myth, but is unlikely to be true. The first great universal library, though neither as great nor as universal as myth would have it, was nevertheless a remarkable achievement, of which nothing now remains. But this also furnishes a tale with a moral.

There were public and private libraries throughout Greece and the Roman Empire, though none as significant, in legend at least, as Alexandria. Scholars and schools had libraries in Greece as early as the fifth century BC: for example, the library of the Hippocratic school in Cos. The first public library in Rome was planned by Caesar and built by his supporters after his death, around 39 BC; Emperor Hadrian founded a public library in Athens in 131 AD. The great libraries of Greece and Rome were destroyed or fell into disuse with the fall of the civilizations they served. In the Middle Ages in Europe, books were largely under control of the Church, more particularly of monasteries. Most monasteries had scriptoria where books (generally religious books) were copied, and many had libraries, though these often contained only a few hundred volumes; however, so valuable were some of these collections that they were chained to the shelves to prevent theft. Private individuals also amassed personal libraries. Printing in the fifteenth century and the birth of the publishing industry brought with them new developments in the provision, organization and preservation of written and

---

14   Uwe Jochum, 'The Alexandrian Library and its Aftermath', originally published in *Library History*, 15 (1999), pp. 5–12; now available in PDF at <www.ub.uni-konstanz. de/fileadmin/Dateien/Fachreferenten/Jochum/alexandria-aftermath.pdf> (accessed 2 October 2007), p. 9.

15   Jochum, 'The Alexandrian Library and its Aftermath', p. 10.

16   Battles, *Library: An Unquiet History*, p. 32.

printed materials, and libraries became larger and more structured. At the same time, books in manuscript and print continued to be discarded, neglected and actively destroyed: some were recycled as materials to bind other books; many were deaccessioned in favour of newer editions.[17]

Many of the great research libraries of today are based upon the collections of monasteries and individuals. The collections of Archbishop Matthew Parker, sixteenth-century antiquary, were vital to the library (named after him) at Corpus Christi College, Cambridge; the British Library's founding collections were those of Sir Hans Sloane, Sir Robert Cotton, Edward and Robert Harley, earls of Oxford, and the Royal Collection given by George II in 1757.[18] When the British army invaded the city of Washington in 1814 and burned the Capitol, including the 3,000-volume Library of Congress, Thomas Jefferson offered his personal library, considered to be one of the finest in the country, as a replacement. He had built it up over 50 years, 'putting by everything which related to America, and indeed whatever was rare and valuable in every science'. The purchase of Jefferson's 6,487 volumes for $23,950 was approved in 1815.[19] From the eighteenth century, commercially profitable circulation libraries and subscription libraries started to appear throughout Britain to satisfy the demands of a growing reading public for cheap access to print; and the nineteenth century saw the rise of the great civic public libraries. As the production of printed books increased, libraries became larger and new legal forces came into play. A law of legal deposit was established, first in France in 1537, with other European countries following in the seventeenth century (England in 1610). Where it applied, the law was designed to develop and preserve a national collection, with one copy of every book published in a country deposited in that country's national library. The great national and research libraries of today are large and growing; and they hold much more than books. The British Library, for instance, claims to hold 'over 13 million books, 920,000 journal and newspaper titles, 57 million patents, 3 million sound recordings, and so much more'.[20] As of 2006, the Library of Congress holds 134,517,714 unique items, more than 20 million books, almost 60 million manuscripts, and large holdings of recorded materials,

---

17   See Neil R. Ker, *Fragments of Medieval Manuscripts Used as Pastedowns in Oxford Bindings, with a Survey of Oxford Bindings c. 1515–1620* (1954; reprinted, Oxford: Oxford Bibliographical Society, 2004); and David Pearson, *Oxford Binding 1500–1640* (Oxford: Oxford Bibliographical Society, 2000), pp. 140–42.

18   See R.I. Page, *Matthew Parker and his Books* (Kalamazoo, MI: Medieval Institute Publications, 1993); C.J. Wright (ed.), *Sir Robert Cotton as Collector: Essays on an Early Stuart Courtier and his Legacy* (London and Toronto: The British Library and University of Toronto Press, 1997).

19   Library of Congress, <http://www.loc.gov/about/history/> (accessed 1 February 2008).

20   British Library website, <www.bl.uk> (accessed 14 September 2007).

film, images, and so on.[21] In Britain, the Legal Deposit Act was amended in 2003 to include non-print materials, and in most countries of the world where legal deposit operates, similar amendments have been made.

***

When libraries became sufficiently sizable that their total collections could not be known intimately, management functions such as bibliographic description, cataloguing and classification were adopted. Such practices are partly objective and partly subjective. Objective, in that a book is in some degree self-describing, carrying with it information about itself – title, author, format, publication details, date, and so on; subjective, in that classification depends, in the traditional model, on a human agent deciding what a book is 'about', in consequence bringing a human perspective to assigning it to one or other category. Bibliographic description and library cataloguing are shorthand methods for managing and organizing information about verbose textual objects, books. They have been developed over centuries as the tersest means of describing books in their absence: that is, as the most abbreviated and least ambiguous way of conveying to the reader the necessary information for finding and using or determining between books. Library management functions are of such complexity that a whole discipline, nowadays called library and information science, grew out of their development. Methods for cataloguing and classification existed as early as the earliest libraries, but the major systems as we know them today were established towards the end of the nineteenth century.[22]

Since the management of many and various text objects is an enormous task, librarians have long sought to mechanize routine processes. Vannevar Bush is generally credited with first proposing automated information retrieval in the 1940s in his design for a theoretical system called the Memex (MEMory EXtender);[23] but his work was preceded by that of information scientists like Emanuel Goldberg and Paul Otlet. Goldberg developed high resolution microfilm and also the technology underlying microdots in the 1920s. In 1932 he wrote a paper describing the design of a microfilm selector using a photoelectric cell, later claimed as 'the first paper on electronic document retrieval'.[24] In 1934 Otlet published *Traité de Documentation*,

---

21   Library of Congress, <http://www.loc.gov/about/reports/> (accessed 17 September 2007).

22   For developments in early modern catalogues, see McKitterick, *Print, Manuscript and the Search for Order, 1450–1830*, pp. 12–17. Many eighteenth-century libraries catalogued books by size. The widespread use of the card catalogue and Dewey's decimal classification system can both be dated to the nineteenth century.

23   Vannevar Bush, 'As We May Think', *Atlantic Monthly* (August 1945), pp. 101–8.

24   M.K. Buckland, 'Emanuel Goldberg, Electronic Document Retrieval, and Vannevar Bush's Memex', *Journal of the American Society for Information Science*, 43 (1992), p. 288.

pronounced 'perhaps the first systematic, modern discussion of general problems of organizing information ... one of the first information science textbooks'.[25]

Computerization in Libraries

Computers were first used in libraries for catalogue record creation, initially to produce printed cards or slips for manual filing, which would be referred to by staff and users in locating library resources. These catalogues could easily be duplicated in various formats, multiple copies could be distributed and new sequencing of information could be generated from the same data. Because bibliographic description is so highly structured, more extensive computerization of catalogues in the form of databases was a significant and inevitable next step from early mechanization initiatives. As a corollary of the increasing automation of library functions, co-operative schemes emerged to aggregate effort across several libraries: many libraries hold copies of the same book, and cataloguing, an expert task, is time-consuming and expensive. In the 1960s, a group of libraries in Ohio founded the Ohio College Library Center (OCLC) to develop a computerized system in which the libraries of Ohio academic institutions could share resources and reduce costs. This has since grown to a cataloguing and resource sharing co-operative of 57,000 libraries worldwide, now simply known as OCLC.

By the 1990s, almost every library in the world (certainly in the developed world) had abandoned card catalogues for recently published materials and was using an OPAC (Online Public Access Catalogue), though card catalogues for earlier holdings were retained. From this point, catalogue information need no longer be consulted in the library; it could be accessed from terminals elsewhere. Retrospective cataloguing since then has also meant that many older materials are now available through OPACs, and because of standardization and co-operation in classification, these records can be shared. OCLC's WorldCat integrated database provides records for almost 90 million items searchable through the Web, and it points the user to the closest geographic copy. WorldCat records items in a variety of media: books, manuscripts, images, maps, sound files and multimedia content.[26] In an unpredicted consequence, librarians have found that the Web has caused a surge in book use:

> In the first iteration of a World Wide Web, they [books] remained all but hidden on library shelves, and, unsurprisingly, circulation numbers dipped. That led some to surmise that the book was languishing in the throes of obsolescence. But

    25   W.B. Rayward, 'Visions of Xanadu: Paul Otlet (1868–1944) and Hypertext', *Journal of the American Society for Information Science*, 45 (1994), pp. 237–8.

    26   OCLC's WorldCat, <http://www.oclc.org/worldcat/> (accessed 17 September 2007).

as search technology improved and books became more discoverable through online library catalogs and keyword searches on the wider web, circulation surged back, by double-digit margins in many libraries. Overnight, books that went untouched for years were getting into patrons' hands again. Almost any librarian today will tell you their book circulation is going strong.[27]

By the 1990s, too, technology had advanced to the point where the cost of scanning documents was no longer an obstacle to digitization, software was becoming available for display and interrogation, and storage capacity was rapidly increasing while its costs also were falling. In a natural development, libraries, sometimes in academic partnerships, began programmes to digitize complete books and manuscripts. Where the aim is the capture of textual content, projects have taken one of two routes: either the imaging of book or manuscript pages as digital facsimiles, sometimes accompanied by transcriptions or automatically generated representations of the texts for searchability and access; or the creation of accurate text by rekeying or corrected optical character recognition (OCR) with the addition of structured metadata and markup (to greater or lesser levels of granularity) to identify individual textual components.

Conservation issues and the status of manuscripts as unique documents make the case for their digitization both compelling and fraught with difficulty. The textual content of a manuscript may not be vastly different from that of a printed book, but restrictions on the use of the container can mark a huge distinction. The conservation issues that normally surround manuscript (by virtue of its uniqueness) tend to intrude upon the value of its textual content in a way that more rarely happens with print (the exceptions being incunabula and other rare or special edition books). This carries over from the analogue to the digital world. Because of the manifest individual labour of manuscript production, we are more likely to be aware that digitization incorporates the representation or translation of a document or physical object as well as of its text. Some of that same high investment informs the surrogate technology: digitization of manuscript carriers and content is rarely as easy or as cheap as book digitization. For example, many more manuscripts are digitized as images without some underlying representation of their texts because the labour involved in preparing fully encoded transcriptions is immense when set beside the possibilities for OCR on printed text. On the other hand, where there are difficulties inherent in the historical technologies of manuscript (and we might extend manuscript to include inscription on papyrus, clay tablets, even stone), if cost and labour are not at issue, the benefits of digitization can be immense. These may include the capacity to display better materials in unwieldy formats – large volumes or maps; the virtual reunification of collections and originals dispersed over time;

27   Andrew Richard Albanese, 'Scan This Book!: An Interview with the Open Content Alliance's Brewster Kahle', *Library Journal*, 15 August 2007, <http://libraryjournal.com/article/CA6466634.html> (accessed 25 September 2007).

the restoration of lost or damaged readings; and the recovery of palimpsests. There can be clear institutional and wide cultural advantages to manuscript digitization, in the shape of excellent accessible surrogates, which make it possible both to conserve fragile or precious originals and display images of unique objects as tools for marketing and promotion.

Manuscript imaging projects come in a variety of forms and serve many purposes. There is mass digitization intended to make large volumes available at low cost: the *Codices Electronici Ecclesiae Coloniensis* (*CEEC*) project in the library of Cologne Cathedral scanned 300 full manuscripts in the five years up to June 2006, a total of 100,000 pages at a cost of a little more than £1 per page;[28] the Manuscriptorium project at the Czech National Library, a consortium of more than 40 Czech and European partners, is carrying out low-cost digitization of many hundreds of manuscripts.[29] Yet other initiatives provide page images of manuscripts with accurate underlying transcriptions; there is a blurred boundary between such projects and the electronic editions we discuss in Chapter 3. At the other end of the scale are expensive, forensically faithful reproductions, such as the British Library's Turning the Pages or the Digital Image Archive of Medieval Music (DIAMM).

For Turning the Pages, images are captured using high-end cameras capable of producing file sizes of hundreds of megabytes, manuscripts are presented to the user as 3-D 'book-like' simulations, and pages turn 'realistically' under the user's control. Tools are provided for annotation and other scholarly functions.[30] Such projects are vastly expensive (though costs are always dropping), and in consequence they are highly selective: using Turning the Pages, the British Library has produced fewer than 20 digital manuscripts in ten years. Over the same period they have of course generated many more digital versions from both manuscript and print originals without Turning the Pages technology. The enhanced treatment appears to denote high value manuscripts, in cultural and now technological terms, but the presumed equivalence of the two sets of values (cultural and technological) may itself become the subject of debate. Does high cultural esteem necessarily equate to high specification gadgetry; or, conversely, do visually appealing manuscripts alone justify the massive costs of digitization? What of the many unique and precious manuscripts without obvious artefactual glamour? The rhetoric used by the British Library to describe the items accorded Turning the Pages treatment (national and international treasures like the Lindisfarne Gospels,

---

28   See Manfred Thaller, 'On Cultural Heritage and the Digital World', presentation given on 5 June 2006 at a seminar on mass digitization organized by the AHRC ICT Methods Network, <http://www.canterburytalesproject.org/massdigit/workshop0606.html> (accessed 1 August 2007).

29   Manuscriptorium, <http://www.manuscriptorium.com/Site/ENG/default_eng.asp> (accessed 1 August 2007).

30   British Library Turning the Pages, <http://www.bl.uk/onlinegallery/ttp/ttpbooks. html> (accessed 1 August 2007).

a William Blake Notebook, the Chinese Diamond Sutra, Mozart's Musical Diary) suggests the ready conspiracy between digitization and cultural exhibitionism: they are 'magnificent', a 'masterpiece', 'superb', produced by a 'genius', the 'oldest', the 'original', 'glorious', 'a landmark', 'stunning'. The technology is particularly seductive because it offers what all might wish but very few in reality achieve: an unparalleled simulation of what it might be like to interact freely with a rare manuscript, to follow our own path through it, to appear to turn its pages. In this precise sense, the digital surrogate is hyper-real, more real than real; for it alone represents to most of us the real properties of the manuscript. But not all are impressed; for one critic interested in animation and video-game theory, page-turning simulations may be no more than a gimmick or marketing device, 'a game of academic scratch-n-sniff' [31] – in other words, an attractive exhibition tool, but far less effective for online interaction, where it appears to impede rather than aid navigation.[32]

In the last ten years, the DIAMM Project[33] has scanned some 350 manuscripts (around 10,000 images). It began as a response to a pressing need: the rapid deterioration of fragmentary medieval music manuscripts held in archives, libraries and religious institutions throughout Britain and mainland Europe. In the Middle Ages, as in any other period, certain genres and styles of music went in and out of fashion. The parchment on which they were recorded was an expensive medium, and as unfashionable works were discarded, it was recycled for other purposes: scraped down to provide a surface for new texts, cut up and used in book bindings, wrappers or even as packing for buildings (some fragments were discovered in the fabric of the roof in New College, Oxford).[34] Digital technology was considered the only way to record these fragile artefacts before they became too unstable for any kind of use. In many cases, the electronic versions have been enhanced to make content more legible: layers of text have been digitally removed, with the result that hitherto unknown pieces of music have since been recovered, transcribed and even performed.

Music manuscripts are not alone in suffering damage, dispersal or dismemberment over centuries. The ravages of time, climate, warfare or deliberate agency have left textual artefacts in varying states of preservation

---

31   Sally Northmore, 'if:book', a Project of the Institute for the Future of the Book, blog, 15 February 2006, <http://www.futureofthebook.org/blog/archives/2006/02/who_really_needs_to_turn_the_p.html> (accessed 25 September 2007).

32   Turning the Pages has been widely adopted by, among others, the British National Archives, the Royal Society, the National Library of Ireland, the Henry Moore Institute, the Zoological Society of London. See <http://www.turningthepages.com/> (accessed 7 May 2008).

33   Digital Image Archive of Medieval Music (DIAMM), <http://www.diamm.ac.uk> (accessed 1 August 2007).

34   Julia Craig-McFeely, 'Digital Image Archive of Medieval Music: The Evolution of a Digital Resource', *Digital Medievalist*, 3 (2008), <http://www.digitalmedievalist.org/journal/3/mcfeely/> (accessed 11 February 2008).

randomly scattered around the world in private and public collections. In all probability these can never be reintegrated, as repatriating originals and recreating their early contexts is not possible physically, economically or politically. But the right digital technology and metadata standards can in many cases allow materials long dispersed to be viewed as virtual wholes. The fourth century *Codex Sinaiticus*, one of the earliest surviving examples of the Bible in Greek, was written as one manuscript but is now divided between four institutions – St Catherine's Monastery, Sinai, the British Library, the University of Leipzig and the National Library of Russia – who have together embarked upon a project to reunify the codex virtually.[35] In the case of an extreme form of text, inscription on stone, digitization at last allows its systematic inclusion within the literary canon. Previously, the publication of stone inscriptions was restricted by the difficulty and expense of including high quality photographs in print collections. In practice, scholars have relied on recycling transcriptions made over a long period of time and divorced from their material surface. Now images, transcriptions, translations and other materials can all be gathered within an online edition.[36]

Such projects are helping to preserve precious cultural artefacts by providing surrogates to stand in for the original and reduce the strain of constant use. They are also, through remediation, making these artefacts accessible to a wider audience, with sometimes paradoxical results: libraries find they have more requests (rather than fewer) for access to originals once they are widely available in digital form. But, however wide their reach, they are unlikely to be as influential as the enormous print conversions now under way. Currently the digitization of printed content is being undertaken by a number of players with diverse goals and interests: scholars with some kind of intellectual rationale, libraries with collection development in mind and commercial companies whose aims are more difficult to determine.

Research libraries have been digitizing their own printed content since the early 1990s, and much of this started, as with manuscript digitization, from a preservation problem: in this case, the rapid deterioration of nineteenth-century books printed on acid paper. Preservation microfilming had been standard practice for such materials since the 1950s. The development of digital photocopy machines in the 1980s, notably the Xerox Docutech, seemed to offer an alternative: books could be copied onto high quality acid-free paper, and because the process was digital, more than one book copy could be produced from the same scan through the machine and the digital files saved for future need. The paradigmatic projects were those at Cornell and Yale in the early 1990s, in partnership with Xerox Corporation; and the great journals digitization project, JSTOR, conceived of by the Andrew W. Mellon Foundation and carried

---

35   'World's Oldest Bible Goes Global: Historic International Digitisation Project Announced', British Library Press Release, 11 March 2005, <http://www.bl.uk/news/2005/pressrelease20050311.html> (accessed 11 February 2008).

36   Charlotte Roueché, 'Digitizing Inscribed Texts', in Deegan and Sutherland (eds), *Text Editing, Print and the Digital World*.

out in partnership with Michigan University. At Cornell and Yale, around one million pages of brittle nineteenth-century volumes were scanned over five to six years, and the originals replaced in the library by surrogates on acid-free paper. During the course of this work, many of the technical standards for high quality digitization were tested and adopted. Processes were shared with other institutions and emerged as a robust methodology which has shaped the architecture for document digitization worldwide. Access to content was provided through the paper surrogates and the digital files; for long-term preservation, methods were developed to inscribe the digital files to microfilm using the COM (Computer Output Microfilm) technology.[37] In 1995, Cornell partnered the University of Michigan to develop targeted collections of digital texts of American materials: the Making of America Project. They were joined in 1999 by the Library of Congress, and some two million pages of American-interest books and journals were digitized over a five-year period.[38]

JSTOR was the brain-child of William G. Bowen, then President of the Andrew W. Mellon Foundation. Begun in the early 1990s as a funded project, it became a not-for-profit corporation in 1995, with the express aim of digitizing and providing worldwide access to complete series of scholarly journals. JSTOR was established to solve the problem of dwindling shelf-space: with guaranteed access to back runs, libraries could confidently dispose of printed originals. It is worth noting that the same digital technology was used by Cornell to fill library shelves with acid-free volumes and by JSTOR to empty them. As of May 2008, JSTOR listed 773 journals provided by 516 participating publishers online: a total of 176,525 journal issues, 24,699,855 pages. The great benefit of the JSTOR model is, of course, its thrift: print technology provides multiple access across institutions by means of multiple copies. Only one digital copy is needed to perform the same service. If for libraries there are economies of scale through cost sharing,[39] for publishers, JSTOR's 'moving wall' policy protects revenue streams. Each publisher sets the limits to the currency of content in the collection and may restrict digital access to more recent issues, with most journals opting for a five-year moving wall. To provide access and searchability to the digital data, JSTOR makes available image files offering an accurate representation of the original, plus uncorrected text produced by OCR (not displayed to the user). Where the quality of the printed originals is relatively good and intelligent searching algorithms are used, this gives surprisingly accurate retrieval, especially when used in conjunction with catalogue information for each article. As with the e-publication of current journals, discussed in Chapter 4, the user is presented with copies of originals which are faithful to the

37   See Anne R. Kenney, *Digital to Microfilm Conversion: A Demonstration Project, 1994–1996*, Final Report to the National Endowment for the Humanities (1996), <http://www.library.cornell.edu/preservation/com/comfin.html> (accessed 3 August 2007).

38   See the report, *The Making of America: A Distributed Digital Library Collaboration*, <http://memory.loc.gov/ammem/ndlpcoop/moahtml/ncpcollab.html> (accessed 3 August 2007).

39   JSTOR, <http://www.jstor.org/about/> (accessed 3 August 2007).

appearance of the books or journals as they previously experienced them, can be cited accurately, and provide the added convenience of rapid retrieval and direct delivery. JSTOR is highly successful, reporting 277,586,546 total accesses in the first half of 2007 alone.[40]

Digitization and Scholarship

Two major commercial digitization projects have had a profound effect on scholarship and teaching over the last ten years: ProQuest's *Early English Books Online (EEBO)* and Thomson Gale's *Eighteenth-Century Collections Online (ECCO)*. *EEBO* makes available 100,000 volumes printed in England, Ireland, Scotland, Wales and British North America, and works in English printed elsewhere from 1473 to 1700; *ECCO* delivers 155,000 volumes printed in England, Ireland, Scotland, Wales and British North America, countries under British colonial rule, and in English elsewhere from 1701 to 1800. Each provides somewhere in excess of 20 million pages. Both grew out of earlier microfilming projects: the first microfilms of Early English books were produced in 1938; Gale's microfilming dates from the 1960s. Both projects had from the outset a clear collection development policy: books in English from a particular period, as listed in respected and comprehensive bibliographic records. These records included Pollard and Redgrave's *Short-Title Catalogue* (1475–1640) and Wing's *Short-Title Catalogue* (1641–1700) and their revised editions, the *Thomason Tracts* (1640–61) collection, the *Early English Books Tract Supplement* and the *English Short Title Catalogue* (1473–1800). None of these may be a perfect work of reference, but all are internationally recognized. Pollard and Redgrave's pioneering *STC* was only published in 1926, but it took shape under the shadow of the First World War when emergency measures required the removal, for safety from air-attack, of rare volumes from the Printed Books Department of the British Museum. An author list, with group headings for anonymous works, of books held in certain British libraries, the printed *STC* is itself a virtual repository or grand archive for what exists in reality only in scattered or in partial form in any particular place. The subsequent filming was a massive undertaking which involved tracking book copies across the world. The films were then sold to libraries worldwide, giving access for the first time to many rare volumes – a more visible witness to Pollard and Redgrave's ideal library. Microfilm may be a good archive medium, but it is a poor delivery mechanism; digitization of the films greatly improves the reading experience. Early online versions of *EEBO* provided page images only with access through bibliographic records, but marked-up text is now being created from a selection of the volumes for enhanced searchability. *ECCO* uses an OCR engine for full-text search across all volumes.

---

40   JSTOR, <http://www.jstor.org/about/facts.html> (accessed 3 August 2007).

The strengths of these two resources lie in their cohesiveness, their declared bibliographic component and their familiarity as a development from well-understood and much-used existing resources. They have brought obvious gains in the form of access to images of early modern English imprints for scholars without easy recourse to research libraries; they have given students in many cases their first encounter with the historical difference and difficulty of the physical appearance of early printings of texts: their strange typography and orthography. But a digital copy of a print copy is never more than a partial copy. However distinguished their pedigrees, we should proceed with caution when we adopt *EEBO* and *ECCO* as our standard of authority. Yet the signs are that most of us, seasoned scholars and students new to historical research, are blind to their inadequacies. The speed of their assimilation as indispensable tools also suggests some of the changes we might perceive over time as our encounters with print shift from book to screen. It is worth reminding ourselves that what underlies *EEBO* is a film surrogate, not print, and that these are books at two removes, their often poor image quality a derivative of the conversion of one substitute technology into another. Inferior imaging and its enhancement by various means – removing paper blemishes or shadows from the verso page, altering colour, page cropping, distorting size – regardless of the best intentions, always impose an interpretative filter, skewing the relationship the medium purports to broker between reader and, in this case, early English text. Microfilm, an intermediate between print and digital, has with rare exceptions never been seen as a satisfactory surrogate: unlike book or computer screen, its technology has remained cumbersome and obtrusive, with the useful consequence that no reader can be under the illusion that what they see on film is the 'real thing'. By contrast, online versions appear to provide a more complete substitution; so much so that digital texts available from *EEBO* are replacing the print object, even where it is relatively easy to access both. What is particularly interesting here is that what appeared obvious in microfilm – the loss of valuable details of the artefactual form of the book – appears far less obvious when film is digitized and delivered as a screen image. (In the microfilm project underlying *EEBO*, texts were systematically shorn of their book carriers.) Though it lacks the physicality of either print or film, the screen image appears as the real thing – to such a degree that the absence of binding, front and end pages, blanks, special front matter (so much of the material that constitutes a book as distinct from its text) goes unnoticed. There is already evidence that a whole generation of scholars (including, ironically, historians of the book) is turning to *EEBO* for early printed books and not even noticing that they are engaging only with texts; that as a project to recover and circulate more widely our early print culture, *EEBO* is compromised.[41]

There is a fallacy or contradiction at the core of *EEBO* and other digital resources which has to do with their substitution of visual data for abstract data.

---

41   For a thoughtful critique of *EEBO*, see Kichuk, 'Metamorphosis: Remediation in *Early English Books Online (EEBO)*', pp. 291–303.

The fallacy being that we assume completeness of information in what we see and incompleteness in the abbreviated formulas we have to work at to translate into sense. Yet the truth is the reverse; the farther the project to record early modern English books has moved from its origins in the rich but compressed data of retrospective enumerative catalogues, the farther it has also shifted from representing with any accuracy or fullness the physical details of printed works. This should give us pause for several reasons: because as a digital library *EEBO* has better credentials than most in the form of its respected bibliographic antecedents; because many more recent initiatives are abandoning rich metadata and relying ever more on the visual evidence of a highly manipulative technology; because the more we come to trust as scholars and students what we see on screen and the limits set for us by search programs, the more we will content ourselves with what has been called 'maimed information'. The charge comes from William Proctor Williams and William Baker, who as long ago as 2001 expressed their anxieties over the scholarly pretensions of *EEBO* and what they saw as the dangerous decline of 'book-in-hand' bibliography. In their words, 'the conversion of all this work ["book-in-hand" bibliography] into electronic form is treading dangerously near the corruption of more than a century's careful work in the field of Early English books'.[42]

There are anomalies and gaps in the evidence as found in *EEBO* that make little sense; when combined with the obvious benefit of immediate transition from bibliographic record to full text digital images, they become dangerously misleading. For example, the catalogue records that underpin works in *EEBO* have not been carried over from printed form into electronic as identical copies but have been adjusted in various undeclared ways; to complicate things further, this adjustment has occurred twice over. Thus, the original *STC* and its second print edition (1971–91) provided reference to copyright entry in the Stationers' Company records for pre-1700 books. This has been removed from the online version, *ESTC*, a database administered in Britain through the British Library. Yet such information as copy entry is vital to our understanding of how the book trade operated before the first copyright act in 1708–09. On the other hand, *ESTC* gives more of some kinds of information than its print 'original': details of pagination, for example. And things get more confused at the next stage: for the catalogue entries in *EEBO* derive in their turn from those in *ESTC*, but again are not identical to them; this time they remove details of format from each item. Not only, then, do the digital images in *EEBO* distort in various ways the actual appearance and size of the print object, but bibliographic evidence that would permit us to arrive at this more accurate physical understanding by other means (details of format – that is, of how sheets are folded and formed into page sequences as folio, quarto, octavo, and so on) has been removed from the metadata. It gets worse: details of pagination,

---

42   William P. Williams and William Baker, '*Caveat Lector*: English Books 1475–1700 and the Electronic Age', *Analytical and Enumerative Bibliography*, n.s., 12 (2001), p. 23.

first included in *ESTC*, have been modified in *EEBO* to represent pages with text only rather than the actual pagination of the book (including blanks). Because there is no facility for moving directly between *ESTC* and *EEBO* (presumably because they represent separately financed projects), it is likely that users of the digital images will rely upon the most imperfect version of the bibliographic records, those in *EEBO*. If, however, they persevere and compare entries for the same item under *ESTC* and *EEBO*, they will find that information (including page numbers) does not tally. The most disturbing thing to note is that *EEBO*, whose strength lies in its capacity to make manifest the appearance of early books, systematically distorts the bibliographic evidence that should support its visualization, providing instead catalogue entries for texts, not books. In some important ways it is far harder to reconstruct the appearance of a book from *EEBO* than from the library catalogues that underlie it. The daftness or ignorance that led to the suppression of such vital material from this particular scholarly project is staggering. It is also a useful warning against putting our faith in digital libraries.[43]

Digital Libraries and Mass Digitization

Out of the many digitization projects active in the 1980s and 1990s grew the concept of the digital library: an ordered, managed collection of digital objects created for specific purposes and integrated with the library's catalogues and its analogue collections to form a hybrid library. Initiatives to develop digital/hybrid libraries have increased in size by several orders of magnitude as technology improves and costs fall. They differ from the kinds of digitization/editorial projects we discuss in Chapter 3 in a number of ways. Generally, libraries and their supply companies digitize in order to do better what they have always done: connect content with readers. They do not, generally, add scholarly value to the materials; that is not their role. In the traditional model, readers come to libraries to consult or borrow books and journals; in the digital library, content is, or can be, delivered directly to the desktop. The danger of this newer model has been that, for some readers, if the book cannot be delivered to the desktop, it may as well not exist, even if there is a printed copy in the nearby library. But what if readers could have all the content from all the world's libraries delivered to the desktop, even content they did not hitherto know existed? What if the utopian vision of the universal library could at last be made real? What if the library of the future could be, as in Roger Chartier's imaginings, 'a library

---

43   See, for example, the omissions and discrepancies in catalogue entries in *ESTC* and *EEBO* for Wing B5557 and Wing B5558 (John Bunyan, *Pilgrim's Progress* (1678), first and second editions). There has been little research to date on how we are using *EEBO*. But see Thea Lindquist and Heather Wicht, 'Pleas'd By a Newe Inuention?: Assessing the Impact of *Early English Books Online* on Teaching and Research at the University of Colorado at Boulder', *Journal of Academic Librarianship*, 33 (2007), pp. 347–60.

without walls ... the library of the future ... inscribed where all texts can be summoned, assembled, and read – on a screen'.[44] What if all this content were free and could be made available in a much shorter time than was ever believed possible? Such were the aims of a number of large-scale digitization projects begun around the new millennium: the Million Book Project (also known as the Universal Library), led by Carnegie Mellon University and started in 2002, after some initial pilot studies; the Google Book Search project (originally known as Google Print), proposed in 2002 by Larry Page, co-founder of Google and started in 2004; and Microsoft's MSN Book Search, announced in 2005.

Until the early 2000s, library and scholarly digitization projects had been driven by library or scholarly needs, and they proceeded cautiously, according to robust, well-tried collection development principles. They did so for reasons both intellectual and economic: materials of perceived intellectual value or widespread interest (or both) were scanned by preference in order to maximize cost benefits and minimize waste of both human effort and expensive processing power. But the increase in storage and the driving down of scanning costs make such selectivity no longer necessary: indeed selection itself has a high cost in a world where mass scanning is carried out almost entirely mechanically, with robotic scanners turning book pages and sometimes even removing books from shelves. Statistics available from 2005 suggest that at that point duplication of digital content was running as high as 40 per cent: a huge waste of effort and resources.[45] Such an increase of the means to digitize arrived unexpectedly and with the kind of dramatic consequences that echo the arrival of the World Wide Web some ten years previously. It, too, appeared to come almost from nowhere; in reality, it built on disparate developments over the previous 40 years which coalesced suddenly in the work of a few physicists who wanted to share ideas and documentation. The reason the Web has grown so fast and so chaotically is that it is simple to create content for it; and when the threshold of expertise is lowered, many more can participate. Because digitization has recently become simpler and cheaper, content is again easy to create. New players are emerging whose motives are not solely or even directly to serve libraries and scholars. The larger of these are commercial organizations with huge funds at their disposal, like Google and Microsoft, whose origins lie in software and hardware development, in engineering rather than publishing or libraries. As with the early Web, mass digitization currently seems chaotic. Rigorous, library-derived collection policies have been discarded in favour of a 'scan everything' approach; and with competing players

---

44   Roger Chartier, *The Order of Books*, trans. L.G. Cochrane (Stanford: Stanford University Press, 1992), p. 89.

45   Quoted in Oya Y. Rieger, *Preservation in the Age of Large-Scale Digitization*, A White Paper (Washington, DC: Council on Library and Information Resources, February 2008), p. 14. This is an extensive and judicious examination of large digital projects, particularly in its attempt to identify issues which might influence the availability and usability of digital books and their impact on library collections over time.

all in the race to scan the same (admittedly large) body of materials, confusion is bound to arise. The financial model, too, has profound implications: unlike *EEBO* and ECCO, whose underlying companies need to recover the huge costs of development through sales and licences, Google and Microsoft sell information (for free) through advertising.

MSN Book Search worked at first with the Open Content Alliance (OCA) and with major libraries, like the British Library, to digitize 'millions of publicly available print materials'.[46] This open agreement soon ended.[47] (Where the Open Content Alliance is a consortium of content and technology providers pledged to make content available according to 'open' principles – that is, content resides in multiple archives worldwide, accessible to multiple search engines[48] – Google and MSN, by contrast, require contributors to agree to make their content unavailable to other commercial search engines.) The Million Book Project, which is working with the OCA, embarked on an initial digitization of one million books (300–500 million pages), and Google's stated goal was 15 million volumes (4.5 billion pages) in six years from 2004. For both, these mind-boggling figures were simply the first tranche. In a statement from the Million Book Project back in 2001:

> The primary long-term objective is to capture all books in digital format. Some believe such a task is impossible. Thus as a first step we are planning to demonstrate the feasibility by undertaking to digitize 1 million books (less than 1% of all books in all languages ever published) by 2005. We believe such a project has the potential to change how education is conducted in much of the world. The project hopes to create a universal digital library free to read any time anywhere by anyone.[49]

As of the first half of 2007 Million Books had scanned 1.4 million books, many of them Indian and Chinese volumes. Google has aspirations to continue beyond its initial 15 million volumes and to 'digitize the world's books'.[50] The name Google, incidentally, derives from a googol, the number represented by the numeral 1 followed by 100 zeros. Such ambitions may sound hubristic but, with shorter term goals like 15 million volumes in six years within reach and rapid increases in rates

46   Press release, 25 October 2005, 'MSN Search Announces MSN Book Search', <http://www.microsoft.com/presspass/press/2005/oct05/10-25MSNBookSearchPR.mspx> (accessed 12 September 2007).

47   Albanese, 'Scan this Book!'.

48   The Open Content Alliance, <http://www.opencontentalliance.org/> (accessed 10 January 2008).

49   Raj Reddy and Gloriana St Clair, 'The Million Book Digital Library Project' (1 December 2001), <http://www.rr.cs.cmu.edu/mbdl.htm> (accessed 12 September 2007).

50   Google Book Search News and Views, <http://www.google.co.uk/googlebooks/ newsviews/index.html> (accessed 3 August 2007).

of digitization, 60 million volumes in less than 20 years is beginning to sound achievable. What concerns us here is how this digital conversion might itself convert into benefits for scholars and the reading public, meeting Million Books' claim that '[t]he result will be a unique resource accessible to anyone in the world 24x7x365, without regard to nationality or socioeconomic background'.[51]

All three are huge endeavours set to change dramatically library provision and access to printed materials. Because of its size and the company's position as one of the world's leading technology providers, Google Book Search (GBS) has received most publicity and been the subject of controversy since its inception, with fierce critical focus on the quality of the materials released, the long-term strategy for access and usability, and attitudes to intellectual property. Google is reluctant to give out figures. Writing in February 2007, Jeffrey Toobin reported that: 'At the University of Michigan, Google's original partner in Google Book Search, tens of thousands of books are processed each week on the company's custom-made scanning equipment.'[52] Even ten thousand books per week add up to half a million per year, so multiples of tens of thousands across a number of libraries is a lot of books. Captured as page images with uncorrected OCR text for searching (the method also used by Million Books and MSN), Google books are presented with brief bibliographic information. If it is out of copyright, the user can download the entire book; with in-copyright works, just the search result with a line or two of context can be viewed, accompanied by links directing the reader to places where they can obtain the volume in libraries or from vendors of new or second-hand books.

The vision behind the project is explained by Eric Schmidt, Google Chief Executive, in headily beneficial terms:

> Imagine the cultural impact of putting tens of millions of previously inaccessible volumes into one vast index, every word of which is searchable by anyone, rich and poor, urban and rural, First World and Third, *en toute langue* – and all, of course, entirely for free. How many users will find, and then buy, books they never could have discovered any other way? How many out-of-print and backlist titles will find new and renewed sales life? How many future authors will make a living through their words solely because the Internet has made it so much easier for a scattered audience to find them?[53]

---

51   Reddy and St Clair, 'The Million Book Digital Library Project'.

52   Jeffrey Toobin, 'Google's Moon Shot: The Quest for the Universal Library', *New Yorker* (5 February 2007), <http://www.newyorker.com/reporting/2007/02/05/070205fa_fact_toobin> (accessed 3 October 2007).

53   Eric Schmidt, 'Books of Revelation', *Wall Street Journal* (18 October 2005), reprinted at <http://googleblog.blogspot.com/2005/10/point-of-google-print.html> (accessed 3 August 2007).

The University of Michigan, one of the founding five libraries in GBS (with the New York Public Library, the Bodleian Library, Oxford, Harvard and Stanford University Libraries), has been involved in digital programmes for the last 20 years, and has long had the ambition to digitize all its seven million holdings. Previous to the Google initiative, Michigan's librarians had estimated that this would take a thousand years. Google's Larry Page, a Michigan alumnus, suggested that GBS would achieve it in six, and at no cost to the institution. For Mary Sue Coleman, University of Michigan president, the entire project is lofty in aspiration and reality:

> a legal, ethical, and noble endeavor that will transform our society ... The University of Michigan's partnership with Google offers three overarching qualities that help fulfill our mission: the preservation of books; worldwide access to information; and, most importantly, the public good of the diffusion of knowledge.[54]

An academic user, working online in Britain, enthuses about the riches available:

> ... no one can play around with Book Search for more than a few minutes without stumbling into intellectual conflict zones that will wake them from the dogmatic doze that might have over-whelmed them in a well-regulated library.[55]

By contrast, the publishing world is divided in its response – more cautious and more sceptical about the benefits. In 2005 the American Association of Publishers and the Authors' Guild filed lawsuits against Google for scanning in-copyright works without partner agreements, even though Google declared such scans would be used for indexing only, with no intention of making full texts available. As a result of the suit, Google temporarily suspended digitization. Other publishers have realized the benefit of GBS as a marketing tool, through its links to libraries and booksellers. Google, in its turn, emphasizes the intention to enhance access to books, not to replace them:

> Some of our critics believe that somehow Google Book Search will become a substitute for the printed word. To the contrary, our goal is to improve access to books – not to replace them. Indeed, we're working closely with publishers to develop new tools and opportunities for selling books online.[56]

---

54   'Google, the Khmer Rouge and the Public Good', Address to the Professional/ Scholarly Publishing Division of the Association of American Publishers, 6 February 2006, transcript available at <http://www.umich.edu/pres/speeches/060206google.html> (accessed 3 August 2007).

55   Jonathan Rée, 'The Library of Google', *Prospect* (February 2007), p. 34.

56   'Google Book Search News and Views: What's the Issue?' <http://www.google.co.uk/googlebooks/newsviews/issue.html> (accessed 31 August 2007).

Where dispute occurs, it hinges on the definition of 'fair use' of in-copyright works.[57] If a publisher is a partner in GBS, up to 20 per cent of a copyright book is available online. It is too early to say whether the concerns of publishers and authors are exaggerated, but at the least they throw into contention issues of who owns what in the digital age and upon what terms. Once a library, traditionally a place for deposit and curation, becomes digital, its capacity to reshape what it stores is more difficult to control. Google and its like are clearly banking on technology repeating its recent trend: in the 1980s, film studios in America fought fiercely the then new technology of the video-cassette recorder, on the grounds that it would spell the end of the film industry. It proved its salvation. Maybe, in the same way, mass digitization will save books. When we think of the world's venerable research libraries, in-copyright books might not seem to represent a significant proportion of their contents. But it is estimated that as much as 80 per cent of everything published is still in copyright; yet only 10 per cent of that exists in print.[58] Google looks set to provide a valuable service for these vast hidden tracts of print. The difficulty is in weighing the likely effect of free access to the information books contain. The superiority of book technology over the computer or print-outs for the moment safeguards the author's investment in some forms of print. On the other hand, the poet Wendy Cope has been angered by the unfair use of her in-copyright poems downloaded, like music files, free from the Internet; novels and other long works, or those whose primary function is not information, appear less likely to suffer this fate – except that the new forms of reading that the Internet encourages may reduce our engagement with all virtual texts to endlessly recycled abstracts and snippets. Information for free seems already an entrenched belief of the digital culture, but this should not be allowed to extend to the products of an individual's creative labour. For the moment, we can see that there is more to a literary text, say, than its potential to be quarried, searched and sifted. But how much individual effort and talent will continue to be protected by this cultural belief, and for how long? Copyright was hammered out, at various points in history, as an issue over books as property (both physical and intellectual) with the interests of writers always hardest squeezed and readers generally unaware of this. There seems reasonable cause for anxiety over the status of in-copyright works once they have been released from the physical constraints of the book. And if your livelihood depends on the copies you sell, are you really likely to be happy that the Internet simply affords you high visibility as a writer?

Cultural disquiet at the universal digital library takes other forms, with vociferous opposition to GBS from France, where even the former President,

---

57   See 'Google Book Search News and Views: Legal Analysis for a Selection of the Opinions in the "Fair Use" Debate', <http://www.google.co.uk/googlebooks/newsviews/legal.html> (accessed 3 August 2007). Following 3 years of litigation brought separately by the Authors' Guild of America and the Association of American Publishers against Google, a settlement was reached in late 2008 – subject to approval by the US courts.

58   Cited in Rieger, *Preservation in the Age of Large-Scale Digitization*, p. 15.

Jacques Chirac, expressed a view. Jean-Noël Jeanneney, President of the Bibliothèque nationale de France, has lodged a spirited critique against American imperialism and the misrepresentation of the world's cultural heritage in the disproportionate preponderance of English language materials in large-scale digital collections. While he may be correct in the first instance, presumably once GBS contains 'all the world's books', the linguistic spread will be more even. Jeanneney proposes a European digitization initiative to redress the balance, in which works of clear cultural significance in the European languages are chosen by experts. This initiative should, he believes, be highly selective, and the French themselves would 'favour the great founding texts of our civilization'.[59] He finds it not unreasonable that up to a million works per year could be digitized throughout Europe. This does not match the rate of digitization proposed by Google, but in his view 'an obsession with numbers should give way to preoccupations with quality'.[60] Currently it seems that private financing, as provided by companies like Google and Microsoft, allows mass digitization to move faster, unhampered by politics and government. But is moving fast necessarily desirable? Google has been criticized from other quarters for privileging speed and volume over quality: some of the scans are unreadable or faulty, underlying searchable text can be so poor as to be almost unusable and metadata is often sparse and inaccurate. Writing for the American Historical Association in April 2007, Robert B. Townsend concludes:

> I am not sure why the rest of us should share the company's sense of haste. Surely the libraries providing the content, and anyone else who cares about a rich digital environment, needs to worry about the potential costs of creating a 'universal library' that is filled with mistakes and an impenetrable smog of information. Shouldn't we ponder the costs to history if the real libraries take error-filled digital versions of particular books and bury the originals in a dark archive (or the dumpster)? And what is the cost to historical thinking if the only

59   Jeanneney, *Google and the Myth of Universal Knowledge*, p. 78.

60   Ibid., p. 76. Funding streams within individual European countries and the European Union are already being drawn upon for digitization. The Norwegian National Library has plans to digitize its entire collection. See 'Digitizing the Collection at the National Library', The National Library of Norway, May 2006, <http://www.nb.no/english/facts/about_the_national_library/digitising_the_collection_at_the_national_library> (accessed 21 August 2007). In parallel with various European projects, President Chirac announced in April 2006 a massive venture to develop a European search engine, to be known as Quaero (Latin 'I search') with a total budget of 450 million euros of public and private funding. See Angelique Chrisafis, 'Chirac Unveils his Grand Plan to Restore French Pride', *Guardian* (26 April 2006), <http://www.guardian.co.uk/technology/2006/apr/26/news.france> (accessed 21 August 2007). Plans now appear to have been shelved. According to Barry Mansfield, 'critics believed that this [budget] would not be enough and that the search engine would be out of date by the time it was launched.' See Barry Mansfield, 'People Power Takes on Google', *Daily Telegraph* (4 August 2007), <http://www.telegraph.co.uk/connected/main.jhtml?xml=/connected/2007/08/04/dlwiki04.xml> (accessed 21 August 2007).

substantive information one can glean out of Google is precisely the kind of narrow facts and dates that make history classes such a bore? The future will be here soon enough. Shouldn't we make sure we will be happy when we get there?[61]

In the early 1990s a project to digitize one million printed pages was considered sizable; the Google promise to scan 4.5 billion pages (15 million books) in six years is a 4,500-fold increase on this.[62] Google is not the only organization, nor is it the first, nor does it necessarily have the most ambitious plans to scan 'all the world's books'. But the universal digital library, from whatever source, is stimulated by Google, producer of the world's most popular search engine and one of the largest and most profitable technology companies. For better or worse, Google is setting the pace and the standards, taking a broad and shallow approach to data: huge quantities of text presented with minimal added value other than searchability and some simple metadata. As a development in digital text creation it looks from certain angles like a step back. Suddenly, even large-scale conventional library projects are dwarfed by comparison; suddenly the assurance provided by conventional library expertise seems redundant. By contrast with Google-like initiatives, the electronic archives or editions, discussed in Chapter 3, are narrow and deep: relatively small volumes of textual data marked up and intensively processed, with considerable added value in the form of multiple witnesses to a textual object, annotations, visual images, glossaries, external links, all presented in complex 'work-sites'. In between these two extremes a substantial volume of electronic text, often in the form of library-sponsored initiatives, is available on websites and in archives throughout the world. Increasingly, in an academic context, these texts are marked up according to robust principles, usually in compliance with the recommendations of the Text Encoding Initiative (TEI) (also discussed in Chapter 3). But such projects are overshadowed by mass digitization, whose intoxicating claims appear to fuel our voracious appetite for digital media, making us ever more impatient of obstacles to the seamless integration of content with commercial search engines – and ever more reluctant to engage closely and critically with what we find electronically.

***

There are various issues to weigh here. At astonishing speed we are shifting the library from a physical space to a virtual environment, and from local institutional

---

61   Robert B. Townsend, 'Google Books: What's Not to Like?', *AHA Today* (30 April 2007), <http://blog.historians.org/articles/204/google-books-whats-not-to-like> (accessed 21 August 2007).

62   The figures require cautious use: Google is digitizing complete holdings of major libraries, with considerable overlap, so that numbers do not equate to unique books. Nevertheless, the sums remain vast.

support, provisioned by experts, to the Internet and a search engine. The world is awash with digital text. If we consider even the most elementary search we might make through a local library catalogue, electronic or paper – to locate and take away a copy of a novel or a play – and then perform the same as a series of Internet searches, the difference in the quality and number of the results is staggering. Across the multifarious collection that is the Internet, searching reveals vast numbers of versions of the works of canonical authors, available in many different formats; texts by non-canonical authors in multiple forms. Let us try three examples. First we search for one specific text object: the Collected Works of the British writer Anna Laetitia Barbauld, published in two volumes in 1825, the year of her death. Barbauld had a successful contemporary writing career, but slipped from view until the 1980s and the rise of feminist literary criticism, when interest revived. An initial search on GBS produced four copies of the 1825 edition and its 1826 reprint. When the same search was performed two months later, six copies were found, from the university libraries of Oxford, Stanford, Harvard, Michigan and California, and the New York Public Library. In an open Internet search, we found the Women Writers Project text, from Brown University, rekeyed and produced in TEI-conformant XML, faithfully representing its chosen original 1825 copy, with page-breaks and layout marked. It is possible to download a fairly accurate 'facsimile' of the text from WWP, but this is not a facsimile in the way that a directly digitized copy would be. It is, however, searchable within genres and by different features within each genre: dramatic texts by prologue, speech or stage direction; poetry by different rhyme schemes.[63] MSN Book Search revealed another full-text copy, scanned from a University of Toronto original.[64] The Miami University, Oxford, Ohio, 'British Women Writers of the Romantic Era' website has page images and TEI-conformant rekeyed text of volume II only;[65] the Anna Laetitia Barbauld website at the University of Saskatchewan has a full digital facsimile that can be browsed, but not searched;[66] there are selections from the Works available at the Electronic Text Centre at the University of Virginia;[67] and individual poems are available in the Chadwyck-Healey Literature Online database. That adds up to nine different full-text copies of Barbauld's Collected Works, plus various selections.

---

63   Women Writers Project, <http://www.wwp.brown.edu/index.html> (accessed 3 September 2007).

64   MSN Live Search Books, <http://search.live.com/results.aspx?q=&mkt=en-us&scope=books&FORM=LIVSOP> (accessed 25 September 2007).

65   British Women Writers of the Romantic Era, Miami University, Oxford, Ohio, <http://www.orgs.muohio.edu/womenpoets/barbauld/index.html> (accessed 3 September 2007).

66   Anna Laetitia Barbauld, University of Saskatchewan, <http://www.usask.ca/english/barbauld/> (accessed 3 September 2007).

67   Special Collections, Electronic Text Centre, University of Virginia, <http://etext.virginia.edu/speccol.html> (accessed 3 September 2007).

Searching for the works of canonical authors unsurprisingly reveals far more. A search on GBS, for example, for author=Shakespeare and title=*King Lear* returns 801 hits, while OCLC's WorldCat, the most extensive collection of book-related metadata in the world, catalogues only 270 items, suggesting that many of those found through Google are duplicates, which is to be expected. Of the texts available for 'full view' in GBS (that is, for which GBS has permission to make full text available, or versions in the public domain) the latest dated edition is 1860. Fully electronic texts of *King Lear* can be found through a straightforward Google search in places too numerous to list: there are marked-up versions in electronic text centres and plain text versions from sites such as Project Gutenberg;[68] hypertexts of the play abound;[69] and there is the highly regarded Thomson Gale *Shakespeare Collection* with its foundation in the Arden Shakespeare, a long-standing and regularly revised scholarly edition. The *Shakespeare Collection* has a scholarly editorial board; it provides electronic versions of modern editions of the plays, alongside historical editions, commentaries and other primary and secondary sources, all with full metadata and information about provenance. There are tools for searching, interrogation and comparison, together with links to resources external to the product itself. What is represented is firmly book-based; the advantage of electronic presentation is the ease with which a plethora of significant book or manuscript sources can be cross-linked and integrated, searched and compared. Little can be done with this that could not be done by conventional means, but the ease of use, the speed of access, and its comprehensiveness and scholarly pedigree make it an impressive product.[70]

Early versions of the works of Barbauld and Shakespeare are long out of copyright. Recent editions, loaded with the latest scholarship and critical insights, of course are not in the public domain; nor are editions of writers still alive or whose work is still in copyright. A search on GBS for our third example, T.S. Eliot, returns 172 results, only one of which is available in full text. Searching the Web one finds that some of Eliot's earlier work is available electronically, the later work is not. A search for T.S. Eliot on MSN Book Search throws up some curious results: the number of hits is not specified, other than to suggest there are 'thousands'. MSN has only full-text search; there are no advanced search facilities and it is not possible to search the metadata. So it is not possible to separate for these purposes works by Eliot himself, books about him or books with random references or quotations. Accordingly, the number of irrelevant or bizarre hits

---

68   Project Gutenberg, <http://www.gutenberg.org/etext/> (accessed 5 September 2007).

69   See the Internet Shakespeare Editions website for a comprehensive listing of Shakespeare resources, <http://internetshakespeare.uvic.ca/index.html> (accessed 5 September 2007).

70   *The Shakespeare Collection: A Global Online Research Environment for Shakespeare Studies*, Thomson Gale, <http://www.galeuk.com/shakespeare> (accessed 7 September 2007).

is high: hit number 248, for example, is a book entitled *Beans: Four Principles for Running a Business in Good Times or Bad*, retrieved because it contains a quotation from Eliot. Eliot died in 1965. For authors whose careers extended later into the twentieth century, there is very little available electronically: searches may return hits but almost nothing in the form of full text.

These limited examples demonstrate some interesting facts about access to electronic versions of literary texts and editions. As one might expect, by far the greatest proportion of material is in the broad and shallow category: this is the cheapest to produce and requires least intellectual input. Despite much scholarly discussion over more than a decade of the merits of electronic editing, there are few extensive electronic editions available, presumably because they are costly of time and money and likely to have highly restricted use. In between, there is a considerable volume of accurately marked-up text, created and made publicly available by academic projects and text archives like the WWP. In all categories, the only texts free for searching and downloading are those that are out of copyright, which effectively means that anything produced after around 1930 is unlikely to be available. This creates a black hole of 70 years or more in which digital access is greatly restricted. The consequences this might have for future scholarship and learning are potentially enormous. With startling speed (the speed of mass digitization) almost the whole of modern literature disappears from sight as we transfer our researches in physical space to the Web. And not just primary works; up-to-date scholarly editions, unless created for electronic delivery, are also largely inaccessible because of the same rights restrictions. Evidence suggests that the Internet is increasingly both first and last recourse of seekers for information. A progressive reliance on online resources will mean that vast swathes of the most recent primary and secondary materials in book form could be ignored unless institutions have access to providers like NetLibrary (discussed in Chapter 4). While online journals and websites are vehicles for some current research, much of the latest thinking about our cultural texts continues to appear for preference in print. So, with scholarship in mind, in using the latest technology we often gain access to content that is superseded, rightly disregarded or unreliable. GBS does reveal current, in-copyright editions of works but they cannot be viewed instantly; they must be ordered from libraries or booksellers (though there are plans to provide in-copyright material for a fee). In the meantime, many users, especially students, are more likely to choose those volumes that can be downloaded than those for which they must wait or pay. The Internet is the pre-eminent tool of instant gratification. It is also, in consequence, resuscitating and recycling dead or stale scholarship.

What, we ask, does an electronic copy or version of a text represent? How is it constituted *qua* text? What do we gain in digitization, and what do we lose? What are the effects of decoupling a text from its physical carrier? What does it mean for a work, a text or a book to be digital, and how are users to make sense of the many different kinds of digital offerings available? What exactly is it that these huge 'universal library' projects are offering and why have our greatest research libraries signed up to them? Among the examples we searched for above are one particular edition of the works of Anna Laetitia Barbauld, and one of Shakespeare's plays, *King Lear*, in any available edition. The WWP version of the Barbauld edition decouples text from book in order to provide sophisticated access, allowing the reader inside the text in new ways. But it also offers the possibility of recoupling text to page by providing all the information necessary to lay the work out as the original, with pagination, lineation, fount information, and so on. At the same time, their text represents not an ideal version of Barbauld's *work*, but one particular copy of that work residing in one particular library; and this is clearly identified in the metadata. Furthermore, the WWP sells printed texts derived from the underlying electronic text versions, and these match the originals as closely as possible. This means that the project is providing a new constitution of a text keyed to and corresponding to its old constitution as a book. In the GBS and other mass digitization projects, what is provided is an image of a copy of the book, a digital photograph of the pages together with very limited, automatically generated search facilities. The images of different copies available on GBS are clearly associated with specific physical copies in selected libraries, identified in the metadata, and marked with signs of usage: they have distinct bindings, library plates, scribbled notes, underlinings. So these multiple copies of the same title are all different too, bearing witness to the vagaries of their material existence as books, even though the accuracy of representation achieved in the image is itself questionable. Some of these visible tokens, it has been suggested, may even provide a false aura of 'quality assurance' for what can be an inferior digital product.[71] GBS represents the book copy itself, the WWP a text of the book copy, but one which does not bear witness to the material existence, given that the reconstituted copy is pristine. Both versions are frozen in time: they will no longer show the accretions of use. Instead, usage will (or might) be tracked by web statistics, download records; it will not be inscribed upon the object itself, or not the object as presented electronically.

The situation with *King Lear* is far more complex, as we might expect from the canonical status of the work and the number of editions or versions available. Our search on GBS returned more than 800 hits; unless the user knows the exact edition she is seeking, these are difficult to sort and sift.[72] However, if she opts for versions available in 'full view', this returns only four hits. Three of the hits point to out-of-copyright editions from 1770, 1811 and 1860; hit number four is clearly a modern typescript published by a press calling itself Plain Label Books. This version is not dated or attributed in any way; it has an ISBN, but a wide search for this yields no results. Plain Label Books does turn up on a website called

---

71   See Paul Duguid, 'Inheritance and Loss? A Brief Survey of Google Books', *First Monday*, 12 (8), August 2007, <http://www.firstmonday.org/issues/issue12_8/duguid/index.html>. (accessed 6 September 2007).

72   A search on MSN, where one cannot restrict the inquiry to author=Shakespeare and title=*King Lear*, returned 6,196 hits, which is so imprecise as to be useless.

cafepress.com, offering a CD-ROM of '444 Books on CD Plus Audio Reader Software for $9.99!'[73] This CD contains a mishmash of works, all in English and most seemingly deriving from North America, a number of which have found their way into GBS. Neither GBS nor Plain Label Books suggests what the history of the texts might be: they are 'plain'; that is, they have no markup, notes or metadata of any kind. A clue to their origins is given by Stephen Leary on a blog posted in April 2007. Leary came across a text on GBS also published by Plain Label Books: *Chess History & Reminiscences* by H.E. Bird. Leary had rekeyed the work some years earlier and uploaded it to Project Gutenberg. He strongly suspected that here was his version, though with header information that might identify its provenance stripped away.[74] Interestingly, Plain Label Books claims copyright in its works – all books have a 'copyrighted material' sign on the bottom of each page – but it seems they have in some if not all instances taken the texts from an uncopyrighted source: Project Gutenberg, if Leary is right. Following the 'publisher' link next to the text of the *King Lear* leads to one 'Daniel Oldis' on the cafepress.com website, and again to the CD of 444 books, along with around 30 printed classics, clearly deriving from underlying texts on the CD.[75] The other three editions of *King Lear* are, like the Barbauld examples, clearly identifiable as related to a particular physical instantiation; they bear the marks of a material life in the form of wear and tear, annotations, library bindings and shelf marks. But what does the Plain Label Books version represent? What text is this of *King Lear*, a highly contested play in its textual forms and status? Who is its implied user/reader? And how does a text move through four centuries of scholarship and become 'plain'? Having no apparatus at all, this version of the play is as far removed as could be from a critical edition. It is the antithesis of the complex electronic editions we discuss in Chapter 3, which groan and creak under the weight of textual variation, annotation, interpretation and interlinking. Will students reach eagerly for the plain e-text, unencumbered by the density of annotation of, say, an Arden edition of Shakespeare? Will it be used as a reading text or for some kind of electronic interrogation? Given that it is 'plain' in every sense, it is not accessible to anything but straightforward word searching. Is this what users now want from electronic text? Google *Book* Search (note our italics) is not providing electronic text, it is providing books, and the status of most of these, deriving as they do from major publishers and libraries, is perfectly clear. Plain Label Books are anomalous as books, and they are anomalous as electronic texts, but they may prove highly popular – much as cheap student paperback editions of

---

73 Plain Label Books, cafepress.com, <http://www.cafepress.com/7391> (accessed 6 September 2007).

74 Stephen Leary, 'Google Books' Plain Label Books', *The Reflective Librarian* (28 April 2007), <http://blog.stephenleary.com/2007/04/google-books-plain-label-books.html> (accessed 6 September 2007).

75 Plain Label Books, cafepress.com, <http://www.cafepress.com/7392?CMP=CJ-CLICK-10462225> (accessed 6 September 2007).

'great works' with no added scholarly value have proved popular. Users wishing to use GBS to obtain the full text of *King Lear* have several choices. They can buy a modern edited text as a print book from the booksellers listed or borrow a copy from a library. If they want to download a free version, the most recent attributed edition is 1860. Finally, they can have the plain text version of dubious provenance and status that may be more recent, or it may not – there is no way of knowing.

According to Kevin Kelly, Google has 'resurrected' the tantalizing possibility of the universal library:

> When Google announced in December 2004 that it would digitally scan the books of five major research libraries to make their contents searchable, the promise of a universal library was resurrected. Indeed, the explosive rise of the Web, going from nothing to everything in one decade, has encouraged us to believe in the impossible again. Might the long-heralded great library of all knowledge really be within our grasp?[76]

Will Google's 'scan everything' approach indeed deliver us the elusive universal library and what will we do with it when we have it? For the user, the promise of all the world's books delivered to the desktop at the touch of a button may seem a seductive one. If we know what book we want, and can get exactly that book and only that book, perhaps finding other interesting and relevant materials along the way, then the saving of time and effort, and the broadening of the span of our intellectual universe, is indeed a dream come true. For educational institutions outside the developed world, the prospect of free access to the riches of major research libraries is an opportunity and benefit beyond price. For research libraries themselves, there is the tantalizing vision of free digital copies of all their content when they have been struggling for years to find funds for local collection developments. But the future may not be quite so sunny. It is clear, for instance, that the licences signed by individual libraries with Google are tightly restrictive in the conditions imposed for making available copies of their own, out-of-copyright works. Libraries may append the Google images and text to their own catalogue records, but these can in many cases only be viewed by members of the institution or by library card holders. The University of Michigan's licence with Google states:

> U of M shall restrict access to the U of M Digital Copy to those persons having a need to access such materials and shall also cooperate in good faith with Google to mutually develop methods and systems for ensuring that the substantial portions of the U of M Digital Copy are not downloaded from the services offered on U of M's website or otherwise disseminated to the public at large.[77]

---

76   Kelly, 'Scan This Book!'

77   Co-operative Agreement Between the University of Michigan and Google, Inc. <http://www.lib.umich.edu/mdp/umgooglecooperativeagreement.html> (accessed 4 October 2007).

The 'public at large', accordingly, can have access to 'the world's books' only through GBS and not through the libraries themselves. And the libraries, though they get the digital content for free, have to access it through the public (Google) system, or spend considerable sums making it available through their own digital library systems. Even then, they cannot make it widely available – public domain content, therefore, once digitized, becomes the intellectual property of large corporations; not a healthy position. It is in some ways comparable to the situation with some photographic images, to which Bill Gates, through his Corbis Corporation, has been buying up the rights for more than ten years. Gates now owns rights to some 100 million images, including the works of the photographer Ansel Adams, the famous images of Marilyn Monroe on the subway grid and Rosa Parks on the bus in Alabama. As one comment has it: 'In some sense, the iconic photograph of Rosa Parks recreating her quiet act of rebellion on a bus in Montgomery, Ala., belongs to every American. But as a practical matter, it belongs to Bill Gates.'[78] Gates' ownership of such a large slice of photographic history has been the subject of intense debate. The bulk of the collection is kept in refrigerated storage under a mountain in rural Pennsylvania: safe but inaccessible. Criticized initially, Gates is now exonerated in some quarters as having done 'the right thing. He has preserved an irreplaceable photographic history.'[79] But photographs, like books, and unlike paintings, say, are intimately bound to their reproductive technologies, which in turn imply access. While Gates has preserved these images, Corbis and its larger rival Getty Images now dominate the market in reproductions. Is this what we want Google and its smaller rivals to do with the digital representations of millions of books?

GBS is largely a library project, but in digitizing complete libraries and making the books (those that are out of copyright) widely available in one vast system, one of the major benefits that libraries bring to the almost boundless intellectual space that is our literate culture is lost: order. What historically the professional librarian offers is organization and interpretation of that mass of cultural materials so that it makes sense to the user. In earlier, smaller projects the professional library approach to organization was seen as integral to the digital process. But early digitization projects of all kinds were costly, and when carried out by libraries, they did not aim at profit or even cost-recovery. At this stage full text digitization was either done manually or using high-priced hardware. Care was taken to select candidates for scanning according to certain clear criteria: books or manuscripts in danger of damage or disintegration; high demand items; coherent collections; items to which

---

78   Katie Hafner, 'A Photo Trove, a Mounting Challenge', *New York Times* (10 April 2007), <http://www.nytimes.com/2007/04/10/business/10corbis.html?n=Top/News/ Business/Companies/Microsoft%20Corporation&_r=1&adxnnl=1&oref=slogin&adxnnlx =1191593819-CP3YAd4n8QCVctwvDjBFsg> (accessed 5 October 2007).

79   Gary Haynes, 'Under Iron Mountain: Corbis Stores "Very Important Photographs" at Zero Degrees Fahrenheit', National Press Photographers Association, *News,* 2005, <http:// www.nppa.org/news_and_events/news/2005/01/corbis_cavehtml> (accessed 7 May 2008).

scanning brought discernible intellectual benefit. Since it was initially cheaper to catalogue and describe items, expert activities that are the daily work of librarians, than to scan them, extensive metadata was carefully produced. Because of general high costs, care was taken not to rescan items for which surrogates might already exist; registers and catalogues of digitized materials were referred to before a new project was undertaken, and decision matrices were consulted to adjudicate between candidate collections or items.[80]

The Internet is a completely different kind of information space from a library. Roger Ebert described it in 1998 as 'a library assembled piecemeal by packrats and vandalized nightly'.[81] The Internet has grown haphazardly because it has always been a 'democratic' space for creation and consumption. It has never been organized or catalogued, but information retrieval technologies have been developed by way of compensation. Current focus is on making the searching and interrogation of large data spaces more intelligent – intelligent machines if not users; we discuss this further in Chapter 6. For the moment, and with books in mind, it is enough to observe that full-text machine searching in a huge unordered mass is not necessarily the best way to direct readers and users to the resources they need. What is curious about some of the newer large-scale digitization projects is that, although the content is being supplied by libraries and publishers, their traditional professional organizational principles do not appear to be carried over. We can understand clearly the purpose of many digitization projects led by libraries, academic teams or their funding bodies. Generally they have stated aims, clear content development policies, good finding aids, explicit technical standards and long-term preservation goals. Less than ten years ago, Dan Hazen, Jeffrey Horrell and Jan Merrill-Oldham summarized the vital criteria as follows:

> The judgments we must make in defining digital projects involve the following factors: the intellectual and physical nature of the source materials; the number and location of current and potential users; the current and potential nature of use; the format and nature of the proposed digital product and how it will be described, delivered, and archived; how the proposed product relates to other digitization efforts; and projections of costs in relation to benefits.[82]

In the current climate of scan everything, such fine discriminations are irrelevant.

---

80   See the decision matrix for digitization in Dan Hazen, Jeffrey Horrell and Jan Merrill-Oldham, *Selecting Research Collections for Digitization* (Washington, DC: Council on Library and Information Resources, 1998), <http://www.clir.org/pubs/reports/hazen/pub74.html> (accessed 12 September 2007).

81   Roger Ebert, *Yahoo! Internet Life* (September, 1998), p.66. This publication is now defunct, but the quotation is to be found at <http://marylaine.com/exlibris/xlib27.html> (accessed 3 March 2008).

82   Hazen, Horrell and Merrill-Oldham, *Selecting Research Collections for Digitization*.

It is instructive that Google, the largest Internet search engine company in existence, should lead and finance the largest print digitization project. Google indexes as much of the visible Web as it can reach, creating an appearance of order where there is no true order. In the physical world of books and libraries, there actually *is* order; but in creating enormous digital collections, GBS and other large projects are producing some degree of chaos out of order. The library of Google offers no catalogue. Among the many often cited 'benefits' of digital data are its democratizing power and its ability to transcend boundaries between countries, institutions, individuals, and indeed the boundaries between and within the data objects themselves. Let us examine the implications of this redistribution.

First of all, democratization: no one would deny the enormous public good inherent in making the content of large research libraries available to those prevented from access by geography or economics. But the collections of research libraries are not easy to navigate, despite the vast array of detailed catalogues, subject classification guides, finding aids, printed guides to the collections and experienced librarians on hand to direct the novice user. Beginning students and members of the general public often need short courses in 'How to use the library' before they enter a reading room or stack; and since the systems of one library are not replicated in another, even experienced scholars and users require help when first set down in an unfamiliar space. When research libraries are not only available on the Internet, but are all accessed together in the universal library, what help will the user need, and what help will she be given? How will communities and educational institutions unfamiliar with a research library as a physical entity know how to find what is of value to them in a virtual collection? Battles points out an obvious but much ignored fact; most books are bad – 'very bad in fact' – and a great deal of energy is expended in 'ferreting out the exceptional books, the ones that shatter paradigms'.[83] How democratizing is it, therefore, to offer a universal library filled with tens of millions of books, most of which are bad, leaving the less-experienced user to work out for themselves which are worth reading? The problem here is that now the paradigm for the universal library is not a library at all, it is the Internet. The implicit question seems to be, 'why can't libraries be more like the Internet, filled with cool information that we can all have for free?' Our response to that is 'why can't the Internet be more like libraries, organized, classified and with powerful filters in place?' Centuries of library management have given way in a matter of years to the search engine, currently the only possible tool for navigating the Internet, given the volumes involved, but not the ideal way of accessing library content, especially when we have long held better ways. The stakes are high, for how libraries are organized ultimately defines how readers think.

Secondly, what are the implications of transcending the boundaries of the printed book? On first sight, this seems like a useful function of the digital: books

---

83   Battles, *Library: An Unquiet History*, pp. 16 and 17.

can be shared across institutional and international borders (licensing, copyrights and fees permitting). They can be interrogated in new ways: footnotes, from being static references on a page, become dynamic links to the full content of the referent; internal components are no longer necessarily seen in the context of the whole book but individual pages or paragraphs or sentences can be relieved of their surrounding text and set down elsewhere, dismembered and recombined endlessly and the recombinations shared as new 'works':

> These snippets will be remixed into reordered books and virtual bookshelves. Just as the music audience now juggles and reorders songs into new albums ... the universal library will encourage the creation of virtual 'bookshelves' – a collection of texts, some as short as a paragraph, others as long as entire books, that form a library shelf's worth of specialized information.[84]

This might work for those books which are in themselves of a fragmentary nature – recipe books, almanacs, encyclopaedias – but for works of sustained fiction or rigorously structured argument, remixing is, in the words of the novelist John Updike, 'a pretty grisly scenario':

> In imagining a huge, virtually infinite wordstream accessed by search engines and populated by teeming, promiscuous word snippets stripped of credited authorship, are we not depriving the written word of its old-fashioned function of, through such inventions as the written alphabet and the printing press, communication from one person to another – of, in short, accountability and intimacy?[85]

For Updike, the very boundedness of books is part of their status as books. When dismembered into 'a sparkling cloud of snippets', they become merely contributions to a conversation composed of electronic chatter. 'Accountability and intimacy' are concepts that should give us pause. If indeed both are at stake through the changes that new technologies are working upon older technologies and the cultural practices they support, we need at least to be aware of what we risk and what transformations beyond the merely technological result from our investment in any technology – how our interactions with the machines we create shape us.

We imagine two possible futures for the universal digital library: both, in a sense, already here. In the first, the Internet grows ever larger and the aspirations of those who wish to create the universal library grow with it. But without filters and guidance as to what is of value, the universal library is potentially worthless. The key to the universal library is not full text searching alone, but full text searching

---

84   Kelly, 'Scan This Book!'

85   John Updike, 'The End of Authorship', *New York Times* (25 June 2006), <http://www.nytimes.com/2006/06/25/books/review/25updike.html> (accessed 4 October 2007).

allied to good cataloguing and the guidance of expert librarians. Unleashing 15, 30 or 60 million books for widespread consumption, without refined aids to their use, is a recipe for intellectual chaos. The British Library, for instance, contains 150 million items, and it is estimated that 'if you see 5 items each day, it would take you 80,000 years to see the whole of the collection'.[86] Those who see the function of the universal library as providing us with increasing amounts of content are faced with the paradoxical problem that they are competing for something that does not and cannot grow: our time and our attention. We live, some suggest, in an 'attention economy' where what we need is not more information, but better filters for the information we already have in order that our precious and finite attention can be used profitably.[87] Currently the universal digital library is a vast hypermarket or palace of consumption, a one-stop shop peddling quick solutions to our needs, facilely merging information searches with a range of electronic services and resources, a mix and match, bounce and flick, cut and paste, hit and run approach, all wrapped round with dubiously relevant advertising. This cheap customization of knowledge is a parody of accountability and intimacy. Without shape but with ever more permeable boundaries and a branded global spread, the digital universal library persuades us to reject the very concept of a library.

In the second, we all become skilled browsers, and search engines become more refined as well as more powerful. Browsing, a term already used to describe our engagement with digitally delivered materials, suggests that reading, too, will fall victim to the impatience the medium appears to instill in all of us to have our information needs satisfied. If we are reading less, we are writing more, and valuing less the power of both to fix things – in the mind and on paper. As a mass reading public came into being in the course of the nineteenth century, some writers worried that the labour represented by their creative effort would go unregarded and unrewarded in the rapidity of its consumption – as mere reading matter. One of the agreed characteristics of great writing, as the capacity to bear re-reading, provided some defence, as did a steadily extended copyright law. As Google and its like deliver to us books as the images of books, they unsettle and reorder our expectations and ownership of reading and writing in many profound ways – ways that we are only beginning to imagine, let alone weigh and consider. What users expect from the virtual library is not books *per se* but the power the retrieval technology provides to pre-extract and (best of all) pre-digest the information within books. And when the virtual library uses cookies[88] to store information

---

86   'Some Facts and Figures', British Library, <http://www.bl.uk/about/didyou.html>, (accessed 4 October 2007).

87   The term 'attention economy' was coined in 1971 by Herbert Simon and is dealt with in some detail by Richard Lanham in *The Economics of Attention: Style and Substance in the Age of Information* (Chicago: University of Chicago Press, 2006).

88   A cookie is a small parcel of data deposited in a user's browser that holds information about that user – without cookies, vital functions such as shopping baskets cannot be implemented. When a website (Amazon, for example) accesses that

about our preferences, as most already do, and all surely will, the pre-extraction and pre-digestion can be done on the basis of our earlier choices – or perhaps the search engine's earlier choices. Recommendations on the basis of past behaviour can be useful in alerting us to new information, but they are no substitute for excellent bibliographic records that allow the reader to make judicious decisions based on the research question in hand.

The biggest difference between the physical and virtual library may not in the end be the enticements of huge size but the passivity induced by rapid retrieval facilities. This is interesting because we have readily substituted the crude power of the search engine for the cataloguing skills of the librarian, even though a very few online searches show us that as things currently stand, this is a poor bargain indeed when it comes to finding expert information. Already we would rather access a book copy remotely than walk across campus to hold it in our hands. So we know the technology delivers something worse when it comes to expert advice and directed searching; but the speed and apparent ease of the delivery, and above all its freedom from the obtrusive intermediation of catalogues, specialist librarians, and so on, is so seductive that we are not likely to retreat from the virtual back into the physical library. Quite soon things will be worse: retrieval will get smarter. What we may soon have is not a virtual library that discovers books for us but one that reads them for us, extracting what it 'thinks' we need. In this likely case, ever more powerful search tools will determine not only what *we* find but what we think about what *they* find. The invitation is already here to replace books as voices to be engaged and hermeneutic models to be weighed with pathways, enquiries, hits, rankings and modes of manipulation. As browsing steadily replaces scholarly reading, more of what we think or write will be the product of high-end technical searching. This will determine the shape of much academic research, and more generally the way we interact with and preserve our culture. In this vision of the future, sophisticated searching persuades us that the universal digital library is indeed the perfect realization of the library.

---

information, it can then match the user up with previous choices and therefore offer targeted recommendations of the type 'you bought that, so you might now be interested in this'.

Chapter 6

Durable Futures

The preservation of texts and other works in a physical medium is an external support of biological memory that facilitates creation ... The physical preservation of creative work didn't only extend collective memory in time and space. It also made it possible for the human species to build a creative heritage, thus accelerating human development.[1]

Preservation

Inscribing images and words on durable surfaces makes them accessible beyond the limits of their original expression, giving them a permanence they otherwise lack. The oldest known recordings of human experience are cave paintings; some of those in South-West France date back more than 30,000 years. Many such expressions have been lost through the work of time, neglect, accident and on occasion deliberate destruction; from some periods it is reasonable to assume that most have been lost. Yet if much has perished, much has survived, either through proactive human agency or benign neglect – if nothing deliberately harmful was done to material artefacts, the inherent robustness of stone, parchment, canvas, clay and paper often ensured their endurance. By contrast, digital artefacts require urgent *active* measures to be taken to prevent their loss, for they do not respond well to neglect, benign or otherwise. We know this, yet not only is the digital medium our latest inscription surface and the preferred means of storing much of our contemporary cultural memory, it is also rapidly becoming a substitute means of access and preservation for more proven durable technologies from the past. This seems like an insane exchange.

Central to the problem posed by the new medium is the fact that in our thinking about digital creation in the arts, in science, in the news, we have decoupled two elements that in previous technologies hung together – storage and preservation. The race has been to store more and more, to share and search it more complexly, but the same effort has not been engaged to keep what is stored continuously accessible. Part of our failure can be explained by the fact that we have not sufficiently considered just how different the digital medium is from any that has gone before: in carrying over into the digital age the convergent assumptions about preservation, storage and access that material forms encourage, we are failing to grasp the truly revolutionary aspects of this latest medium. Imagine a storage

---

1 Zaid, *So Many Books*, p.113.

technology as if it were a book whose printed text has to be retranslated every five years just so that it is readable when you open it, and that gives some idea of the problem we face in ensuring our digital culture has even a short-term future – never mind the 500 years that represent something less than the span of printing in the West. If, as some suggest, we now have the capacity to store digitally more data than there is data in the world to store, we must also face the possibility that, without some serious efforts to reintegrate storage with preservation, the throw-away society will also have thrown away much of its cultural memory. We are skimming and searching our heritage in nanoseconds, morphing and remixing it at a dizzying rate, but neither as a society nor as individuals are we banking it with the care we so recently took for granted as a necessity. We are hastening towards what supercomputer designer Danny Hillis has described as a 'digital dark age'.[2]

We noted in Chapter 5 the widespread loss of the literature of Greece and Rome as their great libraries fell into disuse or were destroyed. The ravages of the Vikings in Britain from the eighth century onwards, the dissolution of the monasteries in the sixteenth century, the war in Bosnia in the 1990s, Hurricane Katrina in 2005, all caused widespread loss of books and manuscripts, with precisely unknowable but considerable long-term cultural consequences. The Catholic University of Louvain in Belgium lost 230,000 books and 900 manuscripts during the First and Second World Wars. Some of what has been lost is known and can be replaced, some is known and cannot be replaced, some can only be surmised. It is a telling fact that as writing surfaces have become easier to use and more portable, they have become progressively less durable and less easy to preserve: the clay tablets of the library of Ashurbanipal have survived for millennia, the acid paper of the nineteenth century is crumbling into dust. What is the likely fate of the digital documents of the last 50 years?

Though much cultural content has been lost over time, much survives, and the memory organizations of the world – libraries, archives, museums – are charged with preserving what we have and making it accessible to scholars and the wider society. Unique objects are most at risk: the printed book has a greater chance of survival because of its token status as one among many. Individual manuscripts and rare cultural artefacts once lost are lost forever, unless some kind of copy has been made; even then, unlike the book copy, the surrogate manuscript or the plaster cast of an architectural frieze is no real duplicate. But since it is the best we can do, libraries and archives have been creating surrogates of at-risk materials for centuries. Microfilming of documents, used extensively since the 1930s, enables a photographic reproduction to be created to stand in for some or all of the uses of the original, and microfilm itself can be duplicated relatively easily. The degree to which a surrogate, like microfilm, can substitute for an original depends on the extent to which the features of the original can be captured. A modern printed book with black letter shapes on white paper,

2   Cited in Stewart Brand, 'Escaping the Digital Dark Age', *Library Journal*, 124 (20 June 2003), <http://www.rense.com/general38/escap.htm> (accessed 26 June 2008).

and no illustrations other than black and white line drawings, reproduces well on microfilm; a sumptuously illustrated medieval manuscript reproduces badly, even when colour film is used. Substitution of originals with other objects that simulate their properties and content of course poses its own difficulties. Under what circumstances or for what purposes is a facsimile a satisfactory surrogate for the object itself? This depends on both the needs of the reader or user and the quality of the reproduction; and even when these are satisfied a problem remains. The relationship between any original object and a reproduction is massively compromised by the sheer impossibility of exact iteration. As Walter Benjamin noted with devastating simplicity: 'Even the most perfect reproduction … is lacking in one element: its presence in time and space.'[3] More recently, the textual critic Thomas Tanselle has reminded us that:

> Microfilms and other reproductions can be helpful to scholarship if their proper use is recognized: but equating them with originals undermines scholarship by allowing precision to be replaced with approximation and secondary evidence to be confused with primary. The texts of many documents that once existed are now lost forever, and the texts of others are known only in copies. We use whatever there is; but when there are originals, we must not let substitutes supplant them as the best evidence we can have for recovering statements from the past.[4]

Fundamental to any view of representation must be its non-identity to an original: a representation cannot occupy the space in history of its original or rescue an original from the hazards of a material existence. At best, though, it can fruitfully evoke, by placing rigorous conditions upon the way we imagine it, the object which, for a variety of reasons, is not actually before our eyes.

Increasingly, surrogates of all kinds mediate and define our cultural knowledge. With a scholarly product like *EEBO*, an assumption is set that wherever we are in the world we should have access to rare book collections. Surrogates can never replicate or preserve through representation *everything* about an original object, but if we create no surrogates it could mean that, in the case of fragile or compromised originals, *everything* is lost: brittle books printed on acid-based paper, older newspapers, ancient and medieval books and manuscripts, crumbling sculptures, ruined buildings, photographs on glass plates, explosive nitrate film stock. In the case of rare books or specialist collections, without surrogates, opportunities for consultation are severely restricted. It should follow from this that, provisional status notwithstanding, in accepting their usefulness and value, we should be concerned about the conditions for the preservation and conservation

---

3 Walter Benjamin, 'The Work of Art in an Age of Mechanical Reproduction', in *Illuminations* (London: Fontana Press, 1973), p. 214.

4 G. Thomas Tanselle, 'Reproductions and Scholarship', *Studies in Bibliography*, 42 (1989), reprinted in *Literature and Artifacts* (Charlottesville: The Bibliographical Society of the University of Virginia, 1998), p. 88.

of surrogates too. The crucial questions here are: what is it that we are preserving, for whom and for how long? Are we preserving features of the objects themselves or only the information they contain? Beyond that, how does surrogacy affect the status of an original: does its surrogate existence also denote in some way the further preservation of the thing itself, now sealed away under conditions of greater safety, or does surrogacy imply the exact opposite, releasing its curators from future concern for the original?

It is important to be realistic about what *can* be preserved for the long term, given constraints on space, funds and expertise. Archives and libraries, despite popular misconceptions, do not maintain in perpetuity everything deposited with them: part of their duty is to define and implement responsible policies on the accessioning and de-accessioning of materials. With certain unique, intrinsically valuable works – the Diamond Sutra or the Beowulf manuscript – the object itself and the accretions of its use over time are as important as what it carries or contains. With more ephemeral or banal carriers, such as newspapers or government documents, it is, with rare exceptions, generally the content, and the physical arrangement of that content, which needs to be preserved, rather than the objects themselves – though in some quarters these are matters of much controversy. We discuss in Chapter 2 the furore that ensued when, in 2000, the British Library and the Library of Congress decided, in the face of mounting costs of paper preservation, to de-accession runs of newspapers in favour of microfilm. It is at this point that things get interesting, or confused, depending on one's point of view: because the preservation of originals through the substitution of surrogates, which stand in for some of the uses of the original, is now entangled not only with issues to do with which features of an original are simulated by (and in this sense preserved by) a substitute, but also with what is the expected life of the substitute itself and whether there are grounds for declaring the substitute a preferable preservation medium to the original. In such discussions, the concept of preservation can itself be substituted by other pressing issues to do with access and storage. And when the preservation medium is as fragile as digital, then the question of whether we see it as a provisional means of delivery and access or a long-term substitute becomes of vital importance. And what we must not do is confuse the two purposes.

Not everything offered to archives of historical records is by convention accepted as worthy of preservation for the long term. Over time, libraries and archives discard materials, especially if there are known duplicates elsewhere. Selection of documents to be preserved, on the grounds of some perceived long-term value, is deeply problematic: we can only know what has value now; we cannot predict what will have value in the future, though this is what we expect repositories to attempt to do. As David Holdsworth points out in discussing the preservation of digital information:

> There is always the question of which information will be accessed and which information will never be used. As our current technologies do not encompass digital clairvoyance, the best that can be done today is to make storage costs

so cheap that there is little reluctance to keep things that have only a small possibility of being accessed in the future.

Accountant: People tell me that 90% of this archive will never be looked at again. It seems that there is scope for a major cost saving here.

Digital curator: You tell me which 90% ... and I will delete it.[5]

Sometimes the value of an artefact is perceived only after it has been lost. A topical case is the archiving policy of British television stations during the 1960s and 1970s. While political news was regularly archived, much that was classified under light entertainment – a category sufficiently capacious to embrace children's programmes, dramas, documentaries – has been lost. Though the television work of the dramatist Dennis Potter quickly became a high preservation priority, some early pieces were wiped: for example, the original tape of *Message for Posterity*, transmitted on 3 May 1967 on BBC 1 as part of the Wednesday Play series. A new production was commissioned and transmitted in 1994.[6] The BBC, London Weekend Television (LWT), Granada and all the major stations failed to see the likely social and historical significance of thousands of hours of what we would now describe as classic television recordings.[7] The story of their serendipitous reconstitution, often by appeals to the public for illicit taped copies, is instructive, with *Doctor Who* fans proving a powerful lobby in changing official policy. In 1993 the British Film Institute began a proper programme of recovery, dubbed 'Missing Believed Wiped', which continues; each year it screens some newly recovered treasure. 2006 presented 'Out of the Trees', written by Douglas Adams and Graham Chapman, a 1976 pilot for an undeveloped television series which featured some of the cast of the later, hugely successful radio work *A Hitchhiker's Guide to the Galaxy*. Chapman had recorded the show at home on a primitive video machine. Although the tape was rediscovered, it took two years to build a customized player on which it could be run, and the entire process was filmed in case it dissolved after one playing.[8]

Preservation in the analogue world, where texts are often tightly bound to their containers, is largely a question of maintaining the material substrates upon which

---

5   David Holdsworth, 'Strategies for Digital Preservation', in Marilyn Deegan and Simon Tanner (eds), *Digital Preservation* (London: Facet Publishing, 2006), p. 33.

6   See, too, the story of the lost Dennis Potter play *Shaggy Dog*, from 1968, rediscovered in 2005, <http://news.bbc.co.uk/1/hi/entertainment/tv_and_radio/4172145.stm> (accessed 3 March 2008).

7   'The Lost Treasures of British Television', *Teletronic: The Television History Site*, <http://www.teletronic.co.uk/missing.htm#top> (accessed 29 October 2007).

8   Kevin Young, '"Lost" Gems from the TV Archives', *BBC News Website*, 1 December 2006, <http://news.bbc.co.uk/2/hi/entertainment/6150254.stm> (accessed 29 October 2007).

they are inscribed. In these cases, preserving the container saves the contents. But such preservation can come at a hefty price. According to Gabriel Zaid, in 1989 the British Library estimated that, though the books it receives on legal deposit are free, 'Receiving them, cataloguing them, exhibiting them, and properly caring for them cost fifty pounds per copy, plus one pound per copy per year'.[9] In a world where, despite predictions of obsolescence, books are published in ever greater numbers, these costs place increasing strain on the capacity of public institutions. If, by contrast, preserving digital data is different because that data is not bound to its container in the same way, this difference itself entails new issues of authenticity, currency and ephemerality, with different and unforeseen costs. Material containers for information are capable of direct access and can be managed materially – they are stored in environments best suited to their particular needs, delivered materially to users, and the means of their preservation do not change dramatically over time: once an optimum environment for particular kinds of documents has been achieved, it remains optimum.

What makes digital data, and particularly for our discussions here, digital text, different? Digital data is represented purely as a string of electrical impulses consisting of two binary states, 'on' and 'off', written as '1' or '0'. The basic unit is the 'bit' or 'BInary digiT', combined in blocks of fixed numbers, usually eight bits, called 'bytes'. It takes one byte to encode one character in the Roman alphabet; it takes more than one byte to encode characters from other alphabets (for example, ideograms); and the electrical impulses are stored on magnetic media. This simple underlying infrastructure allows the creation of datasets of great complexity – all the world's texts in any language can be encoded thus, in sequences of characters called bitstreams. Texts can also be represented as digitized images of the textual page, still as bits and bytes, but in this case as dots which may be represented as pure black and white, greyscale or colour, not as strings of characters. Digital data has a number of properties which we need to consider here:

- It only exists when there is electricity to fuel the impulses;
- It is not human-readable and can only be made sense of when a machine is imposed between it and its human interpreter;
- It is not inextricably bound to any one container, but can be moved between containers with ease;
- It can be sent to anywhere and accessed from wherever there is the technology to do so;
- It can be replicated indefinitely almost to infinity;
- Every copy of a digital file is the same as every other copy – there is no degradation between the first copy, the thousandth, the millionth;
- Digital data can be altered with no trace.

---

9   Zaid, *So Many Books*, p. 87.

Accordingly, a digital document is 'virtual' in the sense that we have come to understand the word in the computer environment, defined by the OED as 'not physically existing as such but made by software to appear to do so from the point of view of the program or the user'. It is ephemeral in that it exists as long as the machine is available to read it and has called it into its memory – once removed from memory it is no longer a document, but a stream of symbols on magnetic media. The virtual state can convey huge advantages: this book has been written, for example, by two people working in different countries exchanging documents online and discussing them by email. A manuscript in a library in Prague can be consulted by a scholar in New York; two manuscripts not set side by side for centuries can be compared on-screen to reveal that they were written by the same hand; rare and precious artefacts can be given, simultaneously, online access and highly restricted handling; a document can be sent to many people at the same time. But some of the properties that define the digital also pose real disadvantages. Key among these is fragile authenticity. Digital data can be changed with no trace either by accident or design. In consequence, loss and forgery occur with frightening ease, and expensive technologies sometimes have to be employed to prevent or detect them. By extension, version control is a persistent problem: the oft-cited benefit that digital data can be regularly updated carries with it the responsibility to signal updates formally, since there are none of the built-in clues to identify change that pertain in the analogue world. Illegal copying is rife; in order to counteract it, publishers have sought tighter legal restrictions than apply when copying analogue versions. The most pressing issue with digital data, however, is its long-term survival.

What makes digital data so ephemeral and therefore tricky to preserve is not its intrinsic properties, but rather its reliance on hardware and software that become obsolete in time spans we can measure in years rather than in decades or centuries. By contrast, material data can survive for many centuries if properly looked after – or sometimes, as in the case of the carbonized papyri from Herculaneum or the books in the Cairo geniza, examples discussed in Chapter 5, if not curated at all. It is not only digital data of course that relies on machine interpretation: analogue electronic media – film and video, despite their material casings of celluloid strip and tape – are also at risk from the obsolescence of the machinery that runs them. As a general rule, though, digital preservation must imply a more active and interventionist commitment than the preservation of analogue materials. This alone is sufficient reason why preservation ought to weigh with everyone as the hottest topic in digital technology. It does not. While currently there are many suggested strategies, it cannot be known for years yet which will be the most successful. There is a further distinction to be made here, too, between preservation, which is a strategy to ensure the survival of digital data into an unknown future, and data security, which involves a set of procedures and practices to ensure that data is not corrupted by accident or design: for example, hardware and software checking, virus checking, use of algorithmic techniques for verifying data integrity, and the storage of multiple copies in different sites.[10]

As we have seen throughout this book, digital documents and texts, despite an underlying structure as simple as a string of 1s and 0s, come in different forms and carry varying degrees of complexity; this in turn requires a complex approach to preservation. The first distinction to make is between documents 'born digital', which may or may not have a material instantiation in the form of a printed version, and documents digitized from analogue originals. Scanning from analogue originals that are unique, rare and/or fragile will almost always be done using non-destructive techniques, and though every handling of a document has consequences, it is hoped that these are minimal and outweighed by the benefits of creating a high-quality substitute. In such cases, the original is *always* preserved, and the loss of a surrogate over time may not have grave consequences. The ideal approach to scanning such materials is to scan once and create a surrogate that will last for all time, but this may not always be possible or even desirable. New techniques may lead to better surrogates. In the 1990s, for example, the British Library and Oxford University used the highest resolution cameras then available, costing tens of thousands of pounds, to capture images from ancient and medieval manuscripts, creating files of some 20–40 MB. Today, for the same costs, the highest specification cameras can capture files at ten times these resolutions; so a case can probably be made at some point for rescanning some of these materials.

Scanning from print copies will sometimes be done in a destructive manner (because this is cheaper) and the print copies discarded in favour of good digital surrogates. We point out in Chapter 5 that one of the key aims of the JSTOR journals project was to save shelf space in libraries. However, copyright libraries will almost certainly keep a print copy of record of all their holdings, and no library, we presume, will discard print without first ascertaining that another print copy exists somewhere. In such cases, while analogue copies continue to survive, the loss of digital data might be serious but it is not catastrophic. At the other extreme, it continues to be considered best practice in some areas to create in analogue form on a long-lasting substrate documents which are felt to be of significant long-term value. Vellum (animal skin), probably the most durable documentary preservation medium we know, is still used in Britain, at a cost of over £60,000 per year, to record archive copies of all Acts of Parliament as published in Hansard.[11] By contrast, born digital documents are at particular risk. Nonetheless, more and more data, much of which it is necessary to preserve, is being produced in this category and with no analogue back up: emails, electronic newsletters and other

---

10   LOCKSS (Lots of Copies Keep Stuff Safe), <http://www.lockss.org/lockss/Home> (accessed 29 October 2007).

11   Anne Perkins, 'Speech on Vellum Gets Cook's Goat', *Guardian*, Wednesday 6 November 2002, <http://politics.guardian.co.uk/queensspeech2002/story/0,,835762,00. html> (accessed 26 October 2007).

ephemera, dictionaries and encyclopaedias, computer games, and, probably the most fragile of all, websites.

Digital documents are complex; so too are printed documents. But print complexity does not cause the same problems for either readers or curators. A modern novel, a newspaper, a highly structured scholarly work, such as a critical or variorum edition combining and displaying many different witnesses and levels of apparatus, each requires distinct mental skills from their readers, and may pose particular problems for librarians (large-format originals, like newspapers, have different shelving requirements, for example). But the range of digital documents brings new challenges for presentation, access and preservation. The simplest digital documents are those born digital and composed of alphanumeric characters only, marked up according to international standards such as those supported by the Text Encoding Initiative (TEI), and locally cohesive. At the other end of the scale stand highly complex multimedia editions which may contain many interlinked texts and versions of texts in multiple character sets, with embedded images and possibly even sound and video files, all distributed across a number of sites. In between these two extremes lies a multiplicity of varying forms, all posing their own challenges, among which are documents digitized from some analogue original. Keyed or rekeyed and marked up documents pose relatively few difficulties for long-term preservation; but as digital textual forms increase in complexity, the problems of preservation increase exponentially, especially where there are highly intricate interlinking mechanisms across multiple sites. Also at severe risk are the more ephemeral kinds of publications that, when printed on paper, often survived by accident, but once online will not survive at all unless proactive techniques are used. Print ephemera such as playbills, advertisements, theatre tickets, broadsheet ballads and news-sheets have survived from several centuries, albeit haphazardly, and are now collected, stored, conserved and valued as vital witnesses to political, economic, social, literary and private aspects of the past. Today, equivalent digital ephemera (small society websites, parish announcements, private blogs) may appear on the Web for a matter of days, to disappear from view in the blink of a pixel, as if they had never existed.

The preservation of the documentary heritage in whatever form it might be manifest is a vital matter. The codex, and latterly print, have proved robust technologies in this respect. It is true that paper manufacturing techniques of the nineteenth century lit what have been described by Anne Kenney as 'the "slow fires" of acidic paper', necessitating the large-scale microfilming of millions of pages over decades in order that content should not be lost. But Kenney also warned more than ten years ago that many electronic initiatives have now lit 'the "fast fires" of digital obsolescence'.[12] Why is the matter so urgent? The problem

---

12   Anne R. Kenney, *Digital to Microfilm Conversion: A Demonstration Project, 1994–1996*, p. 2 at <http://www.library.cornell.edu/preservation/com/comfin.html> (accessed 3 August 2007).

is the rate of progress of the new technology, by which digital documents can be almost impossible to read after only ten to twenty years; and this rate of progress, or obsolescence, is constantly increasing. As Jim Barksdale and Francine Berman suggest:

> In the next 100 years, we will go through dozens of generations of computers and storage media, and our digital data will need to be transferred from one generation to the next, and by someone we trust to do it.[13]

In the case of books, preserving the carrier is all that need be done. With digital data, by contrast, the carrier may be in good-as-new condition after 20 years, but it may also be impossible to access on any current technology. Across less than 60 years of electronic development, data has been stored on punched cards, paper tape, magnetic tape, magnetic disk, optical disk and flash memory. Over the same period, the hardware and software have undergone many cycles of development. No single strategy has yet emerged for long-term preservation, though many different techniques are being proposed and tested. These include technology preservation, refreshing, migration and reformatting, emulation, data archaeology and output to analogue media. We consider each below.

Technology preservation is the maintenance, alongside the digital data, of the technology used to create it: the hardware, software, operating system and storage system. This solution might at first thought seem attractive: a method of preserving the original carrier along with the content, just like with a book. But, as Mary Feeney points out: 'any collection manager in charge of a large collection of digital resources who relied solely on this strategy would very soon end up with a museum of ageing and incompatible computer hardware.'[14] And one can imagine a reading room equipped with every computer of the last 50 years, together with an army of aging mechanics and technicians on hand to fix them when they break down, with the numbers increasing as every new generation of technology comes along.

Refreshing is the copying of data from one generation of storage to the next – from hard drive to the next generation of hard drive, from CD-ROM to DVD, and so on – without actually changing the format. Any strategy chosen for digital preservation has to incorporate refreshing, which needs to be carried out in regular cycles.

---

13   Jim Barksdale and Francine Berman, 'Saving Our Digital Heritage', *Washington Post*, 16 May 2007, p. A15, also available at <http://www.washingtonpost.com/wp-dyn/content/article/2007/05/15/AR2007051501873.html> (accessed 22 October 2007).

14   Mary Feeney (ed.), *Digital Culture: Maximising the Nation's Investment* (A synthesis of JISC/NPO studies on the preservation of digital materials) (London: National Preservation Office, 1999), p. 42, available as PDF at <http://www.ukoln.ac.uk/services/elib/papers/other/jisc-npo-dig/>.

Migration and reformatting are the movement of data from one software and hardware platform to another, necessitating changes in the format of the data. Such changes increase over time in complexity and cost as the data itself increases in complexity, and they carry with them serious risk of corruption. The problem with migration and reformatting is that, once data is selected for long-term preservation, all the content selected has to be regularly treated, whether it will ever be needed or not: this is what is known as a just-in-case strategy. There are problems too in reformatting all the features of a complex document: with each successive cycle of migration, function will almost certainly be lost.

Emulation, by contrast, is a just-in-time strategy, by which the functions of one computer system are replicated by a different system as though it *were* the first system, accessing data created *for* that system. It is proposed by some as a better and more cost-effective means of preserving data, given that data is only emulated when needed. Emulation offers a possible solution to the long-term preservation of highly complex documents deposited in libraries or archives but unmaintained by their original creators. It would be impossible, for example, for repositories to keep current the large numbers of complex electronic editions housed with them, but they can ensure that the files are preserved for emulation at some future time. Against this is the fact that emulation is an expensive and complicated form of computer engineering, especially where the specifications of the original systems which created the data or programs have been lost, requiring the earlier generation functions to be inferred from the data itself. Such costliness ensures that emulation will almost certainly only be used for data that is perceived to be of great value. It has been used successfully to recreate vintage computer games developed for machines no longer available; but the computer games market is huge and buoyant, with many devotees who are themselves highly skilled programmers. In this case, writing an emulator to be shared with other gamers is regarded as a profitable game in itself. The comparatively impoverished worlds of libraries and scholarship are rather different. Here an emulator written at great expense for one complex scholarly text might only be of use to a handful of people. An instructive example is provided by the BBC's Domesday Project. A social record of British life in the 1980s, the original project was created in 1986 with a budget of two million pounds to celebrate the 900th anniversary of the 1086 Domesday book. It involved a team of 60 staff and pupils from half the schools in the country (around a million children from 14,000 schools).[15] Developed as innovative multimedia on BBC Microcomputers and delivered using laser disks, the underlying technology was largely obsolete by the end of the 1990s and the project itself had been a commercial disaster: massive irrecoverable development costs and a purchase price of £4,000 that made it too expensive for most libraries and schools. In 2002, an emulator was successfully built to run the Domesday data by the CAMiLEON

---

15 Phil Mellor, 'CAMiLEON: Emulation and BBC Domesday', *The Icon Bar*, 15 January 2003, <http://www.iconbar.com/forums/viewthread.php?newsid=937> (accessed 26 October 2007).

project, as a proof of concept for emulation of complex multimedia. However, it was still not possible to make the emulated data widely available because of the intricate network of intellectual property rights bound up in it. The whole project offers a cautionary tale of time and money spent on a resource that lasted less than 20 years. The original Domesday Book is of course still perfectly preserved and readable, despite being more than 900 years old.[16]

Data archaeology (sometimes called data recovery) describes the rescue of digital data from serious damage, loss or neglect. The process is only applied where data is thought to contain vital information; as in the case of materials recovered after German reunification from the files of the Stasi by the Archives in Koblenz. In this case, 'the format of the information on the tapes was not readily known, the documentation was limited, and the hardware and software had to be identified (or constructed)'.[17] As a strategy it is an expensive last resort and can involve the physical reading of the magnetic tracks on media such as disks, tapes and hard drives with the assistance of a magnetic force microscope. (This possibility might seem to suggest that, contrary to the second of our seven points above, digital data is directly human-readable. In a highly attenuated sense that is so, but no one could interpret what they read without mediation: the pits on the magnetic media would still have to be translated by something.) Despite its inherent difficulties, such extreme rescue has been mooted as a more widely useful digital preservation technique. According to this model, data would be refreshed regularly, but no migration would be performed, and no programs would be preserved for emulation at a later stage. Instead, data archaeologists of the future would be left to puzzle out the data structures and connections in order to re-access the information. One argument made in its favour is that better recovery techniques are likely to be available in the future, and where resources are felt to be of sufficient value, rescue methods are bound to follow. As a long-term strategy this is highly risky.

Output to analogue media is just that: the digital files are output to some material carrier. This could be as simple as printing documents onto paper,

---

16   A group of universities, led by Cornell and Virginia, are collaborating on a project called FEDORA (Flexible Extensible Digital Object Repository Architecture), which shares some similarities with emulation. FEDORA separates complex data objects into their data and 'behaviours', which are either the operations the data performs or those the data has performed on it. One set of 'behaviours' can apply to many different data sets of the same type: a 'book' for instance. To display the object and create links to other objects, small programs called 'disseminators' are written. A kind of emulation that extracts the performances of an object from earlier in its lifecycle than later forms, this procedure could prove viable for preserving complex objects over time. See the Fedora Commons, <http://www.fedora-commons.org/> (accessed 29 October 2007).

17   Seamus Ross and Ann Gow, *Digital Archaeology: Rescuing Neglected and Damaged Data Resources*, a JISC/NPO Study within the Electronic Libraries (eLib) Programme on the Preservation of Electronic Materials (1999), available at <http://eprints.erpanet.org/47/> (accessed 22 October 2007).

though generally for long-term preservation, Computer Output to Microfilm (COM) is used. The COM process involves printing the digital data file directly onto microfilm, with each page of data becoming a separate frame in the film. Trials at Cornell University demonstrated that COM preserves as much detail in suitable documentary originals as direct copying onto microfilm.[18] COM is most successful for large volumes of straightforward alphanumeric text or for bi-tonal images; it is not really suitable for greyscale or colour images, where too much information is lost to consider it for preservation purposes. More complex digital products are likely to be rendered almost meaningless in analogue form (websites, games, interactive fiction, and so on) unless what is stored is the underlying code, plus supporting documentation, from which they can be recreated. This is probably an unrealistic expectation.

As we suggest, preserving digital documents becomes more difficult as those documents become more complex. Websites and the series of organized structures they support or link are a particular category of digital document, and one that crucially defines our sense of the distinctive capabilities of the electronic medium. The least significant website can be no more than a single screenful of text and images, but its potential connectivity is vast: a page to drop into and bounce out from to the vast world of cyberspace. Increasingly, websites showcase the materials of our culture and how we recreate them as we interact with them. Other sub-categories of web activity – blogs and social networking sites like MySpace, for example – now lay claim to significance as part of the narrative of our textual engagement. A great deal of what has appeared on the Web over the last ten years has vanished, but there are initiatives to prevent further loss. The Internet Archive was established in 1996 to take snapshots of websites at regular intervals and preserve them for the long term. It provides a means of viewing these via the WayBack Machine which, in October 2007, claimed it could retrieve 85 billion archived Web pages, though interestingly this does not include many commercial sites, like MySpace, which block access.[19] National and research libraries throughout the world archive websites, usually from their own domains, and there is debate about how comprehensive or selective this should be: whether sites should be specifically chosen for archiving, or whether there should be regular automatic sweeps of the Web. Currently both methods are employed.[20] While Web

---

18   Stephen Chapman, Paul Conway and Anne Kenney, 'Digital Imaging and Preservation Microfilm: The Future of the Hybrid Approach for the Preservation of Brittle Books' (unpublished report, Washington, DC: Council on Library and Information Resources, 1999), p. 14. Available at <http://www.clir.org/pubs/archives/hybridintro.html#full> (accessed 26 October 2007).

19   The Wayback Machine, <http://www.archive.org/web/web.php> (accessed 26 October 2007).

20   'DPC Forum on Web Archiving Report: 12 June 2006', Digital Preservation Coalition, <http://www.dpconline.org/graphics/events/060612web-archiving.html> (accessed 26 October 2007).

archiving is clearly important, the sheer complexity of the underlying organization means it is inevitably flawed: by the impossibility of maintaining function, given the number of external links to and from sites; by the challenges of preserving data accessed in underlying databases or content management systems. Nevertheless, a trawl through the WayBack Machine sheds fascinating light on the history of the Web and our cybertextual heritage.

It is evident that digital data should be preserved; it is also clear that some of it can be preserved; but whose responsibility is it to ensure that it will be preserved? For academics and others who curate and converse with our textual past and present, these ought to be urgent concerns. For, given the long-term and unknowable costs of digital preservation, it is not at all certain what might survive and on what terms into the future. Will complex electronic documentary editions and artefacts, of importance to scholarship but perhaps not to a wider public, be preserved? Who will make these decisions? Is it the responsibility of authors/creators, publishers or libraries to ensure that works survive? In the analogue world the author/creator's roles and responsibilities in relation to the longevity of a work are clearly understood. Authors are little concerned with the format or composition of the carrier, unless they are involved to some degree in choice of type-face, cover design, and so on. Most responsibilities end on the day of publication, by which time the author may already be engaged in a new piece of work. For publishers, their responsibility is to produce a printed volume, ensuring as far as possible the quality of the writing it represents. This is a complex process involving many different tasks: reading and selection, advising, revision, copy-editing, design, typesetting, printing, proofing, marketing and dissemination. Ongoing responsibilities might include reprinting or publishing a new edition, but any role in the long-term survival of the product is minimal. When an edition of a work is out of print, that usually means it is unobtainable from the publisher, who, unless offering print-on-demand versions, is not required to ensure continuing access: that rests with libraries, especially copyright and major research libraries. In their capacity as a nation's repositories of record, copyright libraries receive a copy of every publication produced in a country in any one year; so a published work which is out of print and unavailable anywhere else will almost certainly be locatable in a copyright library, even if that work is more than a hundred years old. Furthermore, that work will be self-describing, accessible and will contain all the explanation needed for its use, even when created according to different principles from those the modern user might expect. Held within the library, the most complex of scholarly editions, deriving from many witnesses, with annotations, commentary, notes, glossary and all the critical apparatus that we expect, will be perfectly comprehensible after decades or centuries.

As the digital world apportions the workload differently, it also creates different sets of responsibilities which in turn beg difficult questions. Where in the analogue world it is clear when a work is finished, in the digital world, a work may never be finished, especially if that work is an edition of a complex, multiple-witnessed text. In this case, there is always more material to be uploaded and more to be said. Electronic text is fluid in a way that printed text is not, and this is both a strength and a weakness: it can be a strength for the author/creator who can adapt and change the edition or the argument as new information becomes available, but a weakness for the user who may not understand what changes have been made, and for the librarian who needs to recognize which version among many becomes the version to be preserved and delivered. Instability of citation is a potentially serious critical challenge; research and scholarship are based upon a fundamental principle of reproducibility. If an experiment is repeated, are the results the same? If a scholar follows a citation, will it lead to a stable referent which is the same referent that every other scholar following that citation is led to?[21] If these certainties no longer apply, then we do not have scholarship, we have anarchy; an anarchy that is well supported by the Internet. And what is to happen to all the vast amounts of data being scanned by the projects we discuss in Chapter 5: Google Book Search, MSN Book Search, the Million Book project? The individual contributing libraries which receive copies of all files scanned from their volumes will, one presumes, have plans for their preservation, but will the companies or projects that provide the integrated Universal Libraries share the same commitment? Google and its like, after all, have no obvious stake in publishing or text curation. Priorities can change and, unthinkable though it might seem in the case of Google and Microsoft, companies can collapse – as many did in the dot.com crisis at the beginning of the 2000s. Or they can simply lose interest and commercial advantage. In Microsoft's case, this second unthinkable prospect has been realized, with the recent announcement that they are shutting down library digitization programmes and withdrawing search software, to the consternation of many partner institutions. Microsoft will now focus on markets with 'high commercial intent', while libraries whose online delivery plans have suddenly shifted from secure to unfounded will need to find other financial investors.[22] As one small but significant consequence of this decision, searches we conducted in MSN for Chapter 5 of this book are now no longer possible.

It is evident, then, that there needs to be an active will to preserve digital content and that constant intervention will be required for the foreseeable future to ensure that all the necessary preservation tasks are carried out. Objects and documents recognized at any particular moment as culturally significant will be conserved and preserved at that moment and for as long as they continue to have value for society. When a society decides they are no longer precious or relevant, or

---

21 For a promising new approach to the maintenance over time of digital editions, see Van den Branden and Vanhoutte, 'Through the Reading Glass: Generating an Editorial Microcosm through Experimental Modelling', and Gabriel Bodard and Juan Garcés, 'Open Source Critical Editions: A Rationale', in Deegan and Sutherland (eds), *Text Editing, Print and the Digital World*.

22 Andrea L. Foster, 'Microsoft's Book-Search Project has a Surprise Ending', *Chronicle of Higher Education*, 29 May 2008, <http://chronicle.com/free/2008/05/3022n. htm> (accessed 22 June 2008).

indeed that they are even dangerous, they may be neglected or destroyed. In March 2001, the Taliban in Afghanistan blew up two sixth-century statues of the Buddha because they were un-Islamic, despite the fact that they were part of the cultural history of the country. Anything can be destroyed or can erode irretrievably. We are more familiar with accidental, thoughtless or simply unimaginative destruction. The wiping of television programmes in the 1960s and 1970s is a case in point. At the time, the financial and space constraints on archiving were not matched by any perceived commercial value in the continuing broadcast content of children's tea-time classic serials, comedy series like *Dad's Army, Till Death Us Do Part* and *Steptoe and Son* or topical satire like *Not Only But Also* and *That Was the Week That Was*. It took the home video revolution of the late 1980s to change the sense of what was worth banking. Now, as Internet TV looms and we become nostalgic for a time, located around 1960, when television viewing was a shared entertainment – the whole family sitting together for sustained periods in the evening around the same set – many of those television classics appear to resonate their social moment more powerfully than the carefully stored local news reports saved at that time for preference. And, in a further unexpected twist of remediation, as digital channels proliferate, there are some where the majority of output is archive materials. It is far from easy to determine a preservation policy that suits more than the interests of those who set it, and even then perhaps only in the short term; far better to plan to save everything – if we can decide what everything is, that is. But, of course, that is unrealistic; so we must make choices and close down possible futures.

The great benefit of the digital format is that material can be replicated easily many times over; if one copy is destroyed, all is not necessarily lost, which is not the case with unique statues. But, unfortunately, the accidental survival of materials not recognized as of 'high' cultural, scholarly, commercial or government value is less likely in the digital world than in the analogue. A BBC television programme on the Edwardians broadcast in April 2007 suggested that our present culture might be visually opaque to future generations because of the ubiquity of the camera phone. We know how ordinary Edwardians looked because the Box Brownie camera, developed by Kodak in 1900, for the first time allowed people to record their lives cheaply. The relatively stable qualities of film mean that many thousands of photographs have survived in family albums which are increasingly finding their way into museums and archives. By contrast, future generations may have representations of public figures only as a guide to twenty-first-century humanity, because these may be all that will survive. A subsequent BBC programme on the history of photography prompted this letter in the *Daily Telegraph* on 27 October 2007:

> Sir – The first programme in the BBC series *The Genius of Photography* on Thursday night argued for the excellence of 'vernacular' photographs by amateurs in the late-19th and early-20th centuries. Many of these are anonymous … but in a hundred years, what vernacular photographs will our descendants be looking at? In my experience, people take plenty of pictures on their digital

cameras, but never print them out. At best, they load them on to their laptops, where they will remain until the machine becomes obsolete. Is this the end of popular photography as a historic record?[23]

Not only photographs, but the diaries and letters of ordinary people from the nineteenth and twentieth centuries regularly come to light, providing precious glimpses into a shared social history: will our day-to-day emails, blogs and digital images survive into the future?

While research into digital preservation continues with many institutions establishing strong preservation policies, there are those who believe that this may all be too little and possibly too late – for some materials anyway. Seamus Ross, a key figure in the world of digital preservation, has pointed out recently that not enough serious experimentation has gone into tackling the problem of preservation on an appropriately large scale, and that, paradoxically, data is *more* at risk because the cultural community is starting to believe that it is making good progress, when, quite simply, it patently is not:

> Preservation risk is real. It is technological. It is social. It is organisational. And it is cultural. In truth, our heritage may now be at greater risk because many in our community believe that we are making progress towards resolving the preservation challenges. ... it is obvious that, although our understanding of the challenges surrounding digital preservation has become richer and *more* sophisticated, the approaches to overcoming obstacles to preservation remain limited.[24]

If Ross is right, and we believe he is, then the relentless advance of the digital could have serious consequences for both scholarship and popular culture.

After Print

We could leave things here: in-built technological obsolescence and the cost, to society's pocket and to our cultural memory, set the preservation challenges of the digital age sufficiently high to give us all pause for thought. But there are other ways of looking at the choices we face; for how we preserve our culture will affect what we make of it and what it makes of us. In earlier chapters of this book we

---

23   'What Photography Will We Be Able to Hand Down?', Letter from Derrick Green, *Daily Telegraph*, 27 October 2007, <http://www.telegraph.co.uk/opinion/main.jhtml?xml=/opinion/2007/10/27/nosplit/dt2701.xml#head12> (accessed 29 October 2007).

24   Seamus Ross, 'Digital Preservation, Archival Science and Methodological Foundations for Digital Libraries', Keynote Address, ECDL2007, Budapest, 17 September 2007, available at <http://www.hatii.arts.gla.ac.uk/news/budapest.html> (accessed 29 November 2007).

have drawn attention to the limitations of arguments that propose a definition of technology within society as either neutral or at the service of real problems. As social critics, moral philosophers, print historians and media gurus all contend, technological changes do more than solve present needs; they transform us.[25] In changing the surface on which we inscribe and store our artefacts, we gain unprecedented access to cultural treasures and all kinds of materials; by the same process we risk our heritage in largely unforeseen and unintended ways. We might say that some of the problems which technological innovation proposes to solve are real: issues of digital preservation and access are compelling in the case of acidified runs of old newspapers and the dwindling storage facilities of designated repositories. Here digitization addressed a need and bestowed a benefit: tools to unlock the full historical scope of the most powerful print form invented; though even in this instance some experts would disagree. Step back from newsprint to printed text in general and the problem that digital technology solves may be no less real (especially if the choice is between no books and electronic access to a whole library), but the solution itself begets a problem which was not there before: a problem of reading. Digitization does not merely give us access to more books, it changes our relationship to books, and in consequence, it has been suggested, our relationship to ourselves.

In *Proust and the Squid*, Maryanne Wolf, a cognitive neuroscientist, examines what it has meant to human beings to learn to read. While the thrust of our study into communication forms has been cultural and historical, Wolf lays stress on the biological. 'We were never born to read', Wolf writes, but through its invention reading 'rearranged the very organisation of our brain, which in turn expanded the ways we were able to think, which altered the intellectual evolution of our species.' The personal and intellectual and the biological are complicit in the development of the reading brain. The act of reading changes the brain physiologically as well as intellectually; much of how and what we think is generated by reading. It is even apparent that different writing systems, such as Chinese ideograms or alphabets, make different uses of the mental circuitry for reading. In a twist on the familiar post-McLuhan arguments for electronic technologies – that they promote a 'secondary' or 'new' age of orality and social participation[26] – Wolf re-addresses Socrates' famous anxiety over the shift from an oral to a written culture to argue in writing's defence. Far from eroding the basis of critical investigation (Socrates' fear), the sheer effort of literacy propels each of us, Wolf suggests, into dynamic and dialogic relationship with what we read and write. Literacy not only provides us with an external memory bank, it shapes us to go beyond the texts we read, the circuits fashioned in the brain in the act of reading promoting our capacity for deeper thought. One of her conclusions is that if Socrates had lived later he might not have seen writing as memory's destruction but as a tool for deeper enquiry:

---

25   See the arguments offered by Raymond Williams, Marshall McLuhan, Gordon Graham and Neil Postman, referenced at pp. 5–11 and 67–8 above.

26   In, for instance, Ong, *Orality and Literacy*, pp. 136–7.

By its ability to become virtually automatic, literacy allowed the individual reader to give less time to initial decoding processes and to allocate more cognitive time and ultimately more cortical space to the deeper analysis of recorded thought. Developmental differences in the circuit systems between a beginning, decoding brain and a fully automatic, comprehending brain span the length and breadth of the brain's two hemispheres. A system that can become streamlined through specialization and automaticity has more time to think. This is the miraculous gift of the reading brain.[27]

Though the brain is not hard wired to read, reading provides Wolf with a privileged example of the brain's capacity to go beyond its original design – something she sees mirrored in the reader's interaction with text: the capacity of reading to provoke thoughts beyond what is given. Relevant here are what she describes as 'delay neurons', whose sole function in the brain 'is to slow neuronal transmission by other neurons for mere milliseconds'. Essential to the reflective capacity of the reading brain, the delay neurons aid comprehension and inference: they help us build new thoughts, which is why in the process of reading we extend and contribute to what we read, making the text richer by what we bring to it. We can expect that the circuits and pathways that the brain fashions in our use of the Internet will differ from those woven by the reading brain. And herein lies the new anxiety: could the instantaneous access of information, the machine processing of text and the kind of visual stimuli and screen absorption that substitute for reading in the digital space jeopardize the reading brain's precious reflective functions? Wolf argues that the cost is too high and the consequences too uncertain for 'our transition generation' to abandon books for screens. If '*time to think beyond* is the reading brain's greatest achievement', with what loss to the individual and our institutions might the 'rearranged brains' of the future function?[28] No one can answer these questions yet, but we would be foolish not to voice them and not to attempt to find means to resist some of their assumptions. Does the evidence from neuroscience suggest that, with reading as with food, maximum nutritional benefit is achieved only under certain conditions? The arguments against fast and highly processed food mount. Do we now need a comparable debate about good reading and, in the case of professional readers, the benefits of slow scholarship?[29]

If new technologies are transformative, they are also bewildering, especially at the stage when we struggle to describe to one another, often within the conceptual frameworks and language of older, familiar technologies, what needs we think they serve or what functions we think they perform. Currently this is the stage in our

---

27 Maryanne Wolf, *Proust and the Squid: The Story and Science of the Reading Brain* (Cambridge: Icon Books Ltd, 2008), p. 216.

28 Ibid., pp. 15, 213–14 and 228–9.

29 Compare the comment by Thomas Sutcliffe, 'Google Books Have No Shelf-Life', *Independent*, 17 December 2004, <http://www.independent.co.uk/opinion/columnists/thomas-sutcliffe/google-books-have-no-shelf-life-691003.html> (accessed 26 June 2008).

thinking about digital communication. Describing how we perceive the durability of digital objects is a case in point. Storage, preservation, access – book technology serves all these purposes well and, crucially, it serves them simultaneously. Digital technology did not emerge by addressing the same purposes better, nor have its developers adequately engaged with the ways in which its distinct technology problematizes what was unproblematic in the old medium of print. Where storage, preservation and access did not require distinct solutions, we did not need to tease out those distinctions in our thinking about print objects. But what was once legitimate is now simply false. To the extent that we carry over the same stock of assumptions into our attitude to digital objects, we risk endangering their very survival. This is a problem that computer scientists, librarians, publishers, scholars and funding agencies must all confront. What constitutes digital preservation? What distinguishes preservation from access, surrogacy or authenticity? How do we even know whether a digital object is authentic?

As we transfer our cultural memory into digital form and transform it into searchable, linkable information, preservation assumes many shapes. What definitions of preservation, for example, might we apply to mass initiatives like Google Book Search or the Internet itself? The major research libraries who sign agreements with Google or Microsoft (in the recent past) provide volumes of print to be scanned and searched by powerful engines. In return they receive copies of files. Google and Microsoft (until the latter withdrew their search software, Live Search Books and Live Search Academic) offer indexing services; preservation quality scans are not their priority. We have to take it on trust that libraries understand the nature of the bargain; that they do not confuse indexing with preservation; that they have robust long-term policies and finances in place to guarantee the survival of their own digital objects long after their commercial partners lose interest. But there are far more abstract and difficult issues of preservation – to do with the use or value of information retrieval and the possible consequences of our reliance on search engines. As Gordon Graham pointed out a decade ago, 'we must assess the advantages of technological innovation in terms of the *value* of the ends to which it is a useful means'.[30]

The Internet is the largest information space in human history and it is quite literally uncharted and unchartered territory – no one knows how big it is, how far it extends or what is available out there. The use of statistical and linguistic tools to add 'intelligence' to documents and to allow seemingly unrelated items of information to be connected in meaningful ways has powerful widely perceived benefits. At the same time, the companies and research groups dedicated to improving searchability in large, unordered sets of data are not primarily focussed on the needs of scholars or those engaged in high cultural activity, but on the commercial, military and surveillance uses of information retrieval. If we imagine the ideal book as a car manual or a telephone directory, we will have a better sense of the parameters within which retrieval currently operates than if we think

---

30   Graham, *The Internet: A Philosophical Inquiry*, p. 49.

of *Paradise Lost* or *Ulysses*. In consequence, though the tools available to the scholar, student and everyday user may appear sophisticated, in reality they are woefully inadequate to the task of finding relevant content in large bodies of unstructured, richly ambiguated full text. As sophisticated book readers know, the precise retrieval of data in an information space of any size or complexity is a skill that requires training. In digital form the problem is compounded: systems with little or poorly understood internal organization, coupled with powerful tools in the hands of untrained users, will not ensure good results. As Marcia Bates pointed out in 2002, even before the advent of mass digitization projects:

> 'Content' has been treated like a kind of soup that 'content providers' scoop out of pots and dump wholesale into information systems. But it does not work that way. Good information retrieval design requires just as much expertise about information and systems of information organization as it does about the technical aspects of systems.[31]

There are some distinctions that we need to be clear about when discussing 'information' and 'content' in the context of the Internet as a whole, and of digital libraries and mass digitiation initiatives. However large-scale and however produced, digital library content is only ever a subset of the larger information universe that is the Internet. This will almost certainly remain the case. Furthermore, in the online environment the boundaries between different kinds of content are fuzzy and unclear: we thought we knew what a book, a journal, a newspaper, a magazine was, but once they are atomized digitally and mashed together as 'information', they become something else, something we are not sure how to classify. Bates' 'kind of soup' might be as good a description as any other in our present state of thinking, as the key problem seems to be that information leaches meaning when deprived of context. When information floats free in this soup, rather than being presented in organizational hierarchies that serve to contextualize it, meaning gets lost. And not only are discrete information objects atomized and available for endless recombination, so too are whole libraries – all of which makes finding useful information even more difficult. Text mining tools developed for commercial use claim to help us recover the particles of information floating in the soup; in fact, their driving purpose is to help online providers attract more visitors to sites and so generate more revenue. The content management company Nstein, for example, has developed a multilingual Text Mining Engine (TME) which offers 'a more engaging experience to online readers by leveraging the "aboutness"' of the content. The results of this for the providers who use the engine (newspapers, magazines, broadcasters and publishers) are clearly stated: 'With deep, wide websites that both attract more unique visitors and enhance

---

31   Marcia J. Bates, 'After the Dot-Bomb: Getting Web Information Retrieval Right This Time', *First Monday*, 7 (7), July 2002, <http://firstmonday.org/issues/issue7_7/bates/index.html> (accessed 15 February 2008).

site stickiness, publishers are then able to increase their advertising inventories rapidly and generate new online revenue opportunities.'[32] In those information spaces where 'aboutness' can be determined by linguistic or statistical methods, these tools are invaluable. Some disciplines may need and may lend themselves to fast information access: medicine and engineering, for example. Industry, the military and newspapers may all benefit. But among Nstein's clients are a number of academic publishers who are making available large textbases of literary works. We question whether text mining tools can really help us to make sense of literature. Our fear is that many believe they will. And what are we to make of 'site stickiness' and ambient advertising?

Studies have shown that most users want tools that are as simple as possible. One reason for Google's pre-eminence in the online retrieval world is the ease of its search interface: the seductive promise of the world of information through a box – just type in what you want to know and all your questions are answered. And indeed, depending on the question, this is true. For certain things, Google is a wonderful resource – looking for a cheap flight? a hotel in Venice? a good camera? These are all desires easily satisfied using Google. But as soon as we want to answer a scholarly query, things become more problematic. Take, for example, a common topic for a student essay in English literature: 'What is the relationship between love and money in the novels of Jane Austen?' A search on Google Web Search for ('jane austen' love money) returns 909,000 hits, with nothing scholarly in the first 20. Worryingly, two of the hits are to services offering for purchase an essay on this very topic. The same search in Google Books returns 632 hits, which, on an initial browse, look much more useful, except that it is not possible to list these hits by date, author, title or any other parameter than what Google has returned – and it is impossible to find what that parameter is. It is presumably a 'relevance' ranking, estimated on the number of times the key terms are used in the books listed. The same search in Google Scholar returns 9,420 hits, and here it *is* clear how they are ranked: by automatically generated citation indexes. Again, an initial browse suggests that these are useful, but there are some odd anomalies: tracking the links to the first few (and therefore most relevant) works retrieved turns up books and articles with an extremely tenuous connection to the subject sought. For example, top of the list is the 2003 Penguin edition of *Mansfield Park* which is cited by 79 other works. The first of these is a 1994 (note the date) book on meteorology entitled *Sea Breeze and Local Winds*, which does indeed quote *Mansfield Park* on the vileness of sea breezes. However, it cites the 1963 Everyman edition, not the much later Penguin text. This example illustrates well the non-specificity of automatically generated linking: the right work, the wrong edition, and a citation that is unlikely ever to be of use to the literary scholar.

We would not deny that relevant material is recovered by even such simple searches, but they also raise a number of problems. First, it is difficult to know

---

32   See <http://www.nstein.com/en/> (accessed 26 June 2008).

what is actually there to be searched. Currently, none of the mass digitization initiatives provides lists of works available, in which subject areas, nor do they offer browsable author-lists along the lines of more constrained and well-documented digital resources such as *EEBO*. So, in assessing the likely value or representativeness of what has been retrieved, one has no idea of the size and coverage of the data. Is it the equivalent of the British Library or the local school library? For the student, this may not matter; for the serious scholar, it is crucial. We need a yardstick against which to measure data retrieved, and a context within which we retrieve it: we would not search for works on history in an online medical library. Secondly, it is a fact that in the plethora of plausible and even useful information returned, much that is pertinent may never appear. In the analogue world, the expert human reader (as opposed to the computer retriever) discovers subtle and creative ways of querying information in texts because, depending on training and instinct, she will understand tacitly the nuanced and coded registers of literary or historical works (or indeed of any kind of texts). She will, however, be unable to express this in any way that might be amenable to Boolean searching. This controversial issue has beset artificial intelligence for many years: the difference between explicit knowledge which can be codified, and therefore rendered computable, and tacit knowledge which cannot, or not easily. Searching in large databases requires explicit codification, but searches constructed explicitly are blunt instruments, returning many thousands of hits ranked by criteria that are not always apparent. This may not create impediments to the retrieval of straightforward factual information, which is relatively easy to express, but it is potentially an enormous problem for scholarly enquiry.

Searching can be improved and is being improved, but it has serious limits when applied to free text, and as the volumes of unstructured textual material grow, the problems grow exponentially. The search engine in the hands of users may be the right tool for information retrieval in some contexts, but we might question whether those include scholarship. What is puzzling is that most of the texts being digitized for scholarly use have good metadata which does not always accompany the digital file, as though full text searching is so self-evidently better that it renders bibliographic information irrelevant. In some textual domains there *is* no metadata and it would be too expensive to create it manually – in historic newspapers, for example. But even in the case of newspapers, algorithmic techniques can be used to create both structural and semantic metadata, which adds precision to the work of the search engines. The Nineteenth-Century Serials Edition (NCSE), for example, has used automated techniques to identify the structural parts of the journals in its collection (articles, advertisements, titles, by-lines, and so on). Within those structural units, keywords (including proper names, personal names, geographical place-names) are extracted using linguistic techniques; these are reviewed by experts before being added to the metadata for a particular item. Searching can then be carried out in a number of ways: using the metadata alone, by using metadata alongside full-text searching or by full-text searching alone. If this is considered necessary for serious research in a resource of 100,000 pages – small by mass digitization standards – resources containing billions of pages are in even greater need of good metadata. It is incomprehensible that, after 20 years of discussion, the critical issues that would give digital libraries maximum scholarly effectiveness – metadata, standards, resource description, resource discovery – are largely disregarded by those institutions and software companies engaged in mass digitization initiatives. The software companies, making money out of others' content, care little, but the libraries whose task it is to guard our culture should care more.

Finding known items in large volumes of material is relatively straightforward and relatively unburdened with irrelevance if the search is itself sufficiently structured and informed; finding information about known items in unknown sources can also be successful. What is more difficult is pinpointing useful, relevant responses to general queries, a problem that grows more acute as sets of data become larger. What seems to have happened in the move online is a levelling or flattening of text so that all text is somehow assumed to be 'the same', and therefore amenable to the same kinds of searching algorithms. If we look for something highly specific and we use the right terms, we can find what we want: a search for bag-free vacuum cleaners in New Zealand, for example, returns only four hits, of which two are useful. Our Jane Austen example, which is tangible but potentially ambiguated, offers useful material intermingled with swathes of irrelevancy that requires much intelligent sifting. A search on something abstract is really not possible in the present state of search technology; and perhaps it never will be. The phrase the 'idea of beauty', for instance, returns many more hits on beauty products than it does on philosophy. And it is not just text that is being levelled, but our engagements with texts.

The average reader of online resources is not expert in information retrieval. Formulating queries that will yield a maximum number of relevant hits with a minimum of irrelevant 'noise' is both crucial and extremely difficult. The signs are that we are not improving our search skills but relying on highly branded search engines to minister to our needs. According to a recent report:

> users make very little use of advanced search facilities, assuming that search engines 'understand' their enquiries. They tend to move rapidly from page to page, spending little time reading or digesting information and they have difficulty making relevance judgements about the pages they retrieve.

It is not only the young, the so-called Google generation, who place confidence in the technology; worryingly, advanced researchers are abandoning a lifetime of training in deep and sceptical paper-based enquiry:

> from undergraduates to professors, people exhibit a strong tendency towards shallow, horizontal, 'flicking' behavior in digital libraries. Power browsing and viewing appear to be the norm for all. The popularity of abstracts among older researchers rather gives the game away. Society is dumbing down.

'Power browsing' is defined as a new form of 'reading', 'horizontally through titles, contents pages and abstracts going for quick wins'.[33]

It is likely that there are some kinds of knowledge that come only as we read, page by careful page, in a reflective, expansive, circuitous and time-demanding way. If, instead, we merely address the items the machine retrieves, our engagement will settle at a superficial level. There will be a gain in speed: we will reach something plausibly sophisticated or, at least esoteric, more quickly, but the really complex insight will not be made this way, and the danger is that things will shift into a 'good enough' middle ground. Good enough for what: for the essay my tutor expects tomorrow? for the chapter I promised to write in that edited volume due in next week? Yes, probably; but, equally probably, not good enough if we look beyond the short term, to what is worth knowing and carrying forward. The heart of a discipline like English Studies, for example, is good reading, which is reading thoughtfully, suspiciously, and in the round, and not being easily tricked or seduced. Literary texts bear a cultural burden; they are more than information sites to be plundered. We do not just consume literary works; our responses to them are crucial to the way they circulate, are reproduced, and continue to live. Abandoning the kinds of judgements inherent in good reading for targeted searching erodes the very basis of our subject and of its value to society. We are all now familiar with the kinds of essays, articles and even books produced by googling. They skim and swoop, flicker and dart – associatively from point to point. The fortuitous connections by which information is generated on the Internet are coming to determine much scholarly writing: thanks to the speed of searching, the sporadic, serendipitous and fragmentary energy that characterizes annotation rather than sustained argument is a preferred model. In this case, and without the underpinning of a certain kind of labour and reflective capacity, new knowledge may do no more than remix the old – parasitically and parodically. Skilled in the habits of a digital and non-reading mindset, we will be adept at locating, transferring and appropriating at an ever faster rate entries (expert or merely tangentially relevant) from larger sets of information that we no longer need understand. Indeed, relevance rankings will bolster our utilitarian failure of curiosity as we succumb ever more to the contemporary pressure to convert everything into output. We will have replaced a hermeneutic model by a transforming and recycling model. By contrast, the digital knowingness of the good blog – a form in which technology dominates content to playful and ironic result – can make clever creative use of the snippets, summary judgements, free associations and links picked, chosen or plundered to keep the online conversation going and the blogger noticed. Blogs do

---

33   *Information Behaviour of the Researcher of the Future*, a study carried out by the CIBER research team, University College London, released 11 January 2008, pp. 14, 19 and 10, <http://www.ucl.ac.uk/slais/research/ciber> (accessed 11 February 2008).

not effect the reflective change that print can bring about, but on occasion they do grab wide attention and influence public opinion.[34]

The way we preserve our culture affects what we make of it and what it makes of us. The digitized search seems set further to entrench our current disengagement from evaluative judgements by confounding the trivial and the worthwhile as the relationship between information and its authority becomes increasingly difficult to weigh. If the human brain cannot match the computer in its capacity for storage and instant retrieval or sharing, its capacity for complex association is far more intricate. Only humans combine information in subtle and creative ways, and we should not lightly renounce or arrogate this competence to the computer. Deep thinking, to return to Wolf, is linked to deep reading, and neither is promoted by the impatience and restless functions the Internet serves – instant accessibility, multi-linking, multi-tasking and limited immersion in any one space – or by the ever tightening cycles of repetition its use induces.[35]

We enter the future backwards, as Paul Valéry remarked. Not only is there never a clean slate but things rarely work out in the way we imagine they will. In this age of transition the computer offers a window onto our textual world of print – a sufficiently disorientating bargain of gains and losses, perhaps; but, despite early predictions, resolutely text-based nonetheless. With reduced institutional filters, the present digital world of text mixes the old conventions of written and spoken discourse, redefines libraries, publishing, authorship and mass communication. It is all too easy for studies such as this to represent the past by its highest achievements and predict the future in terms of its worst. On the other hand, there is an assumption among technophiles that change means progress, and if not yet then soon because what now looks like confusion or banality or worthlessness will quickly improve. Who is to say whether we are dissolving or remaking our communication forms? There is plenty of evidence to suggest, in the words of Susan Herring, that we are simply 'slouching toward the ordinary'.[36] In a recent book, *The Future of the Internet – And How to Stop It*, Jonathan Zittrain argues that it is in our own hands to avoid the abuse and destruction, and the mindless passive consumption, that in various ways threaten the future of the Internet as a great experiment in openness and interactivity. We face a choice: to retain the Internet as a quintessentially 'generative' technology – one that invites innovation and accepts any contribution – or to abandon such freedom (which currently implies unexpected positive inventiveness *and* viruses,

---

34   See Sarah Boxer, 'Blogs', *New York Review of Books*, 14 February 2008, pp. 16–20.

35   See, also, Nicholas Carr, 'Is Google Making Us Stupid?', *Atlantic Monthly*, July/August 2008. <http://www.theatlantic.com/doc/200807/google> (accessed 26 June 2008); and Tara Brabazon, *The University of Google: Education in a (Post)Information Age* (Aldershot: Ashgate, 2007).

36   Susan C. Herring, 'Slouching Toward the Ordinary: Current Trends in Computer-Mediated Communication', *New Media & Society*, 6 (2004), pp. 26–36.

spam and identity theft) in favour of security. We need controls and protection: for preference, in the shape of active collaboration from 'good hackers' creating tools to keep the Internet 'on a constructive trajectory', and from good content providers ('artistically and intellectually skilled people of goodwill to serve as true alternatives to a centralized, industrialized information economy that asks us to identify only as consumers of meaning rather than makers of it'); but, if necessary, as a form of centralized regulation and even lock-down.[37] The warning is timely; the proposals have a familiar ring to them.

---

37   Jonathan Zittrain, *The Future of the Internet – And How to Stop It* (New Haven and London: Yale University Press, 2008), pp. 245–6.

Bibliography

Ahrens, Frank, 'A Newspaper Chain Sees Its Future, And It's Online and Hyper-Local', *Washington Post*, 4 December 2006, <http://www.washingtonpost.com/wp-dyn/content/article/2006/12/03/AR2006120301037.html>.

Albanese, Andrew Richard, 'Scan this Book!: An Interview with the Open Content Alliance's Brewster Kahle', *Library Journal*, 15 August 2007, <http://libraryjournal.com/article/CA6466634.html>.

Anderson, Benedict, *Imagined Communities: Reflections on the Origin and Spread of Nationalism* (1983; London and New York: Verso, 1991).

Anderson, Chris, *The Long Tail* (London: Random House Business Books, 2006).

Baker, Nicholson, 'Deadline: The Author's Desperate Bid to Save America's Past', *New Yorker*, 24 July 2000, pp. 42–61.

Baker, Nicholson, *Double Fold: Libraries and the Assault on Paper* (New York: Random House, 2001).

Barksdale, Jim, and Francine Berman, 'Saving Our Digital Heritage', *Washington Post*, 16 May 2007, p. A15, also available at <http://www.washingtonpost.com/wp-dyn/content/article/2007/05/15/AR2007051501873.html>.

Barthes, Roland, *S/Z* (1970); trans. Richard Miller (New York: Hill and Wang, 1974).

Barthes, Roland, 'From Work to Text', in *Image-Music-Text*, essays selected and translated by Stephen Heath (London: Fontana, 1977), pp. 155–64.

Barthes, Roland, 'Roland Barthes by Roland Barthes', in Susan Sontag (ed.), *Barthes: Selected Writings* (London: Fontana, 1982), pp. 418–19.

Bates, Marcia J., 'After the Dot-Bomb: Getting Web Information Retrieval Right This Time', *First Monday*, 7 (7), July 2002, <http://firstmonday.org/issues/issue7_7/bates/index.html>.

Battles, Matthew, *Library: An Unquiet History* (London: Vintage, 2004).

Benjamin, Walter, 'The Work of Art in an Age of Mechanical Reproduction', in *Illuminations* (London: Fontana Press, 1973).

Berrie, Phillip, 'A New Technique for Authenticating Content in Evolving Marked-up Documents', *Literary and Linguistic Computing*, 22 (2007), pp. 17–25.

Birkerts, Sven, *The Gutenberg Elegies: The Fate of Reading in an Electronic Age* (New York: Ballantine Books, 1994).

Bodard, Gabriel and Juan Garcés, 'Open Source Critical Editions: A Rationale', in Marilyn Deegan and Kathryn Sutherland (eds), *Text Editing, Print and the Digital World* (Aldershot: Ashgate, 2009).

Bolter, Jay David, *Writing Space: The Computer, Hypertext, and the History of Writing* (Hillsdale, NJ: Erlbaum, 1991).

Bolter, Jay David and Richard Grusin, *Remediation: Understanding New Media* (Cambridge, MA: MIT Press, 1999).

The Book History Reader, David Finkelstein and Alistair McCleery (eds) (London: Routledge, 2002).

Bowers, Fredson, *Textual and Literary Criticism: The Sandars Lectures in Bibliography 1957–8* (Cambridge: Cambridge University Press, 1966).

Boxer, Sarah, 'Blogs', *New York Review of Books*, 14 February 2008, pp. 16–20.

Brabazon, Tara, *The University of Google: Education in a (Post)Information Age* (Aldershot: Ashgate, 2007).

Brand, Stewart, 'Escaping the Digital Dark Age', *Library Journal*, 124 (20 June 2003), <http://www.rense.com/general38/escap.htm>.

Bree, Linda, and James McLaverty, 'The Cambridge Edition of the Works of Jonathan Swift and the Future of the Scholarly Edition', in Marilyn Deegan and Kathryn Sutherland (eds), *Text Editing, Print and the Digital World* (Aldershot: Ashgate, 2009).

Breede, Manfred, 'Plus ça Change … Print-on-Demand Reverts Book Publishing to its Pre-Industrial Beginnings', in Bill Cope and Angus Phillips (eds), *The Future of the Book in the Digital Age* (Oxford: Chandos Publishing, 2006), pp. 27–45.

Brooke, Rupert, *The Prose of Rupert Brooke*, ed. Christopher Hassall (London: Sidgwick & Jackson, 1956).

Buckland, M.K., 'Emanuel Goldberg, Electronic Document Retrieval, and Vannevar Bush's Memex', *Journal of the American Society for Information Science*, 43 (1992), pp. 284–94.

Burrell, Ian, 'The Future of Newspapers', *Independent*, 13 November 2006, <http://news.independent.co.uk/media/article1963543.ece>.

Bush, Vannevar, 'As We May Think', *Atlantic Monthly* (August 1945), pp. 101–8.

Carr, Nicholas, 'Is Google Making Us Stupid?', *Atlantic Monthly*, July/August 2008, <http://www.theatlantic.com/doc/200807/google>.

Chapman, Stephen, Paul Conway and Anne Kenney, 'Digital Imaging and Preservation Microfilm: The Future of the Hybrid Approach for the Preservation of Brittle Books' (unpublished report, Washington, DC: Council on Library and Information Resources, 1999), available at <http://www.clir.org/pubs/archives/hybridintro.html#full>.

Chartier, Roger, *The Order of Books*, trans. L.G. Cochrane (Stanford: Stanford University Press, 1992).

Chernaik, Warren, Marilyn Deegan and Andrew Gibson (eds), *Beyond the Book: Theory, Culture and the Politics of Cyberspace* (Oxford: Office for Humanities Communication Publications, 1996).

Chrisafis, Angelique, 'Chirac Unveils his Grand Plan to Restore French Pride', *Guardian* (26 April 2006), <http://www.guardian.co.uk/technology/2006/apr/26/news.france>.

Cloud, Random, 'Fiat Flux', in Randall McLeod (ed.), *Crisis in Editing: Texts of the English Renaissance* (New York: AMS Press, Inc., 1994), pp. 61–172.

Conner, Patrick, 'Lighting out for the Territory: Hypertext, Ideology, and *Huckleberry Finn*', in Kathryn Sutherland (ed.), *Electronic Text: Investigations in Method and Theory* (Oxford: Clarendon Press, 1997), pp. 67–105.

Cope, Bill, and Angus Phillips (eds), *The Future of the Book in the Digital Age* (Oxford: Chandos Publishing, 2006).

Cox, Richard J.,'The Great Newspaper Caper: Backlash in the Digital Age', *First Monday*, 5, (12), 4 December 2000, http://firstmonday.org/htbin/cgiwrap/bin/ojs/index.php/fm/article/view/822/731.

Craig-McFeely, Julia, 'Digital Image Archive of Medieval Music: The Evolution of a Digital Resource', *Digital Medievalist*, 3 (2008), <http://www.digitalmedievalist.org/journal/3/mcfeely/>.

Cramer, Florian, 'Digital Code and Literary Text', *BeeHive Archive*, 4 (2001); and at <http://beehive.temporalimage.com/archive/43arc.html>.

Crow, David, 'Newspapers Look to the Digital Edition in Battle Against Decline', *The Business*, 14 February 2007, <http://www.thebusinessonline.com/Document.aspx?id=C9C1342F-42DA-4D0E-B220-0583C2152C10&doc_page=1>.

Dahlström, Mats, 'How Reproductive is a Scholarly Edition?' *Literary and Linguistic Computing*, 19 (2004), pp. 17–33.

Dane, Joseph A., *The Myth of Print Culture: Essays on Evidence, Textuality, and Bibliographical Method* (Toronto: University of Toronto Press, 2003).

Deegan, Marilyn, and Simon Tanner, *Digital Futures: Strategies for the Information Age* (London: Library Association Publishing, 2002).

Dekhtyar, A., and I.E. Iacob, 'A Framework for Management of Concurrent XML Markup', *Data and Knowledge Engineering*, 52 (2), pp. 185–215.

DeRose, S-J., David Durand, E. Mylonas and Allen Renear, 'What Is Text, Really?', *Journal of Computing in Higher Education*, 1 (1990), pp. 3–26. Reprinted in the ACM/SIGDOC *Journal of Computer Documentation*, 21 (1997), pp. 1–24.

D'Souza, Sebastian, 'Fishing For The News', *Time Magazine*, 19 September 2005, <http://www.time.com/time/magazine/article/0,9171,501050926-1106460,00.html>.

Duguid, Paul, 'Material Matters: The Past and the Futurology of the Book', in Geoffrey Nunberg (ed.), *The Future of the Book* (Berkeley and Los Angeles: University of California Press, 1996), pp. 63–101.

Duguid, Paul, 'Inheritance and Loss? A Brief Survey of Google Books', *First Monday*, 12 (8), August 2007, <http://www.firstmonday.org/issues/issue12_8/duguid/index.html>.

Eggert, Paul, 'Text-encoding, Theories of the Text, and the "Work-Site"', *Literary and Linguistic Computing*, 20 (2005), pp. 425–35.

Eisenstein, Elizabeth, *The Printing Press as an Agent of Change*, 2 vols, (Cambridge: Cambridge University Press, 1979).

Epstein, Jason, 'The Future of Books', *Technology Review*, January 2005, <http://www.technologyreview.com/Infotech/14064/page3/>.

Febvre, Lucien, and Henri-Jean Martin, *The Coming of the Book* (1958; translated into English, 1976; London: Verso, 1997).

Feeney, Mary, *Digital Culture: Maximising the Nation's Investment* (London: National Preservation Office, 1999).

Flanders, Julia, 'Renaissance Women, Text Encoding, and the Digital Humanities: An Interview', 8 February 2007, <http://www.academiccommons.org/library/julia-flanders>.

Foster, Andrea L., 'Microsoft's Book-Search Project has a Surprise Ending', *Chronicle of Higher Education*, 29 May 2008, <http://chronicle.com/free/2008/05/3022n.htm>.

Foucault, Michel, 'What Is an Author?', in Josué V. Harari (ed.), *Textual Strategies: Perspectives in Post-Structuralist Criticism* (Ithaca, NY: Cornell University Press, 1979), pp. 141–60.

Franzen, Jonathan, 'The Reader in Exile', *New Yorker*, 71 (2) (6 March 1995); reprinted in *How To Be Alone: Essays* (London: Fourth Estate, 2002), pp. 164–78.

Gants, David, 'Drama Case Study: The Cambridge Edition of the Works of Ben Jonson', in Lou Burnard, Katherine O'Brien O'Keefe and John Unsworth (eds), *Electronic Textual Editing* (New York: Modern Language Association of America, 2006), pp. 122–37.

Garside, Peter, James Raven, and Rainer Schöwerling (eds), *The English Novel 1770–1829: A Bibliographical Survey of Prose Fiction Published in the British Isles*, 2 vols (Oxford: Oxford University Press, 2000).

Gaskell, Philip, *A New Introduction to Bibliography* (Oxford: Clarendon Press, 1972).

Godwin, William, *Thoughts on Man, His Nature, Productions, and Discoveries* (London: Effingham Wilson, 1831).

Graham, Gordon, *The Internet: A Philosophical Inquiry* (London: Routledge, 1999).

Grigely, Joseph, *Textualterity: Art, Theory, and Textual Criticism* (Ann Arbor: University of Michigan Press, 1995).

Grossman, Lev, 'Power to the People', *Time Magazine*, 17 December 2006, <http://www.time.com/time/magazine/article/0,9171,1570816-11,00.html>.

Hafner, Katie, 'A Photo Trove, a Mounting Challenge', *New York Times* (10 April 2007), <http://www.nytimes.com/2007/04/10/business/10corbis.html?n=Top/News/Business/Companies/Microsoft%20Corporation&_r=1&adxnnl=1&oref=slogin&adxnnlx=1191593819-CP3YAd4n8QCVctwvDjBFsg>.

Hanna, Ralph, 'The Application of Thought to Textual Criticism in All Modes, with Apologies to A.E. Housman', *Studies in Bibliography*, 53 (2000), pp. 163–72.

Harkness, Bruce, 'Bibliography and the Novelistic Fallacy', *Studies in Bibliography*, 12 (1959), pp. 59–73.

Harnad, Stephen, 'Publish or Perish – Self-Archive to Flourish: The Green Route to Open Access', *Ercim News online edition*, 64, January 2006, <http://www.ercim.org/publication/Ercim_News/enw64/harnad.html>.

Harvey, David, *The Condition of Postmodernity: An Enquiry into the Origins of Cultural Change* (Cambridge, MA, and Oxford: Blackwell, 1990).

Hayles, N. Katherine, *My Mother Was a Computer: Digital Subjects and Literary Texts* (Chicago: University of Chicago Press, 2005).

Haynes, Gary, 'Under Iron Mountain: Corbis Stores "Very Important Photographs" at Zero Degrees Fahrenheit', National Press Photographers Association *News*, 2005, <http://www.nppa.org/news_and_events/news/2005/01/corbis_cavehtml>.

Hazen, Dan, Jeffrey Horrell and Jan Merrill-Oldham, *Selecting Research Collections for Digitization* (Washington, DC: Council on Library and Information Resources, 1998), <http://www.clir.org/pubs/reports/hazen/pub74.html>.

Hellinga, Lotte and J.B. Trapp (eds), *The Cambridge History of the Book in Britain, vol. 3, 1400–1557*, (Cambridge: Cambridge University Press, 1999).

Herring, Susan C., 'Slouching Toward the Ordinary: Current Trends in Computer-Mediated Communication', *New Media & Society*, 6 (2004), pp. 26–36.

Hinchcliffe, Peter, 'The Relentless Decline of Paid-for Newspapers', *OhmyNews*, 17 February 2007, <http://english.ohmynews.com/articleview/article_view.asp?at_code=393125>.

Holdsworth, David, 'Strategies for Digital Preservation', in Marilyn Deegan and Simon Tanner (eds), *Digital Preservation* (London: Facet Publishing, 2006), pp. 32–59.

Jeanneney, Jean-Noël, *Google and the Myth of Universal Knowledge: A View from Europe*, trans. Teresa Lavender Fagan (Chicago and London: The University of Chicago Press, 2006).

Jed, Stephanie H., *Chaste Thinking: The Rape of Lucretia and the Birth of Humanism* (Bloomington and Indianapolis: Indiana University Press, 1989).

Jennett, Seán, *The Making of Books* (1951; reprinted London: Faber & Faber, 1956).

Jochum, Uwe, 'The Alexandrian Library and its Aftermath', *Library History*, 15 (1999), pp. 5–12; available in PDF at <www.ub.uni-konstanz.de/fileadmin/Dateien/Fachreferenten/Jochum/alexandria-aftermath.pdf>.

Johns, Adrian, *The Nature of the Book: Print and Knowledge in the Making* (Chicago: University of Chicago Press, 1998).

Jones, Alison, 'The Many Uses of Newspapers', 2005, <http://dlxs.richmond.edu/d/ddr/proinfo/papers.html>.

Jonscher, Charles, *Wired Life: Who Are We in the Digital Age?* (London: Anchor, 2000).

Jordison, Sam, 'Literature for the MySpace Generation', *Guardian*, 7 February 2007, <http://books.guardian.co.uk/departments/generalfiction/story/0,,2007744,00.html>.

Justice, George L., and Nathan Tinker (eds), *Women's Writing and the Circulation of Ideas: Manuscript Publication in England, 1550–1800* (Cambridge: Cambridge University Press, 2002).

Keen, Andrew, *The Cult of the Amateur: How Today's Internet is Killing Our Culture and Assaulting Our Economy* (London and Boston: Nicholas Brealey Publishing, 2007).

Kelly, Kevin, 'Scan This Book!', *New York Times*, 14 May 2006, <http://www.nytimes.com/2006/05/14/magazine/14publishing.html?_r=1&oref=slogin>.

Kenney, Anne R., *Digital to Microfilm Conversion: A Demonstration Project, 1994-1996* (1996) <http://www.library.cornell.edu/preservation/com/comfin.html1>.

Ker, Neil R., *Fragments of Medieval Manuscripts Used as Pastedowns in Oxford Bindings, with a Survey of Oxford Bindings c. 1515–1620* (1954; reprinted, Oxford: Oxford Bibliographical Society, 2004).

Kichuk, Diana, 'Metamorphosis: Remediation in *Early English Books Online* (*EEBO*)', *Literary and Linguistic Computing*, 22 (2007), pp. 291–303.

Kiernan, K., J.W. Jaromczyk, A. Dekhtyar, et al., 'The ARCHway Project: Architecture for Research in Computing for Humanities through Research, Teaching, and Learning', *Literary and Linguistic Computing*, 20 (Suppl. 1) (2005), pp. 69–88.

Kinross, Robin, *Modern Typography: An Essay in Critical History* (London: Hyphen Press, 1992).

Knight, Charles, *William Caxton, the First English Printer: A Biography* (London: Charles Knight and Co., 1844).

Kristeva, Julia, 'Word, Dialogue, and Novel', in Toril Moi (ed.), *The Kristeva Reader*, trans. Seán Hand et al. (Oxford: Blackwell, 1986), pp. 34–61.

Kular, Christopher, 'The Venues for Vanity: Methods and Means for Self-Published Books', in Bill Cope and Angus Phillips (eds), *The Future of the Book in the Digital Age* (Oxford: Chandos Publishing, 2006), pp. 57–67.

Landow, George P., *Hypertext: The Convergence of Contemporary Critical Theory and Technology* (Baltimore and London: Johns Hopkins University Press, 1992).

Lanham, Richard A., *The Electronic Word: Democracy, Technology, and the Arts* (Chicago: University of Chicago Press, 1993).

Lanham, Richard, *The Economics of Attention: Style and Substance in the Age of Information* (Chicago: University of Chicago Press, 2006).

Lavagnino, John, 'When Not to Use TEI', in Lou Burnard, Katherine O'Brien O'Keefe and John Unsworth (eds), *Electronic Textual Editing* (New York: Modern Language Association of America, 2006), pp. 334–8.

Leary, Patrick, 'Googling the Victorians', *Journal of Victorian Culture*, 10 (1) (Spring 2005), pp. 72–86.

Lerner, Fred, *The Story of Libraries: From the Invention of Writing to the Computer Age* (New York: Continuum, 1998).

Lindquist, Thea, and Heather Wicht, 'Pleas'd By a Newe Inuention?: Assessing the Impact of *Early English Books Online* on Teaching and Research at the University of Colorado at Boulder', *Journal of Academic Librarianship*, 33 (2007), pp. 347–60.

Love, Harold, *The Culture and Commerce of Texts: Scribal Publication in Seventeenth-Century England* (1993; reissued by Amherst: University of Massachusetts Press, 1998).

MacIntyre, Donald, 'The People's News Source', *Time Magazine*, 29 May 2005, <http://www.time.com/time/magazine/article/0,9171,1066945,00.html>.

Mansfield, Barry, 'People Power Takes on Google', *Daily Telegraph,* 4 August 2007, <http://www.telegraph.co.uk/connected/main.jhtml?xml=/connected/2007/08/04/dlwiki04.xml>.

Martinson, Jane, 'China Censorship Damaged Us, Google Founders Admit', *Guardian Unlimited*, 27 January 2007, <http://business.guardian.co.uk/davos2007/story/0,,1999994,00.html>.

McFarlane, Neil, 'Let's Forget About Citizen Journalism', <http://www.completetosh.com/weblog/2005/07/lets_forget_abo.html>.

McGann, Jerome J., 'Theory of Texts', *London Review of Books*, 18 February 1988, pp. 20–21.

McGann, Jerome J., *The Textual Condition* (Princeton: Princeton University Press, 1991).

McGann, Jerome, 'The Rationale of Hypertext', in Kathryn Sutherland (ed.), *Electronic Text: Investigations in Method and Theory* (Oxford: Clarendon Press, 1997), pp. 19–46; reprinted in *Radiant Textuality*, pp. 53–74.

McGann, Jerome J., *Radiant Textuality: Literature after the World Wide Web* (New York and Basingstoke: Palgrave, 2001).

McGann, Jerome J., 'Marking Texts of Many Dimensions', in Susan Schreibman, Ray Siemens and John Unsworth (eds), *A Companion to Digital Humanities*, (Oxford: Blackwell, 2004), pp. 198–217.

McGrath, Charles, 'Can't Judge an E-Book by Its Screen? Well, Maybe You Can', *New York Times*, 24 November 2006.

MacIntyre, Donald, 'The People's News Source', *Time Magazine,* 29 May 2005, <http://www.time.com/time/magazine/article/0,9171,1066945,00.html>.

McKenzie, D.F., *Bibliography and the Sociology of Texts* (1986; republished Cambridge: Cambridge University Press, 1999).

McKitterick, David, (ed.), *Do We Want to Keep Our Newspapers?* (London: Office for Humanities Communication, King's College London, 2002), pp. 1–18.

McKitterick, David, *Print, Manuscript and the Search for Order 1450–1830* (Cambridge: Cambridge University Press, 2003).

McLuhan, Marshall, *The Gutenberg Galaxy: The Making of Typographic Man* (Toronto: University of Toronto Press, 1962).

McLuhan, Marshall, *Understanding Media: The Extensions of Man* (London: Routledge and Kegan Paul, 1964).

McLuhan, Marshall, *The Medium is the Massage: An Inventory of Effects* (Harmondsworth: Penguin, 1967).

Mellor, Phil, 'CAMiLEON: Emulation and BBC Domesday', *The Icon Bar*, 15 January 2003, <http://www.iconbar.com/forums/viewthread.php?newsid=937>.

Miller, J. Hillis, *Illustration: Essays in Art and Culture* (Cambridge, MA: Harvard University Press, 1992).

Murray, H[ugh], *Morality of Fiction; or, An Inquiry into the Tendency of Fictitious Narratives, with Observations on Some of the Most Eminent* (Edinburgh: A. Constable and Co. and J. Anderson ; London : Longman, Hurst, Rees and Orme, 1805).

Naughton, John, 'Websites that Changed the World', *Observer*, 13 August 2006, <http://observer.guardian.co.uk/review/story/0,,1843263,00.html#article_continue>.

Needham, Paul, *The Printer and the Pardoner: An Unrecorded Indulgence Printed by William Caxton for the Hospital of St Mary Rounceval, Charing Cross* (Washington: Library of Congress, 1986).

Negroponte, Nicholas, *Being Digital* (London: Hodder and Stoughton, 1995).

Nelson, Theodore Holm, 'Complex Information Processing: A File Structure for the Complex, the Changing and the Indeterminate', *Proceedings of the 20th National Conference of the Association for Computing Machinery* (New York, NY: ACM, 1965), pp. 84–100.

Nelson, Theodore H., 'XML.com: Embedded Markup Considered Harmful', 2 October 1997, <http://www.xml.com/pub/a/w3j/s3.nelson.html>.

Niles, Robert, 'Fake Grassroots Don't Grow ...', *Online Journalism Review*, 11 January 2007, <http://www.ojr.org/ojr/stories/070112niles/>.

Niles, Robert, 'The Silliest, and Most Destructive, Debate in Journalism', <http://www.ojr.org/ojr/stories/070103niles/>.

Nunberg, Geoffrey, 'The Place of Books in the Age of Electronic Reproduction', *Representations*, 42 (1993), pp. 13–37.

Nunberg, Geoffrey, 'Farewell to the Information Age', in Geoffrey Nunberg (ed.), *The Future of the Book* (Berkeley and Los Angeles: University of California Press, 1996), pp. 103–38.

O'Hara, Kieron, *Plato and the Internet* (Cambridge: Icon Books Ltd, 2002).

Ong, Walter J., *Orality and Literacy: The Technologizing of the Word* (London: Methuen, 1982).

Page, R.I., *Matthew Parker and his Books* (Kalamazoo, MI: Medieval Institute Publications, 1993).

Pearson, David , Letter, *Times Literary Supplement,* 8 September 2000.

Pearson, David, *Oxford Binding 1500–1640* (Oxford: Oxford Bibliographical Society, 2000).

Perkins, Anne, 'Speech on Vellum Gets Cook's Goat', *Guardian*, Wednesday 6 November 2002, <http://politics.guardian.co.uk/queensspeech2002/story/0,,835762,00.html>.

Pickering, John, 'Hypermedia: When Will They Feel Natural?', in Warren Chernaik, Marilyn Deegan and Andrew Gibson (eds), *Beyond the Book: Theory, Culture and the Politics of Cyberspace* (Oxford: Office for Humanities Communication Publications, 1996), pp. 43–55.

Postman, Neil, *Technopoly: The Surrender of Culture to Technology* (New York: Vintage Books, 1993).

Powell, Julie, *Julie and Julia: My Year of Cooking Dangerously* (London: Penguin Books, 2005).

Rayward, W.B., 'Visions of Xanadu: Paul Otlet (1868–1944) and Hypertext', *Journal of the American Society for Information Science*, 45 (1994), pp. 235–50.

Rée, Jonathan, 'The Library of Google', *Prospect* (February 2007), pp. 32-35.

Renear, Allen, 'Out of Praxis: Three (Meta)Theories of Textuality', in Kathryn Sutherland (ed.), *Electronic Text: Investigations in Method and Theory* (Oxford: Clarendon Press, 1997), pp. 107–26.

Renear, Allen H., 'Text Encoding', in Susan Schreibman, Ray Siemens and John Unsworth (eds), *A Companion to Digital Humanities* (Oxford: Blackwell, 2004), pp. 218–39.

Rieger, Oya Y., *Preservation in the Age of Large-Scale Digitization*, A White Paper (Washington, DC: Council on Library and Information Resources, February 2008).

Riverbend, *Baghdad Burning: Girl Blog from Iraq* (New York: Feminist Press, 2005).

Riverbend, *Baghdad Burning II* (New York: Feminist Press, 2006).

Robinson, Peter, 'Ma(r)king the Electronic Text: How, Why and For Whom?', in Joe Bray, Miriam Handley and Anne C. Henry (eds), *Ma(r)king the Text: The Presentation of Meaning on the Literary Page* (Aldershot: Ashgate, 2000), pp. 309–28.

Robinson, Peter, 'Where We Are With Electronic Scholarly Editions, and Where We Want To Be', *Jahrbuchs fur Computerphilogie*, 5 (2003), pp. 126–46.

Ross, Seamus, and Ann Gow, *Digital Archaeology: Rescuing Neglected and Damaged Data Resources*, a JISC/NPO Study within the Electronic Libraries (eLib) Programme on the Preservation of Electronic Materials, (1999), <http://eprints.erpanet.org/47/>.

Roueché, Charlotte, 'Digitizing Inscribed Texts', in Marilyn Deegan and Kathryn Sutherland (eds), *Text Editing, Print and the Digital World* (Aldershot: Ashgate, 2009).

Said, Edward W., 'Traveling Theory', in *The World, the Text, and the Critic* (London: Faber and Faber, 1984).

Sartre, Jean-Paul, *Words* (*Les Mots*) (1964), trans. Irene Clephane (1964), (Harmondsworth: Penguin Books, 1967).

Scarry, Elaine, *Dreaming by the Book* (Princeton, NJ: Princeton University Press, 2001).

Schmidt, Eric, 'Books of Revelation', *Wall Street Journal* (18 October 2005), reprinted at <http://googleblog.blogspot.com/2005/10/point-of-google-print.html>.

Schuchard, Ronald, 'Why I Go to Colindale', in David McKitterick (ed.), *Do We Want to Keep Our Newspapers?* (London: Office for Humanities Communication, King's College London, 2002), pp. 49–58.

Shillingsburg, Peter L., *From Gutenberg to Google: Electronic Representations of Literary Texts* (Cambridge: Cambridge University Press, 2006).

Smith, Martha Nell, 'Electronic Scholarly Editing', in Susan Schreibman, Ray Siemens and John Unsworth (eds), *A Companion to Digital Humanities* (Oxford: Blackwell, 2004), pp. 306–22.

St Clair, William, *The Reading Nation in the Romantic Period* (Cambridge: Cambridge University Press, 2004).

Stephens, Mitchell, *A History of News* (New York and Oxford: Oxford University Press, 2007).

Stephens, Mitchell, 'A Short History of News', Center for Media Literacy, <http://www.medialit.org/reading_room/article409.html>.

Steinberg, S.H., *Five Hundred Years of Printing* (1955), edited and revised by John Trevitt (London: British Library, 1996).

Steiner, George, *Real Presences: Is There Anything in What We Say?* (London: Faber and Faber, 1989).

Sutcliffe, Thomas, 'Google Books Have No Shelf-Life', *Independent*, 17 December 2004, <http://www.independent.co.uk/opinion/columnists/thomas-sutcliffe/google-books-have-no-shelf-life-691003.html>.

Sutherland, Kathryn, '"Events ... Have Made Us a World of Readers": Reader Relations 1780–1830', in David B. Pirie (ed.), *The Romantic Period* (Harmondsworth: Penguin Books, 1994), pp. 1–48.

Tanselle, G. Thomas, 'Reproductions and Scholarship', *Studies in Bibliography*, 42 (1989), pp. 25–54; reprinted in *Literature and Artifacts* (Charlottesville: The Bibliographical Society of the University of Virginia, 1998), pp. 59–88.

Taylor, Gary, 'c:\wp\file.txt 05:41 10-07-98', in Andrew Murphy (ed.), *The Renaissance Text: Theory, Editing, Textuality* (Manchester: Manchester University Press, 2000), pp. 44–54.

Tombs, Robert, 'The French Newspaper Collection at the British Library', in David McKitterick (ed.), *Do We Want to Keep Our Newspapers?* (London: Office for Humanities Communication, King's College London, 2002), pp. 59–64.

Toobin, Jeffrey, 'Google's Moon Shot: The Quest for the Universal Library', *New Yorker*, 5 February 2007, <http://www.newyorker.com/reporting/2007/02/05/070205fa_fact_toobin>.

Townsend, Robert B., 'Google Books: What's Not to Like?', *AHA Today* (30 April 2007), <http://blog.historians.org/articles/204/google-books-whats-not-to-like>.

Twyman, Michael, *Printing 1770–1970: An Illustrated History of its Development and Uses in England* (London: The British Library, 1998).

Updike, John, 'The End of Authorship', *New York Times,* 25 June 2006, <http://www.nytimes.com/2006/06/25/books/review/25updike.html>.

Van den Branden, Ron, and Edward Vanhoutte, 'Through the Reading Glass: Generating an Editorial Microcosm through Experimental Modelling', *Literary and Linguistic Computing,* forthcoming.

Vanhoutte, Edward, 'Every Reader his Own Bibliographer – an Absurdity?', in Marilyn Deegan and Kathryn Sutherland (eds), *Text Editing, Print and the Digital World* (Aldershot: Ashgate, 2009).

Watts, Jonathan, 'Backlash as Google Shores up Great Firewall of China', *Guardian Unlimited,* 25 January 2006, <http://www.guardian.co.uk/china/story/0,,1694293,00.html>.

Williams, Raymond, *Marxism and Literature* (Oxford: Oxford University Press, 1977).

Williams, William P. and William Baker, '*Caveat Lector*: English Books 1475–1700 and the Electronic Age', *Analytical and Enumerative Bibliography,* n.s., 12 (2001), pp. 1–29.

Wilson, R.M., *The Lost Literature of Medieval England* (1952; 2nd edn, London: Methuen, 1970).

Wolf, Maryanne, *Proust and the Squid: The Story and Science of the Reading Brain* (Cambridge: Icon Books Ltd, 2008).

Woodmansee, Martha, *The Author, Art, and the Market: Rereading the History of Aesthetics* (New York: Columbia University Press, 1994).

Wright, C.J. (ed.), *Sir Robert Cotton as Collector: Essays on an Early Stuart Courtier and his Legacy* (London and Toronto: The British Library and University of Toronto Press, 1997).

Young, Kevin, '"Lost" Gems from the TV Archives', *BBC News Website,* 1 December 2006, <http://news.bbc.co.uk/2/hi/entertainment/6150254.stm>.

Zaid, Gabriel, *So Many Books: Reading and Publishing in an Age of Abundance* (Philadelphia, PA: Paul Dry Books, 2003).

Zittrain, Jonathan, *The Future of the Internet – And How to Stop It* (New Haven and London: Yale University Press, 2008).

Zweig, Ronald W., 'Lessons from the *Palestine Post* Project', *Literary and Linguistic Computing,* 13 (1998), pp. 89–94.

Index

Note: Numbers in brackets preceded by *n* are footnote numbers.